D1600873

The proceeds from the sale of this book will be used to support the mission of Library of America, a nonprofit organization that champions the nation's cultural heritage by publishing America's greatest writing in authoritative new editions and providing resources for readers to explore this rich, living legacy.

Molière
THE COMPLETE RICHARD WILBUR TRANSLATIONS
VOLUME 2

Molière

THE COMPLETE RICHARD WILBUR TRANSLATIONS

VOLUME 2

The Misanthrope

Amphitryon

Tartuffe

The Learned Ladies

A LIBRARY OF AMERICA *Special Publication*

MOLIÈRE: THE COMPLETE RICHARD WILBUR TRANSLATIONS
VOLUME 2

Published in the United States by Library of America.
Visit our website at www.loa.org.

Distributed to the trade in the United States by Penguin Random
House Inc. and in Canada by Penguin Random House Canada Ltd.

Library of Congress Control Number: 2021938734
ISBN 978–1–59853–708–6

1 3 5 7 9 10 8 6 4 2

Printed in the United States of America

Molière: The Complete Richard Wilbur Translations
is published and kept in print with support from

THE FLORENCE GOULD FOUNDATION

Contents

Foreword

BY ADAM GOPNIK

Indispensable translations mark the intersection, and some-times the head-on collision, of two sensibilities, and usually two eras. In English, the King James Version of the Bible, most obviously, brings Solomon's time and Shakespeare's into direct overlap, while Alexander Pope's Homer is a still more extreme, inspired collision of archaic Greece and eighteenth-century London. Even Scott Moncrieff's version of Proust, though made close in time to the original, marks a distinct space between the severe French symbolist sounds of Proust's *fin de siècle* and the somewhat more glossily aestheticized sen-sibility of the English one—so that Proust's austere title *In Search of Lost Time* becomes the more self-consciously poetic (and Shakespearean) *Remembrance of Things Past*.

Yet for a translation of a classic to remain impressive in our minds, the original and the new version need somehow to rise from an allied point of view. Some secret concord needs to exist between the two eras for the translation to remain golden. The King James Bible triumphs because it was trans-lated into English at a time when elaborate metaphoric rhet-oric and polysyndeton, extended composition through the simple dignity of "ands," were natural to English style. Pope's Homer was united with Homer's Homer by a shared love in their audiences for large-scale poetic storytelling, and more patience than we have today for long speeches in high diction and endless-seeming lists. The same taste that could put up with all the minor dunces in *The Dunciad* was necessary to put up with all the lists of ships in *The Iliad*.

No translations mark the intersection of two authors and two ages more strikingly than do Richard Wilbur's trans-lations of ten comedies by the seventeenth-century French playwright Molière (1622–1673). Wilbur's first translation, *The Misanthrope*, published in 1955, was soon followed by his *Tartuffe* in 1963, with the last, *Lovers' Quarrels*, appearing more than a half century later, in 2009. All are now collected here by Library of America in two volumes.

Miraculously theatrical in ways that more academic translations are not, Wilbur's Molière is nonetheless miraculously authentic to the original, written in a flowing, vigilantly smooth version of Molière's rhyming couplets, instead of in the lumpy prose of previous English translations. At once readable and stage-friendly, his translations achieve the improbable end of making seventeenth-century French prosody completely playable in English, while remaining true to the essentials of French *grand siècle* style. Wilbur took Molière's Alexandrines, the eleven-syllable rhymed line of classic French theatre and turned it into a more English-friendly iambic pentameter, the ten-syllable heroic couplet of Pope. To do this, he drew on living resources in the American language of his time, particularly on the reality that American ears had become accustomed, both in the then-booming business of light verse and in ambitious musical theater—of which Wilbur himself was to write a supreme example in his lyrics for Leonard Bernstein's *Candide*—to accepting easy rhyme as an aid to emotion.

Well, a better playwright than Molière does not exist, and a better translation of a great writer's plays does not exist—but though that is nearly *that*, all that need be said, it is not quite that. The intersection of author and translator is something far more than a library or even a theatrical triumph. The overlap between Wilbur and Molière is social as much as stylistic. To put it simply—or perhaps to state it as simply as a complicated case can be put—though Molière made his life in and around courts, his role was to become the first great comic poet of the emerging and ascendant middle classes, portraying their domestic concentrations, their appetite for erudition, their constant insecurities, and their easy readiness to be wowed by fashions and trends. Wilbur came to Molière at a moment when that same bourgeoise in America was newly ascendant in another way—when a highly educated postwar GI culture had taken happy possession of a European cultural heritage then undermined on its own ground, a time when all the heritage of European culture seemed in need of American succor and American support. Clive James recalled a Wilbur visit to London in 1962, the height of the period, as offering "the epitome of cool . . . somehow it seemed plausible that the traditional high culture of Europe should be represented . . . by an American who looked like a jet jockey. . . . The internationalization of a mind like Wilbur's, its seemingly relaxed roaming in the European tradition, fitted the picture perfectly." James, writing in 1972, felt obliged to dilute his admiration with a tincture of derision; later on, he would have muted the tone. But the basic picture is sound; much of the confidence and optimism of that postwar epoch is still caught, however improbably, in Wilbur's translations. Wilbur's Molière lives both as masterpieces of the translator's art and as witness to a hopeful (and still not quite finished) American moment.

Wilbur tells us that he had first come upon the idea of translating Molière in 1948, when he saw a production of Cyrano at the Comédie-Française. Wilbur had been one of the great generations of GI aesthetes, those young boys who unthinkingly and instantly threw themselves into the draft and the war, making for a democratized experience of the military alien to post-Vietnam generations—but also meaning that the experience of the war in Europe could offer a sentimental education in European culture, if you survived. (Two great American art historians of Picasso and Rodin respectively, William Rubin and Albert Elsen, would recall in later life how they met on a troopship leaving New York, when they were the only soldiers too aesthetically fastidious to rush to the other side of the deck to look at the Statue of Liberty.) This European education could take very odd forms indeed. The great critic Randall Jarrell came away infatuated with the German romantic culture that had been to some degree causal of the worst of nationalist excess.

Wilbur, instead, became a Francophile. With his elegant

French hand-tooled on the soldiers' road to Paris, he was known as a master craftsman already, after the publication of his shimmeringly precisionist first collection of poetry, *The Beautiful Changes* (1947). But the craftsmanship was metrical and largely expressed in unrhymed verse, and so his decision to write Molière over in English rhyme was far from self-evident. English has, famously but truly, a scarcity of rhyme words, even as it lends itself almost too easily to alliteration. Anyone who dips even a big toe in versification starts to recognize the limited familiar repertory of rhyme words tumbling toward the listener: every chance will produce a romance, and then a dance. An instant, illuminating, ironic illustration of this truth about the scarcity of rhyme in English: a search for rhymes for that word, "scarcity," in English provides . . . precisely zero true rhymes. (You could toy with "ferocity" or the like, or go the Larry Hart route and rhyme it, playfully mis-stressed, with a word pair: i.e., "There's always such a scary scarcity / of honest folks here in our fair city.") The French word for scarcity, by contrast, *rareté*, has such an abundance of rhymes that it makes an English rhymester weep, with *engagé*, *écarté*, and *retardé* leading the charge and many more coming up behind. In French, as in Italian and the other Romance languages, rhyme comes so easy that it can just sneak by our attention on its way to speech. That's how Molière uses it. Not quite invisible, it simply adds the artful tone that iambs do in English.

Rhyme in its nature stylizes and distances an emotion. It's why even the most Francophile of English speakers find something puzzling in Racine: that much rhyming seems "off" for the tragic passions. A Cleopatra who says, in effect, "Give me that knife from off the shelf / Now I have to kill myself" is inescapably comic. Pope's rhetorical exercises in rhyming pathos—his "Eloisa to Abelard"—are DOA to modern readers, as much as his epistles are alive. In English, rhyme belongs almost exclusively to extravagant humor, with Gilbert and Sullivan being both the apotheosis and the cul de sac of this truth. You can't go further in that direction without becoming wholly mechanized.

Wilbur accepted this circumstance of the difficulty of English rhyme, and its inherent bend to the comic, by ingeniously underplaying it. There is not much showy rhyme in Wilbur's Molière, hardly a moment when one is self-consciously impressed by the ingenuity of the rhyme scheme. Scrolling down a random page of his version of *The School for Wives*, one finds all the standards: *care* and *there*, *bliss* and *this*, *two* and *you*, *role* and *soul*. (One rhyme alone—you would be / and nonentity—is witty, and works.)

The rhymes themselves can be commonplace, because the act of rhyming is not. Wilbur knows that whereas in French, rhyme is neutral, in English, rhyme, smoothly and consistently appliquéd, injects a rolling comic energy irresistibly into the text. Its simple presence is enough to produce an effect of ingenuity. Wilbur himself speaks of the importance of making the repetitions in Molière, which are part of the high style of aphoristic argument, land as elegance rather than irritate as overemphasis—Wilbur points out that there is scarcely a metaphor in all of Molière's writing—and that the rhymed couplet is essential to this task.

Yet if rhyming in English is inherently comic, the art and wit of rhyming in English is, as Ogden Nash understood, to land self-consciously on a "find" when you find one. Impressive on every page, Wilbur's wit is particularly so when stretched out across dialogue, so that the exchanges are both perfectly unstilted and idiomatic, and still delight with the ingenuity of each line "tag." Take, for instance, the moment when Alceste, in *The Misanthrope*, responds to the miserable sonnet of Oronte. In French, Oronte says, "Je voudrais bien, pour voir, que de votres manière / Vous en composassiez sur la même matière," and Alceste replies, "Je'n pourrais, par malheur, faire d'aussi méchants; / Mais je me garderais de les montrer aux gens." This exchange becomes, in Wilbur, "Come now, I'll lend you the subject of my sonnet / I'd like to see you try to improve upon it," with Alceste's rejoinder rendered as "I might by chance write something just as shoddy / But then I wouldn't show it to everybody." It is typical of Wilbur's skill that the translation is both nearly literal, word for word, and still inspired: Molière's unemphatic rhyme of *gens* and *méchants* is expressed as the Cole Porterish, more self-consciously inventive, "shoddy" and "everybody"—a rhyme that, it seems fair to say, has rarely, if ever, been found in English before, and gives us wit along with point.

The insistence on rhyme, particularly the play of invisible, "perfect" rhyme with marked "foregrounded" rhyme, that one finds in Wilbur's Molière was part of a larger, though still select, "return to rhyme" in American literary culture in the fifties and sixties, part of a mini–*rappel à l'ordre*, a recall to order, of the time. Ignited by the American Auden's long, neoclassical poems of the forties—particularly his wartime meditation written in Swiftian couplets, "New Year Letter," and the slightly later satiric masterpiece "Under Which Lyre"—rhyme for a period of twenty years or so seemed a vital affirmation of tradition that also, in its self-conscious artifice, had a modernist twang: it guyed the undue inaccessibility of high modernism while, with the elegant knowingness of its revivalist urge, remaining under its umbrella of self-conscious irony. Couplets were as romantic as couples. John Updike, who saw himself first as a light-verse writer, wrote in praise of rhyme, with Wilbur perhaps in the back of his mind, in the early sixties. Updike said that "by rhyming, language calls attention to its own mechanical nature and relieves the represented reality of seriousness. . . . Light verse, an isolated acolyte [isolated, that is, from the main ground of modernism], tends the thin flame of formal magic and tempers the inhuman darkness of reality with the comedy of human artifice." The composer and lyricist Stephen Sondheim, another exact contemporary of Wilbur's, insisted in a parallel way on rejecting in theatre music the increasingly slack—and differently expressive—diction of American pop music, which would lead at last to the sixties revolution in lyric writing. Bob Dylan could, eventually, win the Nobel Prize for Literature while rhyming, in one famous song, "divorced" and "force." Sondheim insisted on lyric writing in favor of true rhyme schemes, seeing in "perfect" rhyme the same kind of formal magic, imposed by the sheer obdurate

resistance of rhyme to easy composition—a sign of the resistance of intelligence to kitsch. To this day Broadway circles
are the last place in American culture where a prosodic distinction has religious force, with the true-rhyme/near-rhyme
distinction inspiring bitter quarrels and feuds. (One major
Broadway composer came away from the great and rap-based
Hamilton indignant and unhappy at Lin Manuel Miranda's
rhyme of "country" and "hungry" in the now famous line
"I'm like my country / I'm young, scrappy and hungry.")

It is no accident, as the academics say, but an act of fra-
ternity that Sondheim, in his slightly perverse way, placed
Wilbur's one-time-only Broadway lyrics, for *Candide*, along-
side those of Heywood Dubose, the one-time-only lyricist
for *Porgy and Bess*, at the very top of the American theatrical
pile. So Wilbur's is a period style in the best sense. A smooth
surface of unostentatious rhyme could suggest a sensibility
at once firmly modernist and still comfortably classicized,
rather like the glittering windowed surfaces of fifties sky-
scrapers, the Seagram Building and Lever House, gleaming
daughters of the Bauhaus at home among the Beaux-Arts
buildings on Park Avenue.

———— ❖ ————

Yet Wilbur's Molière reaches us for more profound reasons
than its skillful surface. Wilbur himself has neatly articulated
Molière's universality: his subject is what happens to social
groups—the microsociety of a family or the larger society of
a social class—when an unbalanced figure appears within it.
And Molière could speak to an American audience because
the moral pluses and minuses were remarkably unaltered.
Having an uncomfortable truth seeker and teller in our midst
provokes the same mixture of exasperation and admiration in
1952 Cambridge as it might in seventeenth-century Paris. The
writer Larry David has made a brilliant career as a comedian
on just this basis, as the man who will innocently say the
uncomfortable truth—that a parent's death suddenly creates
an all-purpose excuse for avoiding obligatory socializing. An

unplugged fanatic like Tartuffe is always going to have an unsettling effect on a family—though today our fanatic may as easily be a yoga enthusiast or a New Age seer as a puritanical hypocrite. (There is no more memorable description of a modern Tartuffe than that in Michael Downing's *Shoes Outside the Door*, of the Zen roshi who, dazzling his adepts with Americanized Zen, turned out to have a lecherous interest in women students.)

Both timeless and timebound, Molière is not our contemporary in some facile and fatuous way: he is not a radical, certainly, in our sense, nor even a romantic, in the nineteenth-century sense—he is a common-sense realist, opposed to putting ideas and obsessions and *idées fixes* in place of people and relationships, and believing not in an ordered but a balanced world. What he is almost uniquely good at doing—perhaps only Jane Austen among the world's masters equals him here—is conveying the quality that Wilbur celebrates in his poetry, that quality of unschooled intelligence we call common sense. Common sense these days is condemned as a conspiracy by the privileged against the excluded; the suspicious circles of what counts as "common" are, we're told, an indictment against the sense. But Molière reaches out across the centuries to remind us that in truth common sense has legs as long as laughter itself. The model of patriarchal order in the plays is not merely impotent; the common sense of the other characters, their knowledge of actual human possibility, leaves it instantly disregarded as absurd. The plays are filled with patriarchal impositions, but the patriarchal figure is always ridiculous, and quickly shown to be completely incompetent and ineffective. In both *The School for Wives* and *The School for Husbands* the protagonists are men so terrified of femininity and the power of women's minds that they bend their worlds right out of shape in order to keep their wards or fiancées ignorant and subordinate. Molière's point, first made in *The School for Husbands* and italicized in *The School for Wives*, is that this is not only a repugnant activity but a ludicrous one, doomed to comic failure. The repressed, cloistered women are instinctively aware of their own repression, and respond to it by making their own clear-eyed choices of suitors and potential husbands. Sganarelle and Ariste, in *The School for Husbands,* are counterpoised as bad and good suitors, a grand siècle Goofus and Gallant: Sganarelle treats his intended as both prey and potential danger; Ariste treats his intended as a full human being; one relationship ends absurdly, the other happily. In *The School for Wives,* Arnolphe's paranoia about feminine choice is so extreme that it compels him to have isolated his object of desire since she was a child. Both Arnolphe and Sganarelle get schooled by the very women they thought they were schooling. The common sense of the women X-rays the patriarchal hypocrisies and then obliterates their absurdities.

Molière's great theme is the folly of fanaticism of every kind: the religious fanaticism in *Tartuffe,* where a self-seeking pseudo-holy man warps a family's life, or the social fanaticism in *The Misanthrope,* where the proudly plainspoken Alceste has to be instructed by his mistress and his friends that too much candor is egocentric and vain, not admirable. Molière is no philistine; he is the *poet* of common sense, not merely in his ridicule of the idea that life can be lived by a rule of excessive piety or in his exposure of erudition for its own sake, but by being most fully alive on the stage when dramatizing their opposite. He holds what every professor wants for a satirist: a set of positive ideas made more positive by not being ideas. Molière loves natural actions and affections, including that of lust. In *The Learned Ladies,* Molière's feminist point is not that the ladies should not be learned, but that their natural wit, all that they know already from their own experience, is more profound than what their lecherous tutors, with their extravagantly abstract ideas, wish to teach them. Molière escapes fatuity in his candor that what restores a universe unbalanced by intellectual obsession is, most often, normal erotic appetite. In Molière, sex is always the rejuvenating juice of common sense. Alceste loves Célimène, in part because she is clearly his only intellectual equal in the play, but also because he is sexually infatuated with her, and the intensity of his desire, though it makes him miserable, humanizes him. She, in turn, cannot understand his raging jealousy at the attraction she offers to other men; she is not being flirtatious—or not merely flirtatious, or "coquettish"— in her insistence that her plethora of suitors is not a sign of bad faith but exactly an extension of the same sincerity of affect that Alceste claims to admire as a virtue, and cultivates in himself. Being flirtatious with many, she is being true to herself. Tartuffe is shown as a hypocrite in his lecheries, but a human being in his appetites. It's the purpose of comedy to restore energy to sanity—to make common sense come alive to our dramatic imagination by making the pious certitudes that censure common sense look as loony as they are.

Those values are Wilbur's values, too, yet expressed in his poetry more often in an elegiac and wistfully observant key than in a satiric or wholly comic one. Molière releases Wilbur's lyricism into laughter. There's no harm in small white lies; it's egocentric to give way to undue passion; what matters in life is not hierarchical order but emotional ease. Easy does it, Molière says, and our romantic-trained minds still rebel a little against the fatuity of the injunction. But he's right. A more truly radical feminism, a better form of family piety, emerge when we recognize the folly of trying to live by maxims and morals and principles and plans, instead of by the equilibrium of actual existence.

A romantic Molière has been the desideratum of some since the romantic period began. Jean-Jacques Rousseau famously said that he could not understand why anyone laughed at Alceste, and many a modern reading of Molière tried to make him "radical" in this sense—readings in which the balancing forces are seen as pernicious and the unbalancing disruptive force benign, or subversive.

Perhaps if there is a backward blessing in this latest and hardest recent disruption, the pandemic of 2020–2021 under which these lines are written, it may be its reminder that domestic balance is in itself a good thing, to the degree it can be achieved. Once again subject to the vagaries of an untamable and vindictive-seeming Nature, we have a keener sense of the values of the circle drawn around us to keep Nature away. On stage as in mid-plague, there is nothing like a mask to regulate our passions. And nothing like high comedy in rhyme, rolling down the page and affirming the primacy of unaffected affection, to blow away our bourgeois blues.

MOLIÈRE

The Complete Richard Wilbur Translations

VOLUME 2

THE MISANTHROPE

COMEDY IN FIVE ACTS, 1666

To Harry Levin

Introduction

The idea that comedy is a ritual in which society's laughter corrects individual extravagance is particularly inapplicable to *The Misanthrope*. In this play, society itself is indicted, and though Alceste's criticisms are indiscriminate, they are not unjustified. It is true that falseness and intrigue are everywhere on view; the conventions enforce a routine dishonesty, justice is subverted by influence, love is overwhelmed by calculation, and these things are accepted, even by the best, as "natural." The cold vanity of Oronte, Acaste, and Clitandre, the malignant hypocrisy of Arsinoé, the insincerity of Célimène, are to be taken as exemplary of the age, and Philinte's philosophic tolerance will not quite do in response to such a condition of things. The honest Éliante is the one we are most to trust, and this is partly because she sees that Alceste's intransigence *A quelque chose en soy de noble & d'héroïque.*

But *The Misanthrope* is not only a critique of society; it is also a study of impurity of motive in a critic of society. If Alceste has a rage for the genuine, and he truly has, it is unfortunately compromised and exploited by his vast, unconscious egotism. He is a jealous friend (*Je veux qu'on me distingue*), and it is Philinte's polite effusiveness toward another which prompts his attack on promiscuous civility. He is a jealous lover, and his "frankness" about Oronte's sonnet owes something to the fact that Oronte is his rival, and that the sonnet is addressed to Célimène. Like many humorless and indignant people, he is hard on everybody but himself, and does not perceive it when he fails his own ideal. In one aspect, Alceste seems a moral giant misplaced in a trivial society, having (in George Eliot's phrase) "a certain spiritual grandeur ill-matched with the meanness of opportunity"; in another aspect, he seems an unconscious fraud who magnifies the petty faults of others in order to dramatize himself in his own eyes.

He is, of course, both at once: but the two impressions predominate by turns. A victim, like all around him, of the moral enervation of the times, he cannot consistently be the Man of Honor—simple, magnanimous, passionate, decisive, true. It is his distinction that he is aware of that ideal, and that he can fitfully embody it; his comic flaw consists in a Quixotic confusion of himself with the ideal, a willingness to distort the world for his own self-deceptive and histrionic purposes. Paradoxically, then, the advocate of true feeling and honest intercourse is the one character most artificial, most out-of-touch, most in danger of that nonentity and solitude which all, in the chattery, hollow world of this play, are fleeing. He must play-act continually in order to believe in his own existence, and he welcomes the fact or show of injustice as a dramatic cue. At the close of the play, when Alceste has refused to appeal his lawsuit and has spurned the hand of Célimène, one cannot escape the suspicion that his indignation is in great part instrumental, a desperate means of counterfeiting an identity.

Martin Turnell (whose book *The Classical Moment* contains a fine analysis of *The Misanthrope*) observes that those speeches of Alceste which ring most false are, as it were, parodies of "Cornelian *tirade*." To duplicate this parody-tragic effect in English it was clearly necessary to keep the play in verse, where it would be possible to control the tone more sharply, and to recall our own tragic tradition. There were other reasons, too, for approximating Molière's form. The constant of rhythm and rhyme was needed, in the translation as in the original, for bridging great gaps between high comedy and farce, lofty diction and ordinary talk, deep character and shallow. Again, while prose might preserve the thematic structure of the play, other "musical" elements would be lost, in particular the frequently intricate arrangements of balancing half-lines, lines, couplets, quatrains, and sestets. There is no question that words, when dancing within such patterns, are not their prosaic selves, but have a wholly different mood and meaning.

Consider, finally, two peculiarities of the dialogue of the play: redundancy and logic. When Molière has a character repeat essentially the same thing in three successive couplets, it will sometimes have a very clear dramatic point; but it will always have the intention of stabilizing the idea against the movement of the verse, and of giving a specifically rhetorical pleasure. In a prose rendering, these latter effects are lost, and the passage tends to seem merely prolix. As for logic, it is a convention of *The Misanthrope* that its main characters can express themselves logically, and in the most complex grammar; Molière's dramatic verse, which is almost wholly free of metaphor, derives much of its richness from argumentative virtuosity. Here is a bit of logic from Arsinoé:

> *Madame, l'Amitié doit sur tout éclater*
> *Aux choses qui le plus nous peuvent importer:*
> *Et comme il n'en est point de plus grande importance*
> *Que celles de l'Honneur et de la Bienséance,*
> *Je viens par un avis qui touche vostre honneur*
> *Témoigner l'amitié que pour vous a mon Coeur.*

In prose it might come out like this: "Madam, friendship should most display itself when truly vital matters are in question: and since there are no things more vital than decency and honor, I have come to prove my heartfelt friendship by giving you some advice which concerns your reputation." Even if that were better rendered, it would still be plain that Molière's logic loses all its baroque exuberance in prose; it sounds lawyerish; without rhyme and verse to phrase and emphasize the steps of its progression, the logic becomes obscure like Congreve's, not crystalline and followable as it was meant to be.

For all these reasons, rhymed verse seemed to me obligatory. The choice did not preclude accuracy, and what follows is, I believe, a line-for-line verse translation quite as faithful as any which have been done in prose. I hasten to say that I am boasting only of patience; a translation may, alas, be faithful on all counts, and still lack quality.

One word about diction. This is a play in which French aristocrats of 1666 converse about their special concerns, and employ the moral and philosophical terms peculiar to their thought. Not all my words, therefore, are strictly modern; I had for example to use "spleen" and "phlegm"; but I think that I have avoided the zounds sort of thing, and that at best the diction mediates between then and now, suggesting no one period. There are occasional vulgarities, but for these there is precedent in the original, Molière's people being aristocrats and therefore not genteel.

If this English version is played or read aloud, the names should be pronounced in a fashion *roughly* French, without nasal and uvular agonies. Damon should be *dah-MOAN*, and for rhythmic convenience Arsinoé should be *ar-SIN-oh-eh*.

My translation was begun in late 1952 in New Mexico, during a fellowship from the Guggenheim Foundation, and finished this year in Rome under grants from the American Academy of Arts & Letters and the Chapelbrook Foundation. To these organizations, and to certain individuals who have befriended the project, I am very grateful.

R. W.
Wellesley, Massachusetts.

CHARACTERS

ALCESTE, in love with Célimène
PHILINTE, Alceste's friend
ORONTE, in love with Célimène
CÉLIMÈNE, Alceste's beloved
ELIANTE, Célimène's cousin
ARSINOÉ, a friend of Célimène's
ACASTE ⎫ marquesses
CLITANDRE ⎭
BASQUE, Célimène's servant
A GUARD of the Marshalsea
DUBOIS, Alceste's valet

PLACE
The scene throughout is in Célimène's house at Paris.

First produced by The Poets' Theatre,
Cambridge, on October 25th, 1955

Act One

SCENE ONE

———•◦•———

Philinte, Alceste

PHILINTE

Now, what's got into you?

ALCESTE, *seated*
      Kindly leave me alone.

PHILINTE

Come, come, what is it? This lugubrious tone . . .

ALCESTE

Leave me, I said; you spoil my solitude.

PHILINTE

Oh, listen to me, now, and don't be rude.

ALCESTE

I choose to be rude, Sir, and to be hard of hearing.

PHILINTE

These ugly moods of yours are not endearing;
Friends though we are, I really must insist . . .

ALCESTE, *abruptly rising*

Friends? Friends, you say? Well, cross me off your list.
I've been your friend till now, as you well know;
But after what I saw a moment ago
I tell you flatly that our ways must part.
I wish no place in a dishonest heart.

PHILINTE

Why, what have I done, Alceste? Is this quite just?

ALCESTE

My God, you ought to die of self-disgust.
I call your conduct inexcusable, Sir,
And every man of honor will concur.
I see you almost hug a man to death,
Exclaim for joy until you're out of breath,
And supplement these loving demonstrations
With endless offers, vows, and protestations;
Then when I ask you "Who was that?", I find
That you can barely bring his name to mind!
Once the man's back is turned, you cease to love him,
And speak with absolute indifference of him!
By God, I say it's base and scandalous
To falsify the heart's affections thus;
If I caught myself behaving in such a way,
I'd hang myself for shame, without delay.

PHILINTE

It hardly seems a hanging matter to me;
I hope that you will take it graciously
If I extend myself a slight reprieve,
And live a little longer, by your leave.

ALCESTE

How dare you joke about a crime so grave?

PHILINTE

What crime? How else are people to behave?

ALCESTE

I'd have them be sincere, and never part
With any word that isn't from the heart.

PHILINTE

When someone greets us with a show of pleasure,
It's but polite to give him equal measure,
Return his love the best that we know how,
And trade him offer for offer, vow for vow.

ALCESTE

No, no, this formula you'd have me follow,
However fashionable, is false and hollow,
And I despise the frenzied operations
Of all these barterers of protestations,
These lavishers of meaningless embraces,
These utterers of obliging commonplaces,
Who court and flatter everyone on earth
And praise the fool no less than the man of worth.
Should you rejoice that someone fondles you,
Offers his love and service, swears to be true,
And fills your ears with praises of your name,
When to the first damned fop he'll say the same?
No, no: no self-respecting heart would dream
Of prizing so promiscuous an esteem;
However high the praise, there's nothing worse
Than sharing honors with the universe.
Esteem is founded on comparison:
To honor all men is to honor none.
Since you embrace this indiscriminate vice,
Your friendship comes at far too cheap a price;
I spurn the easy tribute of a heart
Which will not set the worthy man apart:
I choose, Sir, to be chosen; and in fine,
The friend of mankind is no friend of mine.

PHILINTE

But in polite society, custom decrees
That we show certain outward courtesies. . . .

ALCESTE

Ah, no! we should condemn with all our force
Such false and artificial intercourse.
Let men behave like men; let them display
Their inmost hearts in everything they say;
Let the heart speak, and let our sentiments
Not mask themselves in silly compliments.

PHILINTE

In certain cases it would be uncouth
And most absurd to speak the naked truth;
With all respect for your exalted notions,
It's often best to veil one's true emotions.
Wouldn't the social fabric come undone
If we were wholly frank with everyone?
Suppose you met with someone you couldn't bear;
Would you inform him of it then and there?

ALCESTE

Yes.

PHILINTE

Then you'd tell old Emilie it's pathetic
The way she daubs her features with cosmetic
And plays the gay coquette at sixty-four?

ALCESTE

I would.

PHILINTE

And you'd call Dorilas a bore,
And tell him every ear at court is lame
From hearing him brag about his noble name?

ALCESTE

Precisely.

PHILINTE

Ah, you're joking.

ALCESTE
Au contraire:
In this regard there's none I'd choose to spare.
All are corrupt; there's nothing to be seen
In court or town but aggravates my spleen.
I fall into deep gloom and melancholy

When I survey the scene of human folly,
Finding on every hand base flattery,
Injustice, fraud, self-interest, treachery. . . .
Ah, it's too much; mankind has grown so base,
I mean to break with the whole human race.

PHILINTE
This philosophic rage is a bit extreme;
You've no idea how comical you seem;
Indeed, we're like those brothers in the play
Called *School for Husbands*, one of whom was prey . . .

ALCESTE
Enough, now! None of your stupid similes.

PHILINTE
Then let's have no more tirades, if you please.
The world won't change, whatever you say or do;
And since plain speaking means so much to you,
I'll tell you plainly that by being frank
You've earned the reputation of a crank,
And that you're thought ridiculous when you rage
And rant against the manners of the age.

ALCESTE
So much the better; just what I wish to hear.
No news could be more grateful to my ear.
All men are so detestable in my eyes,
I should be sorry if they thought me wise.

PHILINTE
Your hatred's very sweeping, is it not?

ALCESTE
Quite right: I hate the whole degraded lot.

PHILINTE

Must all poor human creatures be embraced,
Without distinction, by your vast distaste?
Even in these bad times, there are surely a few . . .

ALCESTE

No, I include all men in one dim view:
Some men I hate for being rogues; the others
I hate because they treat the rogues like brothers,
And, lacking a virtuous scorn for what is vile,
Receive the villain with a complaisant smile.
Notice how tolerant people choose to be
Toward that bold rascal who's at law with me.
His social polish can't conceal his nature;
One sees at once that he's a treacherous creature;
No one could possibly be taken in
By those soft speeches and that sugary grin.
The whole world knows the shady means by which
The low-brow's grown so powerful and rich,
And risen to a rank so bright and high
That virtue can but blush, and merit sigh.
Whenever his name comes up in conversation,
None will defend his wretched reputation;
Call him knave, liar, scoundrel, and all the rest,
Each head will nod, and no one will protest.
And yet his smirk is seen in every house,
He's greeted everywhere with smiles and bows,
And when there's any honor that can be got
By pulling strings, he'll get it, like as not.
My God! It chills my heart to see the ways
Men come to terms with evil nowadays;
Sometimes, I swear, I'm moved to flee and find
Some desert land unfouled by humankind.

PHILINTE

Come, let's forget the follies of the times
And pardon mankind for its petty crimes;

Let's have an end of rantings and of railings,
And show some leniency toward human failings.
This world requires a pliant rectitude;
Too stern a virtue makes one stiff and rude;
Good sense views all extremes with detestation,
And bids us to be noble in moderation.
The rigid virtues of the ancient days
Are not for us; they jar with all our ways
And ask of us too lofty a perfection.
Wise men accept their times without objection,
And there's no greater folly, if you ask me,
Than trying to reform society.
Like you, I see each day a hundred and one
Unhandsome deeds that might be better done,
But still, for all the faults that meet my view,
I'm never known to storm and rave like you.
I take men as they are, or let them be,
And teach my soul to bear their frailty;
And whether in court or town, whatever the scene,
My phlegm's as philosophic as your spleen.

ALCESTE

This phlegm which you so eloquently commend,
Does nothing ever rile it up, my friend?
Suppose some man you trust should treacherously
Conspire to rob you of your property,
And do his best to wreck your reputation?
Wouldn't you feel a certain indignation?

PHILINTE

Why, no. These faults of which you so complain
Are part of human nature, I maintain,
And it's no more a matter for disgust
That men are knavish, selfish and unjust,
Than that the vulture dines upon the dead,
And wolves are furious, and apes ill-bred.

ALCESTE

Shall I see myself betrayed, robbed, torn to bits,
And not . . . Oh, let's be still and rest our wits.
Enough of reasoning, now. I've had my fill.

PHILINTE

Indeed, you would do well, Sir, to be still.
Rage less at your opponent, and give some thought
To how you'll win this lawsuit that he's brought.

ALCESTE

I assure you I'll do nothing of the sort.

PHILINTE

Then who will plead your case before the court?

ALCESTE

Reason and right and justice will plead for me.

PHILINTE

Oh, Lord. What judges do you plan to see?

ALCESTE

Why, none. The justice of my cause is clear.

PHILINTE

Of course, man; but there's politics to fear. . . .

ALCESTE

No, I refuse to lift a hand. That's flat.
I'm either right, or wrong.

PHILINTE

      Don't count on that.

ALCESTE

No, I'll do nothing.

PHILINTE
Your enemy's influence
Is great, you know . . .

ALCESTE
That makes no difference.

PHILINTE
It will; you'll see.

ALCESTE
Must honor bow to guile?
If so, I shall be proud to lose the trial.

PHILINTE
Oh, really . . .

ALCESTE
I'll discover by this case
Whether or not men are sufficiently base
And impudent and villainous and perverse
To do me wrong before the universe.

PHILINTE
What a man!

ALCESTE
Oh, I could wish, whatever the cost,
Just for the beauty of it, that my trial were lost.

PHILINTE
If people heard you talking so, Alceste,
They'd split their sides. Your name would be a jest.

ALCESTE
So much the worse for jesters.

PHILINTE
                    May I enquire
Whether this rectitude you so admire,
And these hard virtues you're enamored of
Are qualities of the lady whom you love?
It much surprises me that you, who seem
To view mankind with furious disesteem,
Have yet found something to enchant your eyes
Amidst a species which you so despise.
And what is more amazing, I'm afraid,
Is the most curious choice your heart has made.
The honest Eliante is fond of you,
Arsinoé, the prude, admires you too;
And yet your spirit's been perversely led
To choose the flighty Célimène instead,
Whose brittle malice and coquettish ways
So typify the manners of our days.
How is it that the traits you most abhor
Are bearable in this lady you adore?
Are you so blind with love that you can't find them?
Or do you contrive, in her case, not to mind them?

ALCESTE
My love for that young widow's not the kind
That can't perceive defects; no, I'm not blind.
I see her faults, despite my ardent love,
And all I see I fervently reprove.
And yet I'm weak; for all her falsity,
That woman knows the art of pleasing me,
And though I never cease complaining of her,
I swear I cannot manage not to love her.
Her charm outweighs her faults; I can but aim
To cleanse her spirit in my love's pure flame.

PHILINTE
That's no small task; I wish you all success.
You think then that she loves you?

ALCESTE

Heavens, yes!
I wouldn't love her did she not love me.

PHILINTE

Well, if her taste for you is plain to see,
Why do these rivals cause you such despair?

ALCESTE

True love, Sir, is possessive, and cannot bear
To share with all the world. I'm here today
To tell her she must send that mob away.

PHILINTE

If I were you, and had your choice to make,
Eliante, her cousin, would be the one I'd take;
That honest heart, which cares for you alone,
Would harmonize far better with your own.

ALCESTE

True, true: each day my reason tells me so;
But reason doesn't rule in love, you know.

PHILINTE

I fear some bitter sorrow is in store;
This love . . .

SCENE TWO

———•◦•———

Oronte, Alceste, Philinte

ORONTE, *to Alceste*
The servants told me at the door
That Eliante and Célimène were out,
But when I heard, dear Sir, that you were about,
I came to say, without exaggeration,
That I hold you in the vastest admiration,
And that it's always been my dearest desire
To be the friend of one I so admire.
I hope to see my love of merit requited,
And you and me in friendship's bond united.
I'm sure you won't refuse—if I may be frank—
A friend of my devotedness—and rank.
        (*During this speech of Oronte's, Alceste is abstracted,
        and seems unaware that he is being spoken to. He
        only breaks off his reverie when Oronte says:*)
It was for you, if you please, that my words were intended.

ALCESTE
For me, Sir?

ORONTE
Yes, for you. You're not offended?

ALCESTE
By no means. But this much surprises me. . . .
The honor comes most unexpectedly. . . .

ORONTE
My high regard should not astonish you;
The whole world feels the same. It is your due.

ALCESTE
Sir . . .

ORONTE
Why, in all the State there isn't one
Can match your merits; they shine, Sir, like the sun.

ALCESTE
Sir . . .

ORONTE
You are higher in my estimation
Than all that's most illustrious in the nation.

ALCESTE
Sir . . .

ORONTE
If I lie, may heaven strike me dead!
To show you that I mean what I have said,
Permit me, Sir, to embrace you most sincerely,
And swear that I will prize our friendship dearly.
Give me your hand. And now, Sir, if you choose,
We'll make our vows.

ALCESTE
Sir . . .

ORONTE
What! You refuse?

ALCESTE
Sir, it's a very great honor you extend:
But friendship is a sacred thing, my friend;
It would be profanation to bestow
The name of friend on one you hardly know.
All parts are better played when well-rehearsed;
Let's put off friendship, and get acquainted first.
We may discover it would be unwise
To try to make our natures harmonize.

ORONTE

By heaven! You're sagacious to the core;
This speech has made me admire you even more.
Let time, then, bring us closer day by day;
Meanwhile, I shall be yours in every way.
If, for example, there should be anything
You wish at court, I'll mention it to the King.
I have his ear, of course; it's quite well known
That I am much in favor with the throne.
In short, I am your servant. And now, dear friend,
Since you have such fine judgment, I intend
To please you, if I can, with a small sonnet
I wrote not long ago. Please comment on it,
And tell me whether I ought to publish it.

ALCESTE

You must excuse me, Sir; I'm hardly fit
To judge such matters.

ORONTE
Why not?

ALCESTE
I am, I fear,
Inclined to be unfashionably sincere.

ORONTE

Just what I ask; I'd take no satisfaction
In anything but your sincere reaction.
I beg you not to dream of being kind.

ALCESTE

Since you desire it, Sir, I'll speak my mind.

ORONTE

Sonnet. It's a sonnet. . . . *Hope* . . . The poem's addressed
To a lady who wakened hopes within my breast.

Hope . . . this is not the pompous sort of thing,
Just modest little verses, with a tender ring.

ALCESTE

Well, we shall see.

ORONTE

Hope . . . I'm anxious to hear
Whether the style seems properly smooth and clear,
And whether the choice of words is good or bad.

ALCESTE

We'll see, we'll see.

ORONTE

Perhaps I ought to add
That it took me only a quarter-hour to write it.

ALCESTE

The time's irrelevant, Sir: kindly recite it.

ORONTE, reading
Hope comforts us awhile, t'is true,
Lulling our cares with careless laughter,
And yet such joy is full of rue,
My Phyllis, if nothing follows after.

PHILINTE

I'm charmed by this already; the style's delightful.

ALCESTE, sotto voce, to Philinte
How can you say that? Why, the thing is frightful.

ORONTE
Your fair face smiled on me awhile,
But was it kindness so to enchant me?
'Twould have been fairer not to smile,
If hope was all you meant to grant me.

PHILINTE
What a clever thought! How handsomely you phrase it!

ALCESTE, *sotto voce, to Philinte*
You know the thing is trash. How dare you praise it?

ORONTE
If it's to be my passion's fate
Thus everlastingly to wait,
Then death will come to set me free:
For death is fairer than the fair;
Phyllis, to hope is to despair
When one must hope eternally.

PHILINTE
The close is exquisite—full of feeling and grace.

ALCESTE, *sotto voce, aside*
Oh, blast the close; you'd better close your face
Before you send your lying soul to hell.

PHILINTE
I can't remember a poem I've liked so well.

ALCESTE, *sotto voce, aside*
Good Lord!

ORONTE, *to Philinte*
I fear you're flattering me a bit.

PHILINTE
Oh, no!

ALCESTE, *sotto voce, aside*
What else d'you call it, you hypocrite?

ORONTE, *to Alceste*

But you, Sir, keep your promise now: don't shrink
From telling me sincerely what you think.

ALCESTE

Sir, these are delicate matters; we all desire
To be told that we've the true poetic fire.
But once, to one whose name I shall not mention,
I said, regarding some verse of his invention,
That gentlemen should rigorously control
That itch to write which often afflicts the soul;
That one should curb the heady inclination
To publicize one's little avocation;
And that in showing off one's works of art
One often plays a very clownish part.

ORONTE

Are you suggesting in a devious way
That I ought not . . .

ALCESTE

                        Oh, that I do not say.
Further, I told him that no fault is worse
Than that of writing frigid, lifeless verse,
And that the merest whisper of such a shame
Suffices to destroy a man's good name.

ORONTE

D'you mean to say my sonnet's dull and trite?

ALCESTE

I don't say that. But I went on to cite
Numerous cases of once-respected men
Who came to grief by taking up the pen.

ORONTE

And am I like them? Do I write so poorly?

ALCESTE

I don't say that. But I told this person, "Surely
You're under no necessity to compose;
Why you should wish to publish, heaven knows.
There's no excuse for printing tedious rot
Unless one writes for bread, as you do not.
Resist temptation, then, I beg of you;
Conceal your pastimes from the public view;
And don't give up, on any provocation,
Your present high and courtly reputation,
To purchase at a greedy printer's shop
The name of silly author and scribbling fop."
These were the points I tried to make him see.

ORONTE

I sense that they are also aimed at me;
But now—about my sonnet—I'd like to be told . . .

ALCESTE

Frankly, that sonnet should be pigeonholed.
You've chosen the worst models to imitate.
The style's unnatural. Let me illustrate:

> For example, *Your fair face smiled on me awhile,*
> Followed by, *'Twould have been fairer not to smile!*
> Or this: *such joy is full of rue;*
> Or this: *For death is fairer than the fair;*
> Or, *Phyllis, to hope is to despair*
>   *When one must hope eternally!*

This artificial style, that's all the fashion,
Has neither taste, nor honesty, nor passion;
It's nothing but a sort of wordy play,
And nature never spoke in such a way.
What, in this shallow age, is not debased?
Our fathers, though less refined, had better taste;
I'd barter all that men admire today
For one old love-song I shall try to say:

> *If the King had given me for my own*
> *Paris, his citadel,*
> *And I for that must leave alone*
> *Her whom I love so well,*
> *I'd say then to the Crown,*
> *Take back your glittering town;*
> *My darling is more fair, I swear,*
> *My darling is more fair.*

The rhyme's not rich, the style is rough and old,
But don't you see that it's the purest gold
Beside the tinsel nonsense now preferred,
And that there's passion in its every word?

> *If the King had given me for my own*
> *Paris, his citadel,*
> *And I for that must leave alone*
> *Her whom I love so well,*
> *I'd say then to the Crown,*
> *Take back your glittering town;*
> *My darling is more fair, I swear,*
> *My darling is more fair.*

There speaks a loving heart. (*To Philinte*) You're laughing, eh?
Laugh on, my precious wit. Whatever you say,
I hold that song's worth all the bibelots
That people hail today with ah's and oh's.

ORONTE
And I maintain my sonnet's very good.

ALCESTE
It's not at all surprising that you should.
You have your reasons; permit me to have mine
For thinking that you cannot write a line.

ORONTE
Others have praised my sonnet to the skies.

ALCESTE

I lack their art of telling pleasant lies.

ORONTE

You seem to think you've got no end of wit.

ALCESTE

To praise your verse, I'd need still more of it.

ORONTE

I'm not in need of your approval, Sir.

ALCESTE

That's good; you couldn't have it if you were.

ORONTE

Come now, I'll lend you the subject of my sonnet;
I'd like to see you try to improve upon it.

ALCESTE

I might, by chance, write something just as shoddy;
But then I wouldn't show it to everybody.

ORONTE

You're most opinionated and conceited.

ALCESTE

Go find your flatterers, and be better treated.

ORONTE

Look here, my little fellow, pray watch your tone.

ALCESTE

My great big fellow, you'd better watch your own.

PHILINTE, *stepping between them*

Oh, please, please, gentlemen! This will never do.

ORONTE

The fault is mine, and I leave the field to you.
I am your servant, Sir, in every way.

ALCESTE

And I, Sir, am your most abject valet.

SCENE THREE

Philinte, Alceste

PHILINTE
Well, as you see, sincerity in excess
Can get you into a very pretty mess;
Oronte was hungry for appreciation. . . .

ALCESTE
Don't speak to me.

PHILINTE
What?

ALCESTE
No more conversation.

PHILINTE
Really, now . . .

ALCESTE
Leave me alone.

PHILINTE
If I . . .

ALCESTE
Out of my sight!

PHILINTE
But what . . .

ALCESTE
I won't listen.

PHILINTE
But . . .

ALCESTE
Silence!

PHILINTE
Now, is it polite . . .

Act Two
SCENE ONE

——◆◆——

Alceste, Célimène

ALCESTE

Shall I speak plainly, Madam? I confess
Your conduct gives me infinite distress,
And my resentment's grown too hot to smother.
Soon, I foresee, we'll break with one another.
If I said otherwise, I should deceive you;
Sooner or later, I shall be forced to leave you,
And if I swore that we shall never part,
I should misread the omens of my heart.

CÉLIMÈNE

You kindly saw me home, it would appear,
So as to pour invectives in my ear.

ALCESTE

I've no desire to quarrel. But I deplore
Your inability to shut the door
On all these suitors who beset you so.
There's what annoys me, if you care to know.

CÉLIMÈNE

Is it my fault that all these men pursue me?
Am I to blame if they're attracted to me?
And when they gently beg an audience,
Ought I to take a stick and drive them hence?

ALCESTE

Madam, there's no necessity for a stick;
A less responsive heart would do the trick.
Of your attractiveness I don't complain;
But those your charms attract, you then detain

By a most melting and receptive manner,
And so enlist their hearts beneath your banner.
It's the agreeable hopes which you excite
That keep these lovers round you day and night;
Were they less liberally smiled upon,
That sighing troop would very soon be gone.
But tell me, Madam, why it is that lately
This man Clitandre interests you so greatly?
Because of what high merits do you deem
Him worthy of the honor of your esteem?
Is it that your admiring glances linger
On the splendidly long nail of his little finger?
Or do you share the general deep respect
For the blond wig he chooses to affect?
Are you in love with his embroidered hose?
Do you adore his ribbons and his bows?
Or is it that this paragon bewitches
Your tasteful eye with his vast German breeches?
Perhaps his giggle, or his falsetto voice,
Makes him the latest gallant of your choice?

CÉLIMÈNE

You're much mistaken to resent him so.
Why I put up with him you surely know:
My lawsuit's very shortly to be tried,
And I must have his influence on my side.

ALCESTE

Then lose your lawsuit, Madam, or let it drop;
Don't torture me by humoring such a fop.

CÉLIMÈNE

You're jealous of the whole world, Sir.

ALCESTE

                           That's true,
Since the whole world is well-received by you.

CÉLIMÈNE

That my good nature is so unconfined
Should serve to pacify your jealous mind;
Were I to smile on one, and scorn the rest,
Then you might have some cause to be distressed.

ALCESTE

Well, if I mustn't be jealous, tell me, then,
Just how I'm better treated than other men.

CÉLIMÈNE

You know you have my love. Will that not do?

ALCESTE

What proof have I that what you say is true?

CÉLIMÈNE

I would expect, Sir, that my having said it
Might give the statement a sufficient credit.

ALCESTE

But how can I be sure that you don't tell
The selfsame thing to other men as well?

CÉLIMÈNE

What a gallant speech! How flattering to me!
What a sweet creature you make me out to be!
Well then, to save you from the pangs of doubt,
All that I've said I hereby cancel out;
Now, none but yourself shall make a monkey of you:
Are you content?

ALCESTE

　　　　　　Why, why am I doomed to love you?
I swear that I shall bless the blissful hour
When this poor heart's no longer in your power!
I make no secret of it: I've done my best
To exorcise this passion from my breast;

But thus far all in vain; it will not go;
It's for my sins that I must love you so.

CÉLIMÈNE

Your love for me is matchless, Sir; that's clear.

ALCESTE

Indeed, in all the world it has no peer;
Words can't describe the nature of my passion,
And no man ever loved in such a fashion.

CÉLIMÈNE

Yes, it's a brand-new fashion, I agree:
You show your love by castigating me,
And all your speeches are enraged and rude.
I've never been so furiously wooed.

ALCESTE

Yet you could calm that fury, if you chose.
Come, shall we bring our quarrels to a close?
Let's speak with open hearts, then, and begin . . .

SCENE TWO

Célimène, Alceste, Basque

CÉLIMÈNE

What is it?

BASQUE

Acaste is here.

CÉLIMÈNE

Well, send him in.

SCENE THREE

Célimène, Alceste

ALCESTE

What! Shall we never be alone at all?
You're always ready to receive a call,
And you can't bear, for ten ticks of the clock,
Not to keep open house for all who knock.

CÉLIMÈNE

I couldn't refuse him: he'd be most put out.

ALCESTE

Surely that's not worth worrying about.

CÉLIMÈNE

Acaste would never forgive me if he guessed
That I consider him a dreadful pest.

ALCESTE

If he's a pest, why bother with him then?

CÉLIMÈNE

Heavens! One can't antagonize such men;
Why, they're the chartered gossips of the court,
And have a say in things of every sort.
One must receive them, and be full of charm;
They're no great help, but they can do you harm,
And though your influence be ever so great,
They're hardly the best people to alienate.

ALCESTE

I see, dear lady, that you could make a case
For putting up with the whole human race;
These friendships that you calculate so nicely . . .

SCENE FOUR

Alceste, Célimène, Basque

BASQUE
Madam, Clitandre is here as well.

ALCESTE
Precisely.

CÉLIMÈNE
Where are you going?

ALCESTE
Elsewhere.

CÉLIMÈNE
Stay.

ALCESTE
No, no.

CÉLIMÈNE
Stay, Sir.

ALCESTE
I can't.

CÉLIMÈNE
I wish it.

ALCESTE
No, I must go.
I beg you, Madam, not to press the matter;
You know I have no taste for idle chatter.

CÉLIMÈNE

Stay: I command you.

ALCESTE

No, I cannot stay.

CÉLIMÈNE

Very well; you have my leave to go away.

SCENE FIVE

───── ◆ ─────

Eliante, Philinte, Acaste, Clitandre, Alceste,
Célimène, Basque

ELIANTE, *to Célimène*
The Marquesses have kindly come to call.
Were they announced?

CÉLIMÈNE
Yes. Basque, bring chairs for all.
(*Basque provides the chairs, and exits.*)
(*To Alceste*)
You haven't gone?

ALCESTE
No; and I shan't depart
Till you decide who's foremost in your heart.

CÉLIMÈNE
Oh, hush.

ALCESTE
It's time to choose; take them, or me.

CÉLIMÈNE
You're mad.

ALCESTE
I'm not, as you shall shortly see.

CÉLIMÈNE
Oh?

ALCESTE
You'll decide.

CÉLIMÈNE

You're joking now, dear friend.

ALCESTE

No, no; you'll choose; my patience is at an end.

CLITANDRE

Madam, I come from court, where poor Cléonte
Behaved like a perfect fool, as is his wont.
Has he no friend to counsel him, I wonder,
And teach him less unerringly to blunder?

CÉLIMÈNE

It's true, the man's a most accomplished dunce;
His gauche behavior charms the eye at once;
And every time one sees him, on my word,
His manner's grown a trifle more absurd.

ACASTE

Speaking of dunces, I've just now conversed
With old Damon, who's one of the very worst;
I stood a lifetime in the broiling sun
Before his dreary monologue was done.

CÉLIMÈNE

Oh, he's a wondrous talker, and has the power
To tell you nothing hour after hour:
If, by mistake, he ever came to the point,
The shock would put his jawbone out of joint.

ELIANTE, *to Philinte*

The conversation takes its usual turn,
And all our dear friends' ears will shortly burn.

CLITANDRE

Timante's a character, Madam.

CÉLIMÈNE
                    Isn't he, though?
A man of mystery from top to toe,
Who moves about in a romantic mist
On secret missions which do not exist.
His talk is full of eyebrows and grimaces;
How tired one gets of his momentous faces;
He's always whispering something confidential
Which turns out to be quite inconsequential;
Nothing's too slight for him to mystify;
He even whispers when he says "good-by."

ACASTE
Tell us about Géralde.

CÉLIMÈNE
                    That tiresome ass.
He mixes only with the titled class,
And fawns on dukes and princes, and is bored
With anyone who's not at least a lord.
The man's obsessed with rank, and his discourses
Are all of hounds and carriages and horses;
He uses Christian names with all the great,
And the word Milord, with him, is out of date.

CLITANDRE
He's very taken with Bélise, I hear.

CÉLIMÈNE
She is the dreariest company, poor dear.
Whenever she comes to call, I grope about
To find some topic which will draw her out,
But, owing to her dry and faint replies,
The conversation wilts, and droops, and dies.
In vain one hopes to animate her face
By mentioning the ultimate commonplace;
But sun or shower, even hail or frost
Are matters she can instantly exhaust.

Meanwhile her visit, painful though it is,
Drags on and on through mute eternities,
And though you ask the time, and yawn, and yawn,
She sits there like a stone and won't be gone.

ACASTE

Now for Adraste.

CÉLIMÈNE
                    Oh, that conceited elf
Has a gigantic passion for himself;
He rails against the court, and cannot bear it
That none will recognize his hidden merit;
All honors given to others give offense
To his imaginary excellence.

CLITANDRE

What about young Cléon? His house, they say,
Is full of the best society, night and day.

CÉLIMÈNE

His cook has made him popular, not he:
It's Cléon's table that people come to see.

ELIANTE

He gives a splendid dinner, you must admit.

CÉLIMÈNE

But must he serve himself along with it?
For my taste, he's a most insipid dish
Whose presence sours the wine and spoils the fish.

PHILINTE

Damis, his uncle, is admired no end.
What's your opinion, Madam?

CÉLIMÈNE
                    Why, he's my friend.

PHILINTE

He seems a decent fellow, and rather clever.

CÉLIMÈNE

He works too hard at cleverness, however.
I hate to see him sweat and struggle so
To fill his conversation with bons mots.
Since he's decided to become a wit
His taste's so pure that nothing pleases it;
He scolds at all the latest books and plays,
Thinking that wit must never stoop to praise,
That finding fault's a sign of intellect,
That all appreciation is abject,
And that by damning everything in sight
One shows oneself in a distinguished light.
He's scornful even of our conversations:
Their trivial nature sorely tries his patience;
He folds his arms, and stands above the battle,
And listens sadly to our childish prattle.

ACASTE

Wonderful, Madam! You've hit him off precisely.

CLITANDRE

No one can sketch a character so nicely.

ALCESTE

How bravely, Sirs, you cut and thrust at all
These absent fools, till one by one they fall:
But let one come in sight, and you'll at once
Embrace the man you lately called a dunce,
Telling him in a tone sincere and fervent
How proud you are to be his humble servant.

CLITANDRE

Why pick on us? Madame's been speaking, Sir,
And you should quarrel, if you must, with her.

ALCESTE

No, no, by God, the fault is yours, because
You lead her on with laughter and applause,
And make her think that she's the more delightful
The more her talk is scandalous and spiteful.
Oh, she would stoop to malice far, far less
If no such claque approved her cleverness.
It's flatterers like you whose foolish praise
Nourishes all the vices of these days.

PHILINTE

But why protest when someone ridicules
Those you'd condemn, yourself, as knaves or fools?

CÉLIMÈNE

Why, Sir? Because he loves to make a fuss.
You don't expect him to agree with us,
When there's an opportunity to express
His heaven-sent spirit of contrariness?
What other people think, he can't abide;
Whatever they say, he's on the other side;
He lives in deadly terror of agreeing;
'Twould make him seem an ordinary being.
Indeed, he's so in love with contradiction,
He'll turn against his most profound conviction
And with a furious eloquence deplore it,
If only someone else is speaking for it.

ALCESTE

Go on, dear lady, mock me as you please;
You have your audience in ecstasies.

PHILINTE

But what she says is true: you have a way
Of bridling at whatever people say;
Whether they praise or blame, your angry spirit
Is equally unsatisfied to hear it.

ALCESTE

Men, Sir, are always wrong, and that's the reason
That righteous anger's never out of season;
All that I hear in all their conversation
Is flattering praise or reckless condemnation.

CÉLIMÈNE

But . . .

ALCESTE

No, no, Madam, I am forced to state
That you have pleasures which I deprecate,
And that these others, here, are much to blame
For nourishing the faults which are your shame.

CLITANDRE

I shan't defend myself, Sir; but I vow
I'd thought this lady faultless until now.

ACASTE

I see her charms and graces, which are many;
But as for faults, I've never noticed any.

ALCESTE

I see them, Sir; and rather than ignore them,
I strenuously criticize her for them.
The more one loves, the more one should object
To every blemish, every least defect.
Were I this lady, I would soon get rid
Of lovers who approved of all I did,
And by their slack indulgence and applause
Endorsed my follies and excused my flaws.

CÉLIMÈNE

If all hearts beat according to your measure,
The dawn of love would be the end of pleasure;
And love would find its perfect consummation
In ecstasies of rage and reprobation.

ELIANTE

Love, as a rule, affects men otherwise,
And lovers rarely love to criticize.
They see their lady as a charming blur,
And find all things commendable in her.
If she has any blemish, fault, or shame,
They will redeem it by a pleasing name.
The pale-faced lady's lily-white, perforce;
The swarthy one's a sweet brunette, of course;
The spindly lady has a slender grace;
The fat one has a most majestic pace;
The plain one, with her dress in disarray,
They classify as *beauté négligée*;
The hulking one's a goddess in their eyes,
The dwarf, a concentrate of Paradise;
The haughty lady has a noble mind;
The mean one's witty, and the dull one's kind;
The chatterbox has liveliness and verve,
The mute one has a virtuous reserve.
So lovers manage, in their passion's cause,
To love their ladies even for their flaws.

ALCESTE

But I still say . . .

CÉLIMÈNE

          I think it would be nice
To stroll around the gallery once or twice.
What! You're not going, Sirs?

CLITANDRE AND ACASTE

               No, Madam, no.

ALCESTE

You seem to be in terror lest they go.
Do what you will, Sirs; leave, or linger on,
But I shan't go till after you are gone.

ACASTE

I'm free to linger, unless I should perceive
Madame is tired, and wishes me to leave.

CLITANDRE

And as for me, I needn't go today
Until the hour of the King's *coucher*.

CÉLIMÈNE, *to Alceste*

You're joking, surely?

ALCESTE

Not in the least; we'll see
Whether you'd rather part with them, or me.

SCENE SIX

Alceste, Célimène, Eliante, Acaste, Philinte,
Clitandre, Basque

BASQUE, *to Alceste*
Sir, there's a fellow here who bids me state
That he must see you, and that it can't wait.

ALCESTE
Tell him that I have no such pressing affairs.

BASQUE
It's a long tailcoat that this fellow wears,
With gold all over.

CÉLIMÈNE, *to Alceste*
You'd best go down and see.
Or—have him enter.

SCENE SEVEN

*Alceste, Célimène, Eliante, Acaste, Philinte,
Clitandre, a Guard of the Marshalsea*

ALCESTE, *confronting the guard*
                    Well, what do you want with me?
Come in, Sir.

GUARD
I've a word, Sir, for your ear.

ALCESTE
Speak it aloud, Sir; I shall strive to hear.

GUARD
The Marshals have instructed me to say
You must report to them without delay.

ALCESTE
Who? Me, Sir?

GUARD
                    Yes, Sir; you.

ALCESTE
                    But what do they want?

PHILINTE, *to Alceste*
To scotch your silly quarrel with Oronte.

CÉLIMÈNE, *to Philinte*
What quarrel?

PHILINTE
Oronte and he have fallen out
Over some verse he spoke his mind about;
The Marshals wish to arbitrate the matter.

ALCESTE
Never shall I equivocate or flatter!

PHILINTE
You'd best obey their summons; come, let's go.

ALCESTE
How can they mend our quarrel, I'd like to know?
Am I to make a cowardly retraction,
And praise those jingles to his satisfaction?
I'll not recant; I've judged that sonnet rightly.
It's bad.

PHILINTE
But you might say so more politely. . . .

ALCESTE
I'll not back down; his verses make me sick.

PHILINTE
If only you could be more politic!
But come, let's go.

ALCESTE
I'll go, but I won't unsay
A single word.

PHILINTE
Well, let's be on our way.

ALCESTE
Till I am ordered by my lord the King
To praise that poem, I shall say the thing

Is scandalous, by God, and that the poet
Ought to be hanged for having the nerve to show it.
(*To Clitandre and Acaste, who are laughing*)
By heaven, Sirs, I really didn't know
That I was being humorous.

CÉLIMÈNE
                    Go, Sir, go;
Settle your business.

ALCESTE
                    I shall, and when I'm through,
I shall return to settle things with you.

Act Three

SCENE ONE

Clitandre, Acaste

CLITANDRE

Dear Marquess, how contented you appear;
All things delight you, nothing mars your cheer.
Can you, in perfect honesty, declare
That you've a right to be so debonair?

ACASTE

By Jove, when I survey myself, I find
No cause whatever for distress of mind.
I'm young and rich; I can in modesty
Lay claim to an exalted pedigree;
And owing to my name and my condition
I shall not want for honors and position.
Then as to courage, that most precious trait,
I seem to have it, as was proved of late
Upon the field of honor, where my bearing,
They say, was very cool and rather daring.
I've wit, of course; and taste in such perfection
That I can judge without the least reflection,
And at the theater, which is my delight,
Can make or break a play on opening night,
And lead the crowd in hisses or bravos,
And generally be known as one who knows.
I'm clever, handsome, gracefully polite;
My waist is small, my teeth are strong and white;
As for my dress, the world's astonished eyes
Assure me that I bear away the prize.
I find myself in favor everywhere,
Honored by men, and worshiped by the fair;
And since these things are so, it seems to me
I'm justified in my complacency.

CLITANDRE
Well, if so many ladies hold you dear,
Why do you press a hopeless courtship here?

ACASTE
Hopeless, you say? I'm not the sort of fool
That likes his ladies difficult and cool.
Men who are awkward, shy, and peasantish
May pine for heartless beauties, if they wish,
Grovel before them, bear their cruelties,
Woo them with tears and sighs and bended knees,
And hope by dogged faithfulness to gain
What their poor merits never could obtain.
For men like me, however, it makes no sense
To love on trust, and foot the whole expense.
Whatever any lady's merits be,
I think, thank God, that I'm as choice as she;
That if my heart is kind enough to burn
For her, she owes me something in return;
And that in any proper love affair
The partners must invest an equal share.

CLITANDRE
You think, then, that our hostess favors you?

ACASTE
I've reason to believe that that is true.

CLITANDRE
How did you come to such a mad conclusion?
You're blind, dear fellow. This is sheer delusion.

ACASTE
All right, then: I'm deluded and I'm blind.

CLITANDRE
Whatever put the notion in your mind?

ACASTE

Delusion.

CLITANDRE
What persuades you that you're right?

ACASTE

I'm blind.

CLITANDRE
But have you any proofs to cite?

ACASTE

I tell you I'm deluded.

CLITANDRE
Have you, then,
Received some secret pledge from Célimène?

ACASTE

Oh, no: she scorns me.

CLITANDRE
Tell me the truth, I beg.

ACASTE

She just can't bear me.

CLITANDRE
Ah, don't pull my leg.
Tell me what hope she's given you, I pray.

ACASTE

I'm hopeless, and it's you who win the day.
She hates me thoroughly, and I'm so vexed
I mean to hang myself on Tuesday next.

CLITANDRE

Dear Marquess, let us have an armistice
And make a treaty. What do you say to this?
If ever one of us can plainly prove
That Célimène encourages his love,
The other must abandon hope, and yield,
And leave him in possession of the field.

ACASTE

Now, there's a bargain that appeals to me;
With all my heart, dear Marquess, I agree.
But hush.

SCENE TWO

Célimène, Acaste, Clitandre

CÉLIMÈNE

Still here?

CLITANDRE
T'was love that stayed our feet.

CÉLIMÈNE
I think I heard a carriage in the street.
Whose is it? D'you know?

SCENE THREE

Célimène, Acaste, Clitandre, Basque

BASQUE
Arsinoé is here,
Madame.

CÉLIMÈNE
Arsinoé, you say? Oh, dear.

BASQUE
Eliante is entertaining her below.

CÉLIMÈNE
What brings the creature here, I'd like to know?

ACASTE
They say she's dreadfully prudish, but in fact
I think her piety . . .

CÉLIMÈNE
It's all an act.
At heart she's worldly, and her poor success
In snaring men explains her prudishness.
It breaks her heart to see the beaux and gallants
Engrossed by other women's charms and talents,
And so she's always in a jealous rage
Against the faulty standards of the age.
She lets the world believe that she's a prude
To justify her loveless solitude,
And strives to put a brand of moral shame
On all the graces that she cannot claim.
But still she'd love a lover; and Alceste
Appears to be the one she'd love the best.
His visits here are poison to her pride;
She seems to think I've lured him from her side;

And everywhere, at court or in the town,
The spiteful, envious woman runs me down.
In short, she's just as stupid as can be,
Vicious and arrogant in the last degree,
And . . .

SCENE FOUR

Arsinoé, Célimène, Clitandre, Acaste

CÉLIMÈNE
Ah! What happy chance has brought you here?
I've thought about you ever so much, my dear.

ARSINOÉ
I've come to tell you something you should know.

CÉLIMÈNE
How good of you to think of doing so!
(*Clitandre and Acaste go out, laughing.*)

SCENE FIVE

Arsinoé, Célimène

ARSINOÉ

It's just as well those gentlemen didn't tarry.

CÉLIMÈNE

Shall we sit down?

ARSINOÉ
                    That won't be necessary.
Madam, the flame of friendship ought to burn
Brightest in matters of the most concern,
And as there's nothing which concerns us more
Than honor, I have hastened to your door
To bring you, as your friend, some information
About the status of your reputation.
I visited, last night, some virtuous folk,
And, quite by chance, it was of you they spoke;
There was, I fear, no tendency to praise
Your light behavior and your dashing ways.
The quantity of gentlemen you see
And your by now notorious coquetry
Were both so vehemently criticized
By everyone, that I was much surprised.
Of course, I needn't tell you where I stood;
I came to your defense as best I could,
Assured them you were harmless, and declared
Your soul was absolutely unimpaired.
But there are some things, you must realize,
One can't excuse, however hard one tries,
And I was forced at last into conceding
That your behavior, Madam, is misleading,
That it makes a bad impression, giving rise
To ugly gossip and obscene surmise,
And that if you were more *overtly* good,

You wouldn't be so much misunderstood.
Not that I think you've been unchaste—no! no!
The saints preserve me from a thought so low!
But mere good conscience never did suffice:
One must avoid the outward show of vice.
Madam, you're too intelligent, I'm sure,
To think my motives anything but pure
In offering you this counsel—which I do
Out of a zealous interest in you.

CÉLIMÈNE

Madam, I haven't taken you amiss;
I'm very much obliged to you for this;
And I'll at once discharge the obligation
By telling you about *your* reputation.
You've been so friendly as to let me know
What certain people say of me, and so
I mean to follow your benign example
By offering you a somewhat similar sample.
The other day, I went to an affair
And found some most distinguished people there
Discussing piety, both false and true.
The conversation soon came round to you.
Alas! Your prudery and bustling zeal
Appeared to have a very slight appeal.
Your affectation of a grave demeanor,
Your endless talk of virtue and of honor,
The aptitude of your suspicious mind
For finding sin where there is none to find,
Your towering self-esteem, that pitying face
With which you contemplate the human race,
Your sermonizings and your sharp aspersions
On people's pure and innocent diversions—
All these were mentioned, Madam, and, in fact,
Were roundly and concertedly attacked.
"What good," they said, "are all these outward shows,
When everything belies her pious pose?
She prays incessantly; but then, they say,

She beats her maids and cheats them of their pay;
She shows her zeal in every holy place,
But still she's vain enough to paint her face;
She holds that naked statues are immoral,
But with a naked *man* she'd have no quarrel."
Of course, I said to everybody there
That they were being viciously unfair;
But still they were disposed to criticize you,
And all agreed that someone should advise you
To leave the morals of the world alone,
And worry rather more about your own.
They felt that one's self-knowledge should be great
Before one thinks of setting others straight;
That one should learn the art of living well
Before one threatens other men with hell,
And that the Church is best equipped, no doubt,
To guide our souls and root our vices out.
Madam, you're too intelligent, I'm sure,
To think my motives anything but pure
In offering you this counsel—which I do
Out of a zealous interest in you.

ARSINOÉ

I dared not hope for gratitude, but I
Did not expect so acid a reply;
I judge, since you've been so extremely tart,
That my good counsel pierced you to the heart.

CÉLIMÈNE

Far from it, Madam. Indeed, it seems to me
We ought to trade advice more frequently.
One's vision of oneself is so defective
That it would be an excellent corrective.
If you are willing, Madam, let's arrange
Shortly to have another frank exchange
In which we'll tell each other, *entre nous*,
What you've heard tell of me, and I of you.

ARSINOÉ

Oh, people never censure you, my dear;
It's me they criticize. Or so I hear.

CÉLIMÈNE

Madam, I think we either blame or praise
According to our taste and length of days.
There is a time of life for coquetry,
And there's a season, too, for prudery.
When all one's charms are gone, it is, I'm sure,
Good strategy to be devout and pure:
It makes one seem a little less forsaken.
Some day, perhaps, I'll take the road you've taken:
Time brings all things. But I have time aplenty,
And see no cause to be a prude at twenty.

ARSINOÉ

You give your age in such a gloating tone
That one would think I was an ancient crone;
We're not so far apart, in sober truth,
That you can mock me with a boast of youth!
Madam, you baffle me. I wish I knew
What moves you to provoke me as you do.

CÉLIMÈNE

For my part, Madam, I should like to know
Why you abuse me everywhere you go.
Is it my fault, dear lady, that your hand
Is not, alas, in very great demand?
If men admire me, if they pay me court
And daily make me offers of the sort
You'd dearly love to have them make to you,
How can I help it? What would you have me do?
If what you want is lovers, please feel free
To take as many as you can from me.

ARSINOÉ

Oh, come. D'you think the world is losing sleep
Over that flock of lovers which you keep,
Or that we find it difficult to guess
What price you pay for their devotedness?
Surely you don't expect us to suppose
Mere merit could attract so many beaux?
It's not your virtue that they're dazzled by;
Nor is it virtuous love for which they sigh.
You're fooling no one, Madam; the world's not blind;
There's many a lady heaven has designed
To call men's noblest, tenderest feelings out,
Who has no lovers dogging her about;
From which it's plain that lovers nowadays
Must be acquired in bold and shameless ways,
And only pay one court for such reward
As modesty and virtue can't afford.
Then don't be quite so puffed up, if you please,
About your tawdry little victories;
Try, if you can, to be a shade less vain,
And treat the world with somewhat less disdain.
If one were envious of your amours,
One soon could have a following like yours;
Lovers are no great trouble to collect
If one prefers them to one's self-respect.

CÉLIMÈNE

Collect them then, my dear; I'd love to see
You demonstrate that charming theory;
Who knows, you might . . .

ARSINOÉ

              Now, Madam, that will do;
It's time to end this trying interview.
My coach is late in coming to your door,
Or I'd have taken leave of you before.

CÉLIMÈNE

Oh, please don't feel that you must rush away;
I'd be delighted, Madam, if you'd stay.
However, lest my conversation bore you,
Let me provide some better company for you;
This gentleman, who comes most apropos,
Will please you more than I could do, I know.

SCENE SIX

Alceste, Célimène, Arsinoé

CÉLIMÈNE

Alceste, I have a little note to write
Which simply must go out before tonight;
Please entertain *Madame*; I'm sure that she
Will overlook my incivility.

SCENE SEVEN

Alceste, Arsinoé

ARSINOÉ

Well, Sir, our hostess graciously contrives
For us to chat until my coach arrives;
And I shall be forever in her debt
For granting me this little tête-à-tête.
We women very rightly give our hearts
To men of noble character and parts,
And your especial merits, dear Alceste,
Have roused the deepest sympathy in my breast.
Oh, how I wish they had sufficient sense
At court, to recognize your excellence!
They wrong you greatly, Sir. How it must hurt you
Never to be rewarded for your virtue!

ALCESTE

Why, Madam, what cause have I to feel aggrieved?
What great and brilliant thing have I achieved?
What service have I rendered to the King
That I should look to him for anything?

ARSINOÉ

Not everyone who's honored by the State
Has done great services. A man must wait
Till time and fortune offer him the chance.
Your merit, Sir, is obvious at a glance,
And . . .

ALCESTE

Ah, forget my merit; I'm not neglected.
The court, I think, can hardly be expected
To mine men's souls for merit, and unearth
Our hidden virtues and our secret worth.

ARSINOÉ

Some virtues, though, are far too bright to hide;
Yours are acknowledged, Sir, on every side.
Indeed, I've heard you warmly praised of late
By persons of considerable weight.

ALCESTE

This fawning age has praise for everyone,
And all distinctions, Madam, are undone.
All things have equal honor nowadays,
And no one should be gratified by praise.
To be admired, one only need exist,
And every lackey's on the honors list.

ARSINOÉ

I only wish, Sir, that you had your eye
On some position at court, however high;
You'd only have to hint at such a notion
For me to set the proper wheels in motion;
I've certain friendships I'd be glad to use
To get you any office you might choose.

ALCESTE

Madam, I fear that any such ambition
Is wholly foreign to my disposition.
The soul God gave me isn't of the sort
That prospers in the weather of a court.
It's all too obvious that I don't possess
The virtues necessary for success.
My one great talent is for speaking plain;
I've never learned to flatter or to feign;
And anyone so stupidly sincere
Had best not seek a courtier's career.
Outside the court, I know, one must dispense
With honors, privilege, and influence;
But still one gains the right, foregoing these,
Not to be tortured by the wish to please.

One needn't live in dread of snubs and slights,
Nor praise the verse that every idiot writes,
Nor humor silly Marquesses, nor bestow
Politic sighs on Madam So-and-So.

ARSINOÉ

Forget the court, then; let the matter rest.
But I've another cause to be distressed
About your present situation, Sir.
It's to your love affair that I refer.
She whom you love, and who pretends to love you,
Is, I regret to say, unworthy of you.

ALCESTE

Why, Madam! Can you seriously intend
To make so grave a charge against your friend?

ARSINOÉ

Alas, I must. I've stood aside too long
And let that lady do you grievous wrong;
But now my debt to conscience shall be paid:
I tell you that your love has been betrayed.

ALCESTE

I thank you, Madam; you're extremely kind.
Such words are soothing to a lover's mind.

ARSINOÉ

Yes, though she *is* my friend, I say again
You're very much too good for Célimène.
She's wantonly misled you from the start.

ALCESTE

You may be right; who knows another's heart?
But ask yourself if it's the part of charity
To shake my soul with doubts of her sincerity.

ARSINOÉ

Well, if you'd rather be a dupe than doubt her,
That's your affair. I'll say no more about her.

ALCESTE

Madam, you know that doubt and vague suspicion
Are painful to a man in my position;
It's most unkind to worry me this way
Unless you've some real proof of what you say.

ARSINOÉ

Sir, say no more: all doubt shall be removed,
And all that I've been saying shall be proved.
You've only to escort me home, and there
We'll look into the heart of this affair.
I've ocular evidence which will persuade you
Beyond a doubt, that Célimène's betrayed you.
Then, if you're saddened by that revelation,
Perhaps I can provide some consolation.

Act Four

SCENE ONE

———————•———————

Eliante, Philinte

PHILINTE

Madam, he acted like a stubborn child;
I thought they never would be reconciled;
In vain we reasoned, threatened, and appealed;
He stood his ground and simply would not yield.
The Marshals, I feel sure, have never heard
An argument so splendidly absurd.
"No, gentlemen," said he, "I'll not retract.
His verse is bad: extremely bad, in fact.
Surely it does the man no harm to know it.
Does it disgrace him, not to be a poet?
A gentleman may be respected still,
Whether he writes a sonnet well or ill.
That I dislike his verse should not offend him;
In all that touches honor, I commend him;
He's noble, brave, and virtuous—but I fear
He can't in truth be called a sonneteer.
I'll gladly praise his wardrobe; I'll endorse
His dancing, or the way he sits a horse;
But, gentlemen, I cannot praise his rhyme.
In fact, it ought to be a capital crime
For anyone so sadly unendowed
To write a sonnet, and read the thing aloud."
At length he fell into a gentler mood
And, striking a concessive attitude,
He paid Oronte the following courtesies:
"Sir, I regret that I'm so hard to please,
And I'm profoundly sorry that your lyric
Failed to provoke me to a panegyric."
After these curious words, the two embraced,
And then the hearing was adjourned—in haste.

ELIANTE

His conduct has been very singular lately;
Still, I confess that I respect him greatly.
The honesty in which he takes such pride
Has—to my mind—its noble, heroic side.
In this false age, such candor seems outrageous;
But I could wish that it were more contagious.

PHILINTE

What most intrigues me in our friend Alceste
Is the grand passion that rages in his breast.
The sullen humors he's compounded of
Should not, I think, dispose his heart to love;
But since they do, it puzzles me still more
That he should choose your cousin to adore.

ELIANTE

It does, indeed, belie the theory
That love is born of gentle sympathy,
And that the tender passion must be based
On sweet accords of temper and of taste.

PHILINTE

Does she return his love, do you suppose?

ELIANTE

Ah, that's a difficult question, Sir. Who knows?
How can we judge the truth of her devotion?
Her heart's a stranger to its own emotion.
Sometimes it thinks it loves, when no love's there;
At other times it loves quite unaware.

PHILINTE

I rather think Alceste is in for more
Distress and sorrow than he's bargained for;
Were he of my mind, Madam, his affection
Would turn in quite a different direction,

And we would see him more responsive to
The kind regard which he receives from you.

ELIANTE

Sir, I believe in frankness, and I'm inclined,
In matters of the heart, to speak my mind.
I don't oppose his love for her; indeed,
I hope with all my heart that he'll succeed,
And were it in my power, I'd rejoice
In giving him the lady of his choice.
But if, as happens frequently enough
In love affairs, he meets with a rebuff—
If Célimène should grant some rival's suit—
I'd gladly play the role of substitute;
Nor would his tender speeches please me less
Because they'd once been made without success.

PHILINTE

Well, Madam, as for me, I don't oppose
Your hopes in this affair; and heaven knows
That in my conversations with the man
I plead your cause as often as I can.
But if those two should marry, and so remove
All chance that he will offer you his love,
Then I'll declare my own, and hope to see
Your gracious favor pass from him to me.
In short, should you be cheated of Alceste,
I'd be most happy to be second best.

ELIANTE

Philinte, you're teasing.

PHILINTE

                Ah, Madam, never fear;
No words of mine were ever so sincere,
And I shall live in fretful expectation
Till I can make a fuller declaration.

SCENE TWO

Alceste, Eliante, Philinte

ALCESTE

Avenge me, Madam! I must have satisfaction,
Or this great wrong will drive me to distraction!

ELIANTE

Why, what's the matter? What's upset you so?

ALCESTE

Madam, I've had a mortal, mortal blow.
If Chaos repossessed the universe,
I swear I'd not be shaken any worse.
I'm ruined. . . . I can say no more. . . . My soul . . .

ELIANTE

Do try, Sir, to regain your self-control.

ALCESTE

Just heaven! Why were so much beauty and grace
Bestowed on one so vicious and so base?

ELIANTE

Once more, Sir, tell us. . . .

ALCESTE

My world has gone to wrack;
I'm—I'm betrayed; she's stabbed me in the back:
Yes, Célimène (who would have thought it of her?)
Is false to me, and has another lover.

ELIANTE

Are you quite certain? Can you prove these things?

PHILINTE

Lovers are prey to wild imaginings
And jealous fancies. No doubt there's some mistake. . . .

ALCESTE

Mind your own business, Sir, for heaven's sake.
(*To Eliante*)
Madam, I have the proof that you demand
Here in my pocket, penned by her own hand.
Yes, all the shameful evidence one could want
Lies in this letter written to Oronte—
Oronte! whom I felt sure she couldn't love,
And hardly bothered to be jealous of.

PHILINTE

Still, in a letter, appearances may deceive;
This may not be so bad as you believe.

ALCESTE

Once more I beg you, Sir, to let me be;
Tend to your own affairs; leave mine to me.

ELIANTE

Compose yourself; this anguish that you feel . . .

ALCESTE

Is something, Madam, you alone can heal.
My outraged heart, beside itself with grief,
Appeals to you for comfort and relief.
Avenge me on your cousin, whose unjust
And faithless nature has deceived my trust;
Avenge a crime your pure soul must detest.

ELIANTE

But how, Sir?

ALCESTE

Madam, this heart within my breast

Is yours; pray take it; redeem my heart from her,
And so avenge me on my torturer.
Let her be punished by the fond emotion,
The ardent love, the bottomless devotion,
The faithful worship which this heart of mine
Will offer up to yours as to a shrine.

ELIANTE

You have my sympathy, Sir, in all you suffer;
Nor do I scorn the noble heart you offer;
But I suspect you'll soon be mollified,
And this desire for vengeance will subside.
When some beloved hand has done us wrong
We thirst for retribution—but not for long;
However dark the deed that she's committed,
A lovely culprit's very soon acquitted.
Nothing's so stormy as an injured lover,
And yet no storm so quickly passes over.

ALCESTE

No, Madam, no—this is no lovers' spat;
I'll not forgive her; it's gone too far for that;
My mind's made up; I'll kill myself before
I waste my hopes upon her any more.
Ah, here she is. My wrath intensifies.
I shall confront her with her tricks and lies,
And crush her utterly, and bring you then
A heart no longer slave to Célimène.

SCENE THREE

Célimène, Alceste

ALCESTE, *aside*
Sweet heaven, help me to control my passion.

CÉLIMÈNE
(*Aside*)
    (*To Alceste*)
Oh, Lord. Why stand there staring in that fashion?
And what d'you mean by those dramatic sighs,
And that malignant glitter in your eyes?

ALCESTE
I mean that sins which cause the blood to freeze
Look innocent beside your treacheries;
That nothing Hell's or Heaven's wrath could do
Ever produced so bad a thing as you.

CÉLIMÈNE
Your compliments were always sweet and pretty.

ALCESTE
Madam, it's not the moment to be witty.
No, blush and hang your head; you've ample reason,
Since I've the fullest evidence of your treason.
Ah, this is what my sad heart prophesied;
Now all my anxious fears are verified;
My dark suspicion and my gloomy doubt
Divined the truth, and now the truth is out.
For all your trickery, I was not deceived;
It was my bitter stars that I believed.
But don't imagine that you'll go scot-free;
You shan't misuse me with impunity.
I know that love's irrational and blind;
I know the heart's not subject to the mind,

And can't be reasoned into beating faster;
I know each soul is free to choose its master;
Therefore had you but spoken from the heart,
Rejecting my attentions from the start,
I'd have no grievance, or at any rate
I could complain of nothing but my fate.
Ah, but so falsely to encourage me—
That was a treason and a treachery
For which you cannot suffer too severely,
And you shall pay for that behavior dearly.
Yes, now I have no pity, not a shred;
My temper's out of hand; I've lost my head;
Shocked by the knowledge of your double-dealings,
My reason can't restrain my savage feelings;
A righteous wrath deprives me of my senses,
And I won't answer for the consequences.

CÉLIMÈNE

What does this outburst mean? Will you please explain?
Have you, by any chance, gone quite insane?

ALCESTE

Yes, yes, I went insane the day I fell
A victim to your black and fatal spell,
Thinking to meet with some sincerity
Among the treacherous charms that beckoned me.

CÉLIMÈNE

Pooh. Of what treachery can you complain?

ALCESTE

How sly you are, how cleverly you feign!
But you'll not victimize me any more.
Look: here's a document you've seen before.
This evidence, which I acquired today,
Leaves you, I think, without a thing to say.

CÉLIMÈNE

Is this what sent you into such a fit?

ALCESTE

You should be blushing at the sight of it.

CÉLIMÈNE

Ought I to blush? I truly don't see why.

ALCESTE

Ah, now you're being bold as well as sly;
Since there's no signature, perhaps you'll claim . . .

CÉLIMÈNE

I wrote it, whether or not it bears my name.

ALCESTE

And you can view with equanimity
This proof of your disloyalty to me!

CÉLIMÈNE

Oh, don't be so outrageous and extreme.

ALCESTE

You take this matter lightly, it would seem.
Was it no wrong to me, no shame to you,
That you should send Oronte this billet-doux?

CÉLIMÈNE

Oronte! Who said it was for him?

ALCESTE

                              Why, those
Who brought me this example of your prose.
But what's the difference? If you wrote the letter
To someone else, it pleases me no better.
My grievance and your guilt remain the same.

CÉLIMÈNE

But need you rage, and need I blush for shame,
If this was written to a *woman* friend?

ALCESTE

Ah! Most ingenious. I'm impressed no end;
And after that incredible evasion
Your guilt is clear. I need no more persuasion.
How dare you try so clumsy a deception?
D'you think I'm wholly wanting in perception?
Come, come, let's see how brazenly you'll try
To bolster up so palpable a lie:
Kindly construe this ardent closing section
As nothing more than sisterly affection!
Here, let me read it. Tell me, if you dare to,
That this is for a woman . . .

CÉLIMÈNE

                    I don't care to.
What right have you to badger and berate me,
And so highhandedly interrogate me?

ALCESTE

Now, don't be angry; all I ask of you
Is that you justify a phrase or two . . .

CÉLIMÈNE

No, I shall not. I utterly refuse,
And you may take those phrases as you choose.

ALCESTE

Just show me how this letter could be meant
For a woman's eyes, and I shall be content.

CÉLIMÈNE

No, no, it's for Oronte; you're perfectly right.
I welcome his attentions with delight,
I prize his character and his intellect,

And everything is just as you suspect.
Come, do your worst now; give your rage free rein;
But kindly cease to bicker and complain.

ALCESTE, *aside*

Good God! Could anything be more inhuman?
Was ever a heart so mangled by a woman?
When I complain of how she has betrayed me,
She bridles, and commences to upbraid me!
She tries my tortured patience to the limit;
She won't deny her guilt; she glories in it!
And yet my heart's too faint and cowardly
To break these chains of passion, and be free,
To scorn her as it should, and rise above
This unrewarded, mad, and bitter love.
(*To Célimène*)
Ah, traitress, in how confident a fashion
You take advantage of my helpless passion,
And use my weakness for your faithless charms
To make me once again throw down my arms!
But do at least deny this black transgression;
Take back that mocking and perverse confession;
Defend this letter and your innocence,
And I, poor fool, will aid in your defense.
Pretend, pretend, that you are just and true,
And I shall make myself believe in you.

CÉLIMÈNE

Oh, stop it. Don't be such a jealous dunce,
Or I shall leave off loving you at once.
Just why should I *pretend*? What could impel me
To stoop so low as that? And kindly tell me
Why, if I loved another, I shouldn't merely
Inform you of it, simply and sincerely!
I've told you where you stand, and that admission
Should altogether clear me of suspicion;
After so generous a guarantee,
What right have you to harbor doubts of me?

Since women are (from natural reticence)
Reluctant to declare their sentiments,
And since the honor of our sex requires
That we conceal our amorous desires,
Ought any man for whom such laws are broken
To question what the oracle has spoken?
Should he not rather feel an obligation
To trust that most obliging declaration?
Enough, now. Your suspicions quite disgust me;
Why should I love a man who doesn't trust me?
I cannot understand why I continue,
Fool that I am, to take an interest in you.
I ought to choose a man less prone to doubt,
And give you something to be vexed about.

ALCESTE

Ah, what a poor enchanted fool I am;
These gentle words, no doubt, were all a sham;
But destiny requires me to entrust
My happiness to you, and so I must.
I'll love you to the bitter end, and see
How false and treacherous you dare to be.

CÉLIMÈNE

No, you don't really love me as you ought.

ALCESTE

I love you more than can be said or thought;
Indeed, I wish you were in such distress
That I might show my deep devotedness.
Yes, I could wish that you were wretchedly poor,
Unloved, uncherished, utterly obscure;
That fate had set you down upon the earth
Without possessions, rank, or gentle birth;
Then, by the offer of my heart, I might
Repair the great injustice of your plight;
I'd raise you from the dust, and proudly prove
The purity and vastness of my love.

CÉLIMÈNE

This is a strange benevolence indeed!
God grant that I may never be in need. . . .
Ah, here's Monsieur Dubois, in quaint disguise.

SCENE FOUR

Célimène, Alceste, Dubois

ALCESTE

Well, why this costume? Why those frightened eyes?
What ails you?

DUBOIS

Well, Sir, things are most mysterious.

ALCESTE

What do you mean?

DUBOIS

I fear they're very serious.

ALCESTE

What?

DUBOIS

Shall I speak more loudly?

ALCESTE

Yes; speak out.

DUBOIS

Isn't there someone here, Sir?

ALCESTE

Speak, you lout!
Stop wasting time.

DUBOIS

Sir, we must slip away.

ALCESTE

How's that?

DUBOIS

We must decamp without delay.

ALCESTE

Explain yourself.

DUBOIS

I tell you we must fly.

ALCESTE

What for?

DUBOIS

We mustn't pause to say good-by.

ALCESTE

Now what d'you mean by all of this, you clown?

DUBOIS

I mean, Sir, that we've got to leave this town.

ALCESTE

I'll tear you limb from limb and joint from joint
If you don't come more quickly to the point.

DUBOIS

Well, Sir, today a man in a black suit,
Who wore a black and ugly scowl to boot,
Left us a document scrawled in such a hand
As even Satan couldn't understand.
It bears upon your lawsuit, I don't doubt;
But all hell's devils couldn't make it out.

ALCESTE

Well, well, go on. What then? I fail to see
How this event obliges us to flee.

DUBOIS

Well, Sir: an hour later, hardly more,
A gentleman who's often called before
Came looking for you in an anxious way.
Not finding you, he asked me to convey
(Knowing I could be trusted with the same)
The following message. . . . Now, what *was* his name?

ALCESTE

Forget his name, you idiot. What did he say?

DUBOIS

Well, it was one of your friends, Sir, anyway.
He warned you to begone, and he suggested
That if you stay, you may well be arrested.

ALCESTE

What? Nothing more specific? Think, man, think!

DUBOIS

No, Sir. He had me bring him pen and ink,
And dashed you off a letter which, I'm sure,
Will render things distinctly less obscure.

ALCESTE

Well—let me have it!

CÉLIMÈNE

What *is* this all about?

ALCESTE

God knows; but I have hopes of finding out.
How long am I to wait, you blitherer?

DUBOIS, *after a protracted search for the letter*
I must have left it on your table, Sir.

ALCESTE
I ought to . . .

CÉLIMÈNE
No, no, keep your self-control;
Go find out what's behind his rigmarole.

ALCESTE
It seems that fate, no matter what I do,
Has sworn that I may not converse with you;
But, Madam, pray permit your faithful lover
To try once more before the day is over.

Act Five

SCENE ONE

————— • —————

Alceste, Philinte

ALCESTE

No, it's too much. My mind's made up, I tell you.

PHILINTE

Why should this blow, however hard, compel you . . .

ALCESTE

No, no, don't waste your breath in argument;
Nothing you say will alter my intent;
This age is vile, and I've made up my mind
To have no further commerce with mankind.
Did not truth, honor, decency, and the laws
Oppose my enemy and approve my cause?
My claims were justified in all men's sight;
I put my trust in equity and right;
Yet, to my horror and the world's disgrace,
Justice is mocked, and I have lost my case!
A scoundrel whose dishonesty is notorious
Emerges from another lie victorious!
Honor and right condone his brazen fraud,
While rectitude and decency applaud!
Before his smirking face, the truth stands charmed,
And virtue conquered, and the law disarmed!
His crime is sanctioned by a court decree!
And not content with what he's done to me,
The dog now seeks to ruin me by stating
That I composed a book now circulating,
A book so wholly criminal and vicious
That even to speak its title is seditious!
Meanwhile Oronte, my rival, lends his credit
To the same libelous tale, and helps to spread it!

Oronte! a man of honor and of rank,
With whom I've been entirely fair and frank;
Who sought me out and forced me, willy-nilly,
To judge some verse I found extremely silly;
And who, because I properly refused
To flatter him, or see the truth abused,
Abets my enemy in a rotten slander!
There's the reward of honesty and candor!
The man will hate me to the end of time
For failing to commend his wretched rhyme!
And not this man alone, but all humanity
Do what they do from interest and vanity;
They prate of honor, truth, and righteousness,
But lie, betray, and swindle nonetheless.
Come then: man's villainy is too much to bear;
Let's leave this jungle and this jackal's lair.
Yes! treacherous and savage race of men,
You shall not look upon my face again.

PHILINTE

Oh, don't rush into exile prematurely;
Things aren't as dreadful as you make them, surely.
It's rather obvious, since you're still at large,
That people don't believe your enemy's charge.
Indeed, his tale's so patently untrue
That it may do more harm to him than you.

ALCESTE

Nothing could do that scoundrel any harm:
His frank corruption is his greatest charm,
And, far from hurting him, a further shame
Would only serve to magnify his name.

PHILINTE

In any case, his bald prevarication
Has done no injury to your reputation,
And you may feel secure in that regard.
As for your lawsuit, it should not be hard

To have the case reopened, and contest
This judgment . . .

ALCESTE
                        No, no, let the verdict rest.
Whatever cruel penalty it may bring,
I wouldn't have it changed for anything.
It shows the times' injustice with such clarity
That I shall pass it down to our posterity
As a great proof and signal demonstration
Of the black wickedness of this generation.
It may cost twenty thousand francs; but I
Shall pay their twenty thousand, and gain thereby
The right to storm and rage at human evil,
And send the race of mankind to the devil.

PHILINTE

Listen to me. . . .

ALCESTE
                        Why? What can you possibly say?
Don't argue, Sir; your labor's thrown away.
Do you propose to offer lame excuses
For men's behavior and the times' abuses?

PHILINTE

No, all you say I'll readily concede:
This is a low, dishonest age indeed;
Nothing but trickery prospers nowadays,
And people ought to mend their shabby ways.
Yes, man's a beastly creature; but must we then
Abandon the society of men?
Here in the world, each human frailty
Provides occasion for philosophy,
And that is virtue's noblest exercise;
If honesty shone forth from all men's eyes,
If every heart were frank and kind and just,
What could our virtues do but gather dust

(Since their employment is to help us bear
The villainies of men without despair)?
A heart well-armed with virtue can endure. . . .

ALCESTE

Sir, you're a matchless reasoner, to be sure;
Your words are fine and full of cogency;
But don't waste time and eloquence on me.
My reason bids me go, for my own good.
My tongue won't lie and flatter as it should;
God knows what frankness it might next commit,
And what I'd suffer on account of it.
Pray let me wait for Célimène's return
In peace and quiet. I shall shortly learn,
By her response to what I have in view,
Whether her love for me is feigned or true.

PHILINTE

Till then, let's visit Eliante upstairs.

ALCESTE

No, I am too weighed down with somber cares.
Go to her, do; and leave me with my gloom
Here in the darkened corner of this room.

PHILINTE

Why, that's no sort of company, my friend;
I'll see if Eliante will not descend.

SCENE TWO

Célimène, Oronte, Alceste

ORONTE

Yes, Madam, if you wish me to remain
Your true and ardent lover, you must deign
To give me some more positive assurance.
All this suspense is quite beyond endurance.
If your heart shares the sweet desires of mine,
Show me as much by some convincing sign;
And here's the sign I urgently suggest:
That you no longer tolerate Alceste,
But sacrifice him to my love, and sever
All your relations with the man forever.

CÉLIMÈNE

Why do you suddenly dislike him so?
You praised him to the skies not long ago.

ORONTE

Madam, that's not the point. I'm here to find
Which way your tender feelings are inclined.
Choose, if you please, between Alceste and me,
And I shall stay or go accordingly.

ALCESTE, *emerging from the corner*

Yes, Madam, choose; this gentleman's demand
Is wholly just, and I support his stand.
I too am true and ardent; I too am here
To ask you that you make your feelings clear.
No more delays, now; no equivocation;
The time has come to make your declaration.

ORONTE

Sir, I've no wish in any way to be
An obstacle to your felicity.

ALCESTE

Sir, I've no wish to share her heart with you;
That may sound jealous, but at least it's true.

ORONTE

If, weighing us, she leans in your direction . . .

ALCESTE

If she regards you with the least affection . . .

ORONTE

I swear I'll yield her to you there and then.

ALCESTE

I swear I'll never see her face again.

ORONTE

Now, Madam, tell us what we've come to hear.

ALCESTE

Madam, speak openly and have no fear.

ORONTE

Just say which one is to remain your lover.

ALCESTE

Just name one name, and it will all be over.

ORONTE

What! Is it possible that you're undecided?

ALCESTE

What! Can your feelings possibly be divided?

CÉLIMÈNE

Enough: this inquisition's gone too far:
How utterly unreasonable you are!
Not that I couldn't make the choice with ease;

My heart has no conflicting sympathies;
I know full well which one of you I favor,
And you'd not see me hesitate or waver.
But how can you expect me to reveal
So cruelly and bluntly what I feel?
I think it altogether too unpleasant
To choose between two men when both are present;
One's heart has means more subtle and more kind
Of letting its affections be divined,
Nor need one be uncharitably plain
To let a lover know he loves in vain.

ORONTE
No, no, speak plainly; I for one can stand it.
I beg you to be frank.

ALCESTE
And I demand it.
The simple truth is what I wish to know,
And there's no need for softening the blow.
You've made an art of pleasing everyone,
But now your days of coquetry are done:
You have no choice now, Madam, but to choose,
For I'll know what to think if you refuse;
I'll take your silence for a clear admission
That I'm entitled to my worst suspicion.

ORONTE
I thank you for this ultimatum, Sir,
And I may say I heartily concur.

CÉLIMÈNE
Really, this foolishness is very wearing:
Must you be so unjust and overbearing?
Haven't I told you why I must demur?
Ah, here's Eliante; I'll put the case to her.

SCENE THREE

Eliante, Philinte, Célimène, Oronte, Alceste

CÉLIMÈNE
Cousin, I'm being persecuted here
By these two persons, who, it would appear,
Will not be satisfied till I confess
Which one I love the more, and which the less,
And tell the latter to his face that he
Is henceforth banished from my company.
Tell me, has ever such a thing been done?

ELIANTE
You'd best not turn to me; I'm not the one
To back you in a matter of this kind:
I'm all for those who frankly speak their mind.

ORONTE
Madam, you'll search in vain for a defender.

ALCESTE
You're beaten, Madam, and may as well surrender.

ORONTE
Speak, speak, you must; and end this awful strain.

ALCESTE
Or don't, and your position will be plain.

ORONTE
A single word will close this painful scene.

ALCESTE
But if you're silent, I'll know what you mean.

SCENE FOUR

*Arsinoé, Célimène, Eliante, Alceste, Philinte,
Acaste, Clitandre, Oronte*

ACASTE, *to Célimène*

Madam, with all due deference, we two
Have come to pick a little bone with you.

CLITANDRE, *to Oronte and Alceste*

I'm glad you're present, Sirs; as you'll soon learn,
Our business here is also your concern.

ARSINOÉ, *to Célimène*

Madam, I visit you so soon again
Only because of these two gentlemen,
Who came to me indignant and aggrieved
About a crime too base to be believed.
Knowing your virtue, having such confidence in it,
I couldn't think you guilty for a minute,
In spite of all their telling evidence;
And, rising above our little difference,
I've hastened here in friendship's name to see
You clear yourself of this great calumny.

ACASTE

Yes, Madam, let us see with what composure
You'll manage to respond to this disclosure.
You lately sent Clitandre this tender note.

CLITANDRE

And this one, for Acaste, you also wrote.

ACASTE, *to Oronte and Alceste*

You'll recognize this writing, Sirs, I think;
The lady is so free with pen and ink

That you must know it all too well, I fear.
But listen: this is something you should hear.

"How absurd you are to condemn my lightheartedness in
society, and to accuse me of being happiest in the company
of others. Nothing could be more unjust; and if you do not
come to me instantly and beg pardon for saying such a thing,
I shall never forgive you as long as I live. Our big bumbling
friend the Viscount . . ."

What a shame that he's not here.

"Our big bumbling friend the Viscount, whose name
stands first in your complaint, is hardly a man to my taste;
and ever since the day I watched him spend three-quarters
of an hour spitting into a well, so as to make circles in the
water, I have been unable to think highly of him. As for the
little Marquess . . ."

In all modesty, gentlemen, that is I.

"As for the little Marquess, who sat squeezing my hand
for such a long while yesterday, I find him in all respects the
most trifling creature alive; and the only things of value about
him are his cape and his sword. As for the man with the green
ribbons . . ."

(*To Alceste*)
It's your turn now, Sir.

"As for the man with the green ribbons, he amuses me now
and then with his bluntness and his bearish ill-humor; but
there are many times indeed when I think him the greatest
bore in the world. And as for the sonneteer . . ."

(*To Oronte*)
Here's your helping.

"And as for the sonneteer, who has taken it into his head to be witty, and insists on being an author in the teeth of opinion, I simply cannot be bothered to listen to him, and his prose wearies me quite as much as his poetry. Be assured that I am not always so well-entertained as you suppose; that I long for your company, more than I dare to say, at all these entertainments to which people drag me; and that the presence of those one loves is the true and perfect seasoning to all one's pleasures."

CLITANDRE

And now for me.

"Clitandre, whom you mention, and who so pesters me with his saccharine speeches, is the last man on earth for whom I could feel any affection. He is quite mad to suppose that I love him, and so are you, to doubt that you are loved. Do come to your senses; exchange your suppositions for his; and visit me as often as possible, to help me bear the annoyance of his unwelcome attentions."

It's a sweet character that these letters show,
And what to call it, Madam, you well know.
Enough. We're off to make the world acquainted
With this sublime self-portrait that you've painted.

ACASTE

Madam, I'll make you no farewell oration;
No, you're not worthy of my indignation.
Far choicer hearts than yours, as you'll discover,
Would like this little Marquess for a lover.

SCENE FIVE

———◆•◆———

Célimène, Eliante, Arsinoé, Alceste,
Oronte, Philinte

ORONTE

So! After all those loving letters you wrote,
You turn on me like this, and cut my throat!
And your dissembling, faithless heart, I find,
Has pledged itself by turns to all mankind!
How blind I've been! But now I clearly see;
I thank you, Madam, for enlightening me.
My heart is mine once more, and I'm content;
The loss of it shall be your punishment.
(*To Alceste*)
Sir, she is yours; I'll seek no more to stand
Between your wishes and this lady's hand.

SCENE SIX

Célimène, Éliante, Arsinoé, Alceste, Philinte

ARSINOÉ, _to Célimène_

Madam, I'm forced to speak. I'm far too stirred
To keep my counsel, after what I've heard.
I'm shocked and staggered by your want of morals.
It's not my way to mix in others' quarrels;
But really, when this fine and noble spirit,
This man of honor and surpassing merit,
Laid down the offering of his heart before you,
How _could_ you . . .

ALCESTE

                    Madam, permit me, I implore you,
To represent myself in this debate.
Don't bother, please, to be my advocate.
My heart, in any case, could not afford
To give your services their due reward;
And if I chose, for consolation's sake,
Some other lady, t'would not be you I'd take.

ARSINOÉ

What makes you think you could, Sir? And how dare you
Imply that I've been trying to ensnare you?
If you can for a moment entertain
Such flattering fancies, you're extremely vain.
I'm not so interested as you suppose
In Célimène's discarded gigolos.
Get rid of that absurd illusion, do.
Women like me are not for such as you.
Stay with this creature, to whom you're so attached;
I've never seen two people better matched.

SCENE SEVEN

———— •• ————

Célimène, Eliante, Alceste, Philinte

ALCESTE, *to Célimène*

Well, I've been still throughout this exposé,
Till everyone but me has said his say.
Come, have I shown sufficient self-restraint?
And may I now . . .

CÉLIMÈNE

            Yes, make your just complaint.
Reproach me freely, call me what you will;
You've every right to say I've used you ill.
I've wronged you, I confess it; and in my shame
I'll make no effort to escape the blame.
The anger of those others I could despise;
My guilt toward you I sadly recognize.
Your wrath is wholly justified, I fear;
I know how culpable I must appear,
I know all things bespeak my treachery,
And that, in short, you've grounds for hating me.
Do so; I give you leave.

ALCESTE

           Ah, traitress—how,
How should I cease to love you, even now?
Though mind and will were passionately bent
On hating you, my heart would not consent.
(*To Eliante and Philinte*)
Be witness to my madness, both of you;
See what infatuation drives one to;
But wait; my folly's only just begun,
And I shall prove to you before I'm done
How strange the human heart is, and how far
From rational we sorry creatures are.

(*To Célimène*)
Woman, I'm willing to forget your shame,
And clothe your treacheries in a sweeter name;
I'll call them youthful errors, instead of crimes,
And lay the blame on these corrupting times.
My one condition is that you agree
To share my chosen fate, and fly with me
To that wild, trackless, solitary place
In which I shall forget the human race.
Only by such a course can you atone
For those atrocious letters; by that alone
Can you remove my present horror of you,
And make it possible for me to love you.

CÉLIMÈNE

What! *I* renounce the world at my young age,
And die of boredom in some hermitage?

ALCESTE

Ah, if you really loved me as you ought,
You wouldn't give the world a moment's thought;
Must you have me, and all the world beside?

CÉLIMÈNE

Alas, at twenty one is terrified
Of solitude. I fear I lack the force
And depth of soul to take so stern a course.
But if my hand in marriage will content you,
Why, there's a plan which I might well consent to,
And . . .

ALCESTE

        No, I detest you now. I could excuse
Everything else, but since you thus refuse
To love me wholly, as a wife should do,
And see the world in me, as I in you,
Go! I reject your hand, and disenthrall
My heart from your enchantments, once for all.

SCENE EIGHT

Eliante, Alceste, Philinte

ALCESTE, *to Eliante*
Madam, your virtuous beauty has no peer;
Of all this world, you only are sincere;
I've long esteemed you highly, as you know;
Permit me ever to esteem you so,
And if I do not now request your hand,
Forgive me, Madam, and try to understand.
I feel unworthy of it; I sense that fate
Does not intend me for the married state,
That I should do you wrong by offering you
My shattered heart's unhappy residue,
And that in short . . .

ELIANTE
Your argument's well taken:
Nor need you fear that I shall feel forsaken.
Were I to offer him this hand of mine,
Your friend Philinte, I think, would not decline.

PHILINTE
Ah, Madam, that's my heart's most cherished goal,
For which I'd gladly give my life and soul.

ALCESTE, *to Eliante and Philinte*
May you be true to all you now profess,
And so deserve unending happiness.
Meanwhile, betrayed and wronged in everything,
I'll flee this bitter world where vice is king,
And seek some spot unpeopled and apart
Where I'll be free to have an honest heart.

PHILINTE

Come, Madam, let's do everything we can
To change the mind of this unhappy man.

AMPHITRYON

COMEDY IN THREE ACTS, 1668

For Bill and Sonja

Introduction

———•◆•———

> *I was eleven years old when I read*
> *Molière's* Amphitryon *to myself for the first time;*
> *I laughed so hard that I fell over backward.*
> —VOLTAIRE

Troubled by ill health and by the continuing difficulties of his play *Tartuffe*, a version of which was banned yet again in August, Molière retreated for much of 1667 into a rented house in Auteuil. What came of this retirement was *Amphitryon*, a play very different from his other major comedies. Its characters were not seventeenth-century French people but ancient Greeks and Greek gods with Roman names; its comedy had not the consistent range and tone of, say, *The School for Wives*, but combined the flavors of vaudeville, of fantasy, of high comedy, and even of opera; its medium was not the conventional Alexandrine couplet, but a supple *vers libre* that could modulate easily between the several planes of *Amphitryon*'s comic action and unite them. This novel offering, made all the more exciting by the use of stage machines for "flying" the actors, was first presented at the Palais-Royal in January 1668 and had at once a striking success.

The story of Amphitryon is an ancient one; both of Homer's epics allude to it, and Hesiod recounts it. Essentially, it amounts to this: that the father of the gods (Jupiter, in Molière's play) grows enamored once again of a mortal woman—in this case Alcmena, the wife of the Theban general Amphitryon; that during her husband's absence in the field, Jupiter descends to earth, takes the form of Amphitryon, and is thus received into Alcmena's bed; and that the result of their union is the demigod Hercules. Molière's chief source for *Amphitryon* was a Latin tragicomedy of the second century B.C., the *Amphitruo* of Plautus, and he was influenced as well by Jean Rotrou's prior French adaptation, *Les Sosies* (1636). It is generally agreed that Molière, though borrowing freely, made all borrowings his own, and that he conferred on all his material, old or new, a decisive unity, humanizing the deities of the tale and telling it entirely in the key of comedy.

The plot and subplot of this play tell how two gods, Jupiter and Mercury, usurp the identities of two mortals, Amphitryon and his valet, Sosia. Because that creates a "situation" not only outrageous but (in modern times) incredible, the story belongs to the category of fantastic farce. Nevertheless, this farce has been found, by many readers and scholars, to embody a number of ponderable themes. One such theme, that of entrapment in one's role, is introduced in the prologue by Night's "old-fashioned" insistence on Olympian decorum, and Mercury's praise of Jove's periodic refusal to "let the jeweled bounds of Heaven confine him." The theme of constraint and convention recurs variously throughout the play, and especially in such a character as Sosia's bitter wife, Cleanthis, who, as she twice complains, is the prisoner of her conventional virtue. The title character himself may perhaps be seen as a prisoner of his precious honor.

A second motif, which invites comparisons between *Amphitryon* and Molière's *Don Juan*, is the high-handed amorality of the powerful, and their indifference to truth. Mercury assures Night in the prologue that morals apply only to "those of low degree," and Sosia, in Act Two, Scene One, makes it plain that the great require lies and flattery, and would have all fact and opinion tailored to their advantage. To the overbearing Amphitryon, Sosia says, "I'm the servant and you're the master, Sir; / The truth shall be exactly what you please." Above all, we observe a lordly amorality in Jupiter, who for the sake of a night's pleasure disrupts the happy marriage of Alcmena and Amphitryon. A French critic argues that since we the audience are privy to Jove's imposture from the beginning, we feel superior to the baffled Amphitryon and enjoy a complicity with the god. That may in some measure or at some moments be true, but seigneurial license is not the ideal of the play, and Jupiter's behavior should make us think, in modern terms, of something like Fitzgerald's "vast carelessness" of the rich.

The warping effect of masters on servants is a third theme, and it is introduced at the outset by Mercury, who, despite his divinity, is Jove's overworked and complaining lackey. Like all lackeys, Mercury has surrendered his individuality and exists to execute the will of another; when he boasts, he boasts of his association with the mighty: "I, who in Heaven and on earth am known/As the famed messenger of Jove's high throne." It may be assumed, I think, that in some of Mercury's malicious treatment of Sosia or Amphitryon, he resembles the man who, having been bawled out at the office, comes home and kicks the dog. But of course it is Sosia (the largest part in the play, and the one played by Molière) in whom the psychic cost of servitude is most fully shown. Intelligent but spineless, he clearly sees and says that his existence as "Amphitryon's man" has meant the loss of true personality and a life of servile dissimulation. Not being his own man, Sosia is incapable of a free loyalty or a mature love; his stunted emotional life comprises a solicitude for his physical self, in the form of gluttony, cowardice, and narcissism; he further compensates himself by daydreaming (as when he imagines himself Alcmena's valued courtier) and by the exercise of an insolent wit.

The three pervasive ideas I have mentioned all have to do with role and status, and so does a fourth one—the problem of identity. Identity does indeed become a problem when one is confronted with a living, breathing double, and Amphitryon and Sosia respond to the challenge very differently. Amphitryon sees himself as the world sees him—as an honored military hero and the husband of Alcmena. There is an absolute equation, in his mind, between himself and that image, and anyone else who pretends to it must be an impostor deserving of death. Sosia's response is less simple, because in becoming Amphitryon's mere instrument, and a "performer" in both senses of the word, he has already been estranged from any authentic self. Furthermore, he is more rational than the violent Amphitryon, and so can find himself addressing the question of who he is in a logical, inquiring, and even philosophical way. Despite Sosia's cowardice, his double Mercury cannot quite manage to expropriate his name, and his role as "Amphitryon's man," by brute force alone. In the latter part of Act One, Scene Two, however, the god demonstrates a total knowledge of Sosia's present mission and message, his family history, his unhappy marriage, and his record of petty crimes, leading the surprised Sosia to mutter, "Except by *being* Sosia, how/Could he know so much?" Sosia then studies Mercury's person closely, finding it quite like his own, and discovers by interrogation that Mercury can remember, and claims to have done, a deed that Sosia did "when no one was around." It now seems to Sosia that he has no rational, evidential ground for denying Mercury's claim to his identity. Having made that concession, yet bothered still by the feeling that he "must be someone," Sosia struggles thereafter to maintain that there can be two Sosias in the world. Mercury, meanwhile, treats him as a nonperson who is "on standby," as we say, for an identity which he may have when Mercury is through with it.

One might gather, from what the characters are and say, that in the world of this play, old patterns of being are not viable; that identities are problematical; that the strong are cavalier and unprincipled and their inferiors debased into pawns. In any age, comedy could convert such glum premises into laughter, but they had a special pertinence and bite in Molière's day—a time, in France, of crumbling tradition and of forcefully imposed new order. Nigel Dennis' hilarious novel *Cards of Identity* had a similar pertinence to the painfully transitional state of English society after World War II.

A final concern of *Amphitryon*, and its central one, is love and marriage. Sosia has not the emotional resources for married love, while Cleanthis is starved for tenderness and soured by the want of it; the quarrelsome scenes between this couple (including the one in which Mercury plays Sosia's part) continually counterpoint the amorous dealings of their bet-

ters. Of these betters, the most complex is Jupiter. Though
Mercury says that in his descents to earth, Jupiter "lays his
selfhood by" (*sort tout à fait de lui-même*,) the person we meet
in Act One, Scene Three is quite simply Jupiter in disguise,
pretending to be a Theban general—as Americans abroad
pretend, sometimes, to be French or Italian. What this visitor
seeks is sexual delight, emotional conquest, the opportunity
to playact, and the connoisseur's or tourist's pleasure of sam-
pling human feelings. This last is a chief objective when he
comes onstage in Act Two, Scene Four, uttering the following
aside:

> I'll take this opportunity to appease
> Alcmena, and to banish her vexation,
> And in so doing taste the ecstasies
>   Of happy reconciliation.

Because Jupiter, in posing as a mortal, has taken on no human
limitations, those lines are not an expression of hopeful intent
but a divine fiat; the words of Jove, as he will later say, "are
the decrees of Fate," and in this speech he has ordained what
shall happen in the ensuing scene. Thus, there is no sincerity
or suspense in his suicide threats—how could there be?—but
a great deal of manipulative cruelty, since Alcmena believes
him to be her husband. The purpose of his wholly theatrical
behavior is to enjoy the playing of a scene, and to savor both
"her young tears" and his own mastery.

The one thing in *Amphitryon* that requires a bit of historical explanation is Jupiter's insistent rigmarole about "the
husband" and "the lover." Many of the *précieuses*, or bluestockings, of Molière's day had a proto-feminist disdain for
the slavery of marriage, and for its sensual aspect, and cul-
tivated (instead of marriage, or in addition to it) Platonic
love-relationships of the highest spirituality and refinement.
Molière's *The Learned Ladies* (1672) was to mock this separation of marriage and love, husband and lover, in its portrayal
of Armande. Meanwhile, the first audience of *Amphitryon*
would have been amused to hear a high-minded *précieux* dis-

tinction from one who had just accomplished a sly physical conquest. Does Jupiter suppose that his fancy talk of "husband" and "lover" will appeal to Alcmena? If so, he is, despite his omniscience, very imperceptive as to her character. What such talk clearly does reflect is Jupiter's comically balked desire to appropriate all of Alcmena's love for himself, a thing he can scarcely expect to do while disguised as Amphitryon.

We might almost think, when we first see Amphitryon with Alcmena in Act Two, Scene Two, that Jupiter has preempted his "lover" side and left him nothing but "husband" qualities. He is strangely ready, from the beginning, to encounter some marital dissonance; and, hastening to mistrust his wife's fidelity, he soon arrives at the state of rage (near-tragic in its tone) that he will maintain for the rest of the play. It is a brutal rage based in part on jealousy, and to a greater extent on the loss of his honor. Since the play's action, in which he is a victim throughout, does not show us Amphitryon's more attractive aspects, we must try to remember that he is a handsome young hero, that Alcmena loves him deeply, that he must possess the charm and passion that Jove has imitated in order to deceive her, and that we, in his predicament, might do no better than he. Jules Vuillemin observes that Amphitryon's stature, far nobler than that of the usual figure of comedy, causes his absurd fate to reflect satirically on the general human condition, and on us who witness it. We glimpse in him, perhaps, our derisory relationship to forces greater than ourselves.

Amphitryon's love is possessive, in the sense that Alcmena is essential to his picture of himself. Cleanthis' needy love is also possessive in its hopeless, badgering demand that Sosia do his marital "duty." Jupiter's love—if the word applies to Jupiter at all—is ruthless, exploitative, and (strangely, since he is king of everything) self-aggrandizing. It is Alcmena who, though present in three scenes only and absent from the whole third act, is the standard whereby the play's other lovers are to be measured. She is, quite simply, a perfect wife: beautiful, modest, warm, spirited, sensible, witty, and honest; she conceives of married love as a happy mutual state in which both body and soul are given their due. She says, as Irving Singer puts it, "that she cannot and will not distinguish between lover and husband: her husband is her proper lover, and her lover must provide not only the pleasures of their mutual passion but also the goods of a married life in common." In a play full of users and used, and of manipulative lovers, Alcmena stands for the fact (as Cordelia does in *Lear*) that true and unselfish love can be.

It may seem a gross imbalance of structure that in the play's final scene Alcmena is absent and Amphitryon mute. Yet Alcmena's eloquent absence may serve to underline how little Jupiter's "clearing of her name" could appease her horror at his cold, shallow deception. Amphitryon is speechless because, for all Jove's "sugarcoating" and grand promises, and for all his own concern with prestige and appearances, his chief reaction is that of a violent man who has been stunned by greater power. We may also read into Amphitryon's silence his response, in Act Three, Scene Seven, to Posicles' suggestion that Alcmena may have been quite blamelessly deceived:

> Such errors, in whatever light one views them,
>   Are bound to touch us where we live,
> And though our reason often may excuse them,
>   Our honor and our love will not forgive.

That note of inflexible resentment does not promise a quick and easy mending of Amphitryon's damaged marriage. Nor is the final scene a wholly pleasant one for Jupiter, because his jealousy of Amphitryon is real: he cannot be satisfied with his conquest of Alcmena, since the "tender love" she gave him was given, so she thought, to her husband. There are a number of closing scenes in Molière—those of *Tartuffe* and of *The School for Wives*, for instance—in which the conventional happy ending is both achieved and gently mocked; but the denouement of *Amphitryon*, repeatedly deflated by Sosia, is almost pure mockery.

The reader may wish to pursue the lover/husband notion in René Bray's *La Préciosité et les précieux*, or the dramatic history of the Amphitryon legend in Passage and Mantin-band's *Amphitryon*, or other matters in the fine criticism of Lionel Gossman or J. D. Hubert. But the time has come to remember that this play made Voltaire fall over backward. The themes and behaviors I have been discussing, often in sternly judgmental words such as "amorality" and "spineless," are really there, and yet one could not possibly exaggerate the remoteness of *Amphitryon* from any spirit of preaching or censure. Whatever happens in the piece is framed in a fantasy concerning the incredible intrusions of some gods in whom we do not believe, and who, as the prologue tells, are mere figments of poetic imagination. All of that distances the story from reality, gives it a fairy-tale atmosphere, and ensures that whatever dark things are said or shown will be registered, yet at the same time taken lightly. Beginning with the prologue's midair colloquy, Molière employs all means to envelop the proceedings in lightness and charm, and to that end nothing is more successful than his use of a sparkling and lyrical verse technique.

Vers libre in the French seventeenth century meant a form of poetry in which there was no prescribed rhyme scheme, and the poet could shift at will from one line length to another. This was the form employed by Molière's friend La Fontaine in his *Fables*, and, as Voltaire said, it is not as easy as it sounds. Why? Because it does not work unless there is good expressive reason for each change in line length, and unless the rhyme patterns—like the stanzas of more regular forms—embody the stages of thought. Molière's vers libre in *Amphitryon* is excellent, representing his poetry at its best and most lyric, and the reader will note the numerous ways in which this versatile form enforces one or another tone or comic effect. In many of the speeches of Jupiter and Alc-mena, the baroque opulence of the rhyme combines with an artful redundancy of statement to give an impression of inexhaustible eloquence and gallantry. (The same speeches, in their leisured enlargement of a mood or idea, make one think of arias, though in 1668 the creation of French opera by Lully and Charpentier was still a few years in the future.)

When virtuoso rhyme occurs in the speeches of Sosia, it has a different effect, and becomes the music of quick-witted talk or patter.

There are a variety of line lengths in Molière's text, but verses of twelve or eight syllables are the most common by far; I have tried faithfully to parallel his metrical movement in English measures. In all but one or two lines, I have been able to preserve his rhyme patterns exactly. The intended rhythms of my English lines will best be heard if the reader or actor will honor my occasional stress marks and will treat *Sosia*, *diamond*, and *hellebore* as three-syllable words.

I am indebted to J. D. McClatchy for his suggested textual changes, several of which have been gratefully made. I must also thank, in addition to my wife, William Jay Smith, Sonja Haussmann Smith, and James Merrill for counsel and/or encouragement. Finally, I am obliged to Irving Singer, who kept after me until I undertook this translation.

Richard Wilbur
Cummington, Massachusetts
June 1994

CHARACTERS

MERCURY, messenger of the Gods

NIGHT, a goddess

JUPITER (JOVE), in the guise of Amphitryon

MERCURY, in the guise of Sosia

AMPHITRYON (*am-FIT-ree-un*), general of the Thebans

ALCMENA (*alk-MEE-na*), Amphitryon's wife

CLEANTHIS (*clee-AN-this*), lady's maid to Alcmena,
    and wife of Sosia

ARGATIPHONTIDAS (*ar-gah-tee-FON-tee-das*), NAUCRATES,

POLIDAS, POSICLES: Theban captains

SOSIA (*SO-see-uh*), Amphitryon's manservant

PLACE
The scene: Thebes, in front of Amphitryon's house

Prologue

Mercury, on a cloud*; Night,* in a chariot
drawn through the air by two horses

MERCURY

Whoa, charming Night! I beg you, stop and tarry.
There is a favor I would ask of you.
    I bring you a word or two
    As Jupiter's emissary.

NIGHT

        So it's you, Lord Mercury! Heaven knows,
I scarcely knew you in that languid pose.

MERCURY

Ah me! I was so weary and so lame
From running errands at great Jove's behest,
I sat down on a little cloud to rest
    And wait until you came.

NIGHT

Oh, come now, Mercury. Is it proper for
A god to say that he is tired and sore?

MERCURY

Are we made of iron?

NIGHT

        No; but we must maintain
A tone befitting our divinity.
Some words, if uttered by the gods, profane
    Our lofty rank and high degree,
    And such base language ought to be
Restricted to the human plane.

MERCURY

That's easy enough for you to say;
You have, my sweet, a chariot and a pair
Of splendid steeds to whisk you everywhere
In a most nonchalant and queenly way.
　　　But my life's not like that at all;
And, given my unjust and dismal fate,
　　　I owe the poets endless hate
　　　For their unutterable gall
　　　In having heartlessly decreed,
　　　Ever since Homer sang of Troy,
　　　That each god, for his use and need,
　　　Should have a chariot to enjoy,
　　　While I must go on foot, indeed,
　　　Like some mere village errand boy—
I, who in Heaven and on earth am known
As the famed messenger of Jove's high throne,
　　　And who, without exaggeration,
　　　Considering all the chores I'm given,
　　　Need, more than anyone in Heaven,
　　　To have some decent transportation.

NIGHT

　　　Too bad, but there's no help for it;
　　　The poets treat us as they please.
　　　There's no end to the idiocies
　　　That those fine gentlemen commit.
Still, you are wrong to chide them so severely:
They gave you wingèd heels; that's quite a gift.

MERCURY

　　　Oh, yes: they've made my feet more swift,
　　　But does that make my legs less weary?

NIGHT

　　　Lord Mercury, your point is made.
　　　Now, what's this message that you bear?

MERCURY

It comes from Jove, as you're aware.
He wishes you to cloak him with your shade
While, in a gallant escapade,
He consummates a new affair.
To you, Jove's habits can be nothing new;
You know how often he forsakes the skies;
How much he likes to put on human guise
When there are mortal beauties to pursue,
And how he's full of tricks and lies
That purest maids have yielded to.
Alcmena's bright eyes lately turned his head;
And while, upon the far Boeotian plain,
Amphitryon, her lord, has led
His Thebans in a fierce campaign,
Jove's taken his form and, acting in his stead,
Is eased now of his amorous pain
By the soft pleasures of the lady's bed.
It serves his purpose that the couple were
But lately married; and the youthful heat
Of their amours, their ardor keen and sweet,
Were what inclined the crafty Jupiter
To this particular deceit.
His tactic has succeeded, in this case:
Though, doubtless, such impersonations
Would, with most wives, be vain and out of place;
It isn't always that her husband's face
Will give a woman palpitations.

NIGHT

Jove baffles me, and I have trouble seeing
Why these impostures give him such delight.

MERCURY

He likes to sample every state of being,
And in so doing he's divinely right.
However high the rôle that men assign him,

I'd not think much of him if he
Forever played the awesome deity
And let the jeweled bounds of Heaven confine him.
It is, I think, the height of silly pride
Always to be imprisoned in one's splendor;
Above all, if one would enjoy the tender
Passions, one must set one's rank aside.
Jove is a connoisseur of pleasures, who
Is practiced in descending from on high;
When he would enter into any new
     Delight, he lays his selfhood by,
And Jupiter the god is lost to view.

NIGHT

One might excuse his leaving our high station
To mix with mankind in a lower place,
And sample human passions, however base,
     And share men's foolish agitation,
If only, in his taste for transformation,
He'd join no species save the human race.
     But for great Jupiter to change
     Into a bull, or swan, or snake,
     Is most unsuitable and strange,
And causes tongues to cluck and heads to shake.

MERCURY

     Let critics carp, in their conceit:
     Such metamorphoses are sweet
     In ways they cannot comprehend.
Jove knows what he's about, in all his dealings;
And in their passions and their tender feelings,
Brutes are less brutish than some folk contend.

NIGHT

Let us revert to the current lady-friend.
If Jove's sly trick has proved auspicious,
What does he ask of me? What more can he need?

MERCURY

That you rein in your horses, check their speed,
And thereby satisfy his amorous wishes,
     Stretching a night that's most delicious
     Into a night that's long indeed;
That you allow his fires more time to burn,
And stave the daylight off, lest it awaken
     The man whose place he's taken,
     And hasten his return.

NIGHT

It's not the prettiest of tasks
That Jupiter would have me do!
There's a sweet name for creatures who
Perform the service that he asks!

MERCURY

For a young goddess, you embrace
Old-fashioned notions, it seems to me;
To do such service isn't base
Except in those of low degree.
When one is blessed with high estate and standing,
     All that one does is good as gold,
     And things have different names, depending
     On what position one may hold.

NIGHT

In matters of this dubious kind
You've more experience than I;
I'll trust your counsel, then, and try
To do this thing that Jove's assigned.

MERCURY

Ho! Dearest Madam Night, take care;
Don't overdo it, pray; go easy.
Your reputation everywhere
Is not for being prim and queasy.
In every clime, you've played a shady part

In many a tryst and rendezvous;
As far as morals are concerned, dear heart,
    There's little to choose between us two.

NIGHT

Enough. Let's cease to bicker thus;
Let us maintain our dignities,
And let's not prompt mankind to laugh at us
    By too much frankness, if you please.

MERCURY

Farewell. I must descend now, right away,
And, putting off the form of Mercury,
    So change that I may seem to be
        Amphitryon's valet.

NIGHT

I shall ride on but, as you ask of me,
    I'll often dawdle and delay.

MERCURY

Good day, dear Night.

NIGHT

Good Mercury, good day.

*(Mercury alights from his cloud, and
Night traverses the stage in her chariot.)*

Act One
SCENE ONE

———— •◆• ————

Sosia

SOSIA
Who goes there? At each step, I quake and cower!
    Sirs, I'm a friend to everyone.
    Oh, what a dreadful risk I run,
    Walking abroad at such an hour!
    My master, having won his fight,
    Has charged me with this perilous labor.
If he felt an ounce of charity toward his neighbor,
Would he send me out into so black a night?
To have me herald his return, and say
    The praises of his victory, might
He not have waited for the break of day?
    Behold, poor Sosia, how you are
    Mistreated in your servile state!
    The lot of underlings is far
    More cruel when those we serve are great.
We lesser creatures are designed, they hold,
    To serve their whims until we drop.
By day or night, in wind, hail, heat, or cold,
    They've but to speak, and we must hop.
    With them, long years of servitude
    Will never stand us in good stead.
    Their least caprice, or shift of mood,
    Brings down their wrath upon our head.
    Yet foolishly we cling and cleave
To the empty honor of being at their side,
And strive to feel what other men believe,
That we are privileged and full of pride.
In vain our reason bids us quit our place;
In vain, resentment counsels us the same;
    But when we stand before their face,

They cow us and deflect our aim,
And their least nod, or smile, or show of grace
    Renders us dutiful and tame.
    But now at last, through this dark night,
I see our house, and all my terrors flee.
    I need, for this my embassy,
    Some polished speech I can recite.
I owe Alcmena a tale of martial glory—
Of how our forces thrashed the foe for fair;
    But how can I recount that story
    When, after all, I wasn't there?
No matter; I'll tell of blows and counterblows
    As if I'd witnessed all the fray.
How often battles are described by those
    Who played it safe and stayed away!
    I must rehearse a bit, and groom
    Myself to give this rôle my best.
Let's say that this is the reception room;
    This lantern is Alcmena, to whom
    My eloquence must be addressed.
    (*Sosia places his lantern on the ground, and addresses it.*)
Amphitryon, Madam, my master and your mate,
(Well turned!) whose thoughts are ever of your charms,
    Has chosen me as his delegate
To bring you news of his success in arms,
And say how much he's longed for you of late.
    "Ah, Sosia! My heart's aglow
    With joy to see you back again!"
    I'm the most fortunate of men,
    Madam, if you esteem me so.
(Good answer!) "Tell me how Amphitryon does."
    Madam, he does as brave men do
Whenever there is glory to pursue.
    (Ha! As pretty a speech as ever was!)
"But when will he return, that glorious man,
    And make my happiness entire?"
Madam, he'll come as quickly as he can,
Though far less quickly than he would desire.

(Ha!) "Into what state of mind has the war led him?
How does he speak, or act? I long to know."
Madam, he'd sooner act than speak, and so
    His enemies have cause to dread him.
(Listen to that! Am I not the prince of wits?)
"Have the rebels met the fate they merited?"
They couldn't withstand us, Madam, and as they fled
    We followed, cutting them to bits;
    Their leader, Pterelas, is dead,
And Telebos is taken; it is said
    That everywhere the foe submits.
"My heavens! Who dreamt of a success so great?
Tell me, good Sosia, how the battle went."
Well, Madam, not to brag or overstate,
    I can with certainty relate
    The details of that great event.
    Suppose that Telebos is here,
    Madam—that on this side it lies.
  (*Sosia indicates the locations on his hand, or on the ground.*)
    It is a city which, in size,
    Is big as Thebes, or very near.
        Here's where the river flows.
        This was our camping place,
        While, over there, our foes
        Had occupied that space.
        Up there, upon a height,
        Was their infantry in force;
        Lower, and to the right,
        Was a regiment of horse.
Once we'd addressed our prayers to the gods,
The word came down to engage the enemy.
Our foes, who thought at once to seize the odds,
Sent forth, in three platoons, their cavalry;
But soon we damped their ardor and their zest,
    As I shall now expound.
Here came our vanguard, keen to do their best;
    Here were the royal archers found;
        And here our main force pressed—

(*A noise is heard, from offstage.*)
Forward . . . But wait, that force has had a scare;
   I hear, it seems to me, a noise.

SCENE TWO

Mercury, Sosia

MERCURY, *coming out of Amphitryon's house,*
in the guise of Sosia
Disguised as that damned babbler there,
I'll drive him off ere he destroys
The quiet of this night, and mars the joys
Now savored by our loving pair.

SOSIA, *not seeing Mercury*
No further noises trouble me;
My fears are somewhat pacified.
But, just in case, my colloquy
Had best be finished up inside.

MERCURY, *aside*
Unless you're stronger than Mercury,
Your entry's going to be denied.

SOSIA, *not seeing Mercury*
What a long night! How slow its hours creep!
Given the time I've traveled, trudging on,
My master must have mistaken dusk for dawn,
Or fair-haired Phoebus, having drunk too deep,
    Must lie abed and oversleep.

MERCURY, *aside*
Just listen to that knave defame
A deity! What irreverence!
My arm shall punish him at once,
Leaving him sore in all his frame;
And I'll have sport by stealing from the dunce
Not only his appearance but his name.

SOSIA, *perceiving Mercury from a distance*
Oh, horrors! My anxiety
Was just; my goose is cooked. Look there!
Before my master's house I see
A person whose forbidding air
Is not a pleasant augury.
I think, to cover up my fears,
That I shall sing a bar or two.
(*He sings.*)

MERCURY
Now who, I wonder, is this scoundrel who
Presumes to sing, and to torment my ears?
(*As Mercury speaks, Sosia's voice grows gradually weaker.*)
Perhaps he'd like my fists to work him over?

SOSIA, *aside*
The man, it seems, is not a music lover.

MERCURY
For longer than a week,
I've not had anybody's skull to crack;
My muscles, from disuse, have all grown slack;
I need to break somebody's back,
So as to build up my physique.

SOSIA, *aside*
My gods! What sort of fiend is this?
I feel so terrified that I could die.
But let's not show our cowardice
By trembling; he may be as scared as I.
Such threats may be mere artifice
To hide his inner panic from my eye.
Yes, yes, I mustn't play the frightened mouse.
Though I'm not brave, I can dissimulate.
Come, rise above this timid state:
The man's alone; I'm strong; my master's great,
And here's my master's house.

MERCURY

Who goes there?

SOSIA

I.

MERCURY

Who?

SOSIA

I. (*Aside:*) Bold repartee!

MERCURY

What are you?

SOSIA

I am a man, and so can talk.

MERCURY

Are you master, or servant?

SOSIA

Whichever I choose to be.

MERCURY

Where are you going?

SOSIA

Wherever my feet may walk.

MERCURY

Your tone annoys me.

SOSIA

How that pleases me!

MERCURY

Wretch, I shall make you tell me—and I can,

Despite your insolence and nerve—
Whither you travel tonight, whence you began,
    What you are doing, and whom you serve.

SOSIA

I do both good and ill with verve;
Come here, go there; and am my master's man.

MERCURY

You show some wit, and I can see you're out
To seem a person of superior kind.
To celebrate our meeting, I feel inclined
    To give your head a little clout.

SOSIA

You'd strike me?

MERCURY

    Yes. Here, lest you be in doubt.
    (*Mercury gives Sosia a blow.*)

SOSIA

Ow! That was done in earnest.

MERCURY

        No, in fun,
And in response to all your joking.

SOSIA

My gods, friend! How you batter one!
I'd not said anything provoking.

MERCURY

That blow was the gentlest I can do,
One of my modest little taps.

SOSIA

Had I not more restraint than you,
We'd have an ugly scene, perhaps.

MERCURY

You've not seen anything as yet;
We'll do far better, by and by.
For now, however, let's you and I
Resume our little tête-à-tête.

SOSIA

I quit.

(*Sosia starts to leave.*)

MERCURY, *stopping Sosia*
Just tell me where you're going.

SOSIA

What for?

MERCURY

Come, where are you going? I wish to know.

SOSIA

I'm going to knock upon that door.
What moves you to detain me so?

MERCURY

If you go near that door, you're going to get
A storm of buffets for your impudence.

SOSIA

You mean to keep me, by that threat,
From entering our residence?

MERCURY

"Our residence," eh?

SOSIA

Our residence, yes.

MERCURY

What rot!

You're of that household, so you say.

SOSIA

Of course. It's Amphitryon's household, is it not?

MERCURY

How does that prove your statement, pray?

SOSIA

I'm his man.

MERCURY

You?

SOSIA

I.

MERCURY

His servant?

SOSIA

I am, sincerely.

MERCURY

Amphitryon's servant?

SOSIA

His servant, without a doubt.

MERCURY

And your name's? . . .

SOSIA

Sosia.

MERCURY

How's that?

SOSIA

Sosia.

MERCURY

Now, hear me:
Do you know that this fist is itching to knock you out?

SOSIA

What for? What gives you such a fierce intention?

MERCURY

Tell me, presumptuous rascal, what on earth
Moved you to take the name you mention?

SOSIA

I didn't take it; it's been mine from birth.

MERCURY

What insolence! What brazen falsity!
You dare maintain that Sosia is your name!

SOSIA

Indeed I so maintain, because the same
Was given me by the gods' supreme decree;
It's something I've no power to disclaim;
I can't be someone else than me.

MERCURY

You've earned a thousand cudgel strokes, you whelp,
By all of these effronteries.

SOSIA, *being beaten by Mercury*

Justice, citizens, justice! Save me, please!

MERCURY

So, dog, you whine and cry for help!

SOSIA

Do you expect me not to yelp,
When you deal me a thousand blows like these?

MERCURY

I thrash you thus . . .

SOSIA

It's a tawdry thing to do.
You take advantage of my lack
Of courage, to abuse my smarting back,
And that is most unfair of you.
It's bullying, pure and simple, when
A man takes pleasure in belaboring men
Too craven to retaliate.
To trounce a coward earns one no bravos;
And to prove one's pluck by bashing those
Who have none, is a sorry trait.

MERCURY

Well, are you Sosia still? What do you say?

SOSIA

Your blows have caused no metamorphosis
In me, and the sole effect of all of this
Is that I'm Sosia *frappé*.

MERCURY, *threatening to beat him again*

Such quips will cost you a hundred strokes apiece.

SOSIA

Ah, cease your blows, for the love of heaven.

MERCURY

Then let your insolent prattle cease.

SOSIA

Just as you wish; I'll gladly hold my peace,
For this debate of ours is most uneven.

MERCURY

Are you Sosia still? . . . Speak out, if you wish to live!

SOSIA

I'll be whatever you insist.
Make of me what you will. Your arm and fist
Have gained you that prerogative.

MERCURY

So you thought that you were Sosia, in the past?

SOSIA

Yes, until now the matter seemed quite plain;
But the recent teachings of your cane
Have shown me my mistake at last.

MERCURY

It's I who am Sosia, as all Thebes knows.
Amphitryon's had no other man but me.

SOSIA

You're . . . Sosia?

MERCURY

Yes, I'm Sosia! And he
Who mocks my claim will risk a broken nose.

SOSIA, *aside*

Must I renounce myself, then, and stand by
While this impostor steals my very name?
It's fortunate for him that I

Was born so timid and so tame,
For otherwise, by Jove . . .

MERCURY
                    You're muttering through
Your teeth; is there some meaning in it?

SOSIA
No; but, by all the gods, I beg of you
That I may speak to you for a minute.

MERCURY
Speak, then.

SOSIA
            But promise me, I pray,
That you'll not beat me in reply.
Let's sign a truce.

MERCURY
            Come, say your say.
Your truce I hereby ratify.

SOSIA
Tell me, what put this mad whim into your head?
What use is my name to you, for Heaven's sake?
And, even if you were a demon, how could you make
Me not myself, but someone else instead?

MERCURY, *raising his stick*
So! Once again, you—

SOSIA
            Wait! Take care!
To break our truce would not be fair.

MERCURY

You weasel, you impostor! . . .

SOSIA
As for such
Harsh names, you may apply them
Freely; they don't hurt much,
And I'm not bothered by them.

MERCURY

You say that you're Sosia?

SOSIA
Yes. All this absurd . . .

MERCURY

Watch out: I'll break our truce—take back my word—

SOSIA

No matter. I can't annul myself for you,
Or listen to more fantasy and sham.
How can you be the person that I am?
      Can I cease to be myself? Not true!
Has anyone ever heard of such a thing?
Can one dismiss a sea of evidence?
      Am I dreaming? Am I slumbering?
Have visions addled my intelligence?
      Am I not coolly reasoning,
      And wide awake in every sense?
Was I not ordered by Amphitryon
To come here where his bride, Alcmena, lives,
Convey his love in warm superlatives,
And tell her of the martial deeds he's done?
Did I not walk here from the port, of late?
      Is not a lantern in my hand?
Did I not find you here before our gate?
Was not my manner courteous and bland?

Did you not then exploit my cowardice,
    And bar my entrance to our dwelling?
Have you not thrashed me with such emphasis
    That my back's bruised beyond all telling?
All that I've said is all too true, alas;
    I would to Heaven it were not!
Cease to abuse a poor wretch. Let me pass
To do the humble duties which are my lot.

MERCURY

Halt! If you take one step, it will attract
The lightning of my wrath to strike your spine.
    The tale you've told me is, in fact,
    Save for the blows, entirely mine.
'Twas I who, as Amphitryon's deputy,
Arrived this very minute from the coast;
I who shall greet Alcmena, and shall boast
Of how her brave lord brought us victory,
And slew the leader of the enemy host.
I'm Sosia, I may say with certitude,
    Son of the shepherd Davus, and
Brother of Harpax, dead in a foreign land;
    Husband, moreover, of the prude
    Cleanthis, whose moods I cannot stand;
I have been flogged in Thebes full many a time
    For deeds of which I shall not speak,
And branded on my backside for the crime
    Of getting caught at . . . hide-and-seek.

SOSIA, *sotto voce, aside*

He's right. Except by *being* Sosia, how
Could he know so much? And it's truthful, all of it!
This fellow's words astonish me, and now
I'm starting to believe the man a bit.
What's more, as I look closer now, I see
That he has my bearing, shape, and countenance.
    I'll ask him a question which, perchance,
    May clarify this mystery.

(*Aloud:*)
Out of the booty taken from our foes,
What did Amphitryon choose as his fair share?

MERCURY
Five massive diamonds were what he chose,
Set in a brooch their chief was wont to wear.

SOSIA
Who shall receive this gift so richly wrought?

MERCURY
His wife, to complement her glowing charms.

SOSIA
In what container shall the gift be brought?

MERCURY
A casket, sealed with my master's coat-of-arms.

SOSIA, *aside*
There's not one lie in all of his discourse,
And I feel shaken. He has already made me
Admit that he is Sosia by brute force;
Now reason, too, seems likely to persuade me.
Yet when I pinch myself, or calmly ponder,
    It seems to me that I am I.
Is there not some decisive test, I wonder,
    That I can be enlightened by?
Yes! What I've done when no one was around
Cannot be known, of course, unless by me!
I've thought now of a question which is bound
To stump him altogether. We shall see.
             (*Aloud:*)
During the battle, you hid in the Theban tents.
    What did you do there, while you waited?

MERCURY

From a ham . . .

SOSIA, *aside*

That's it!

MERCURY

                    . . . which I'd appropriated,
I bravely cut two slices, both immense,
      On which I gorged till I was sated.
I washed them down with someone's rare old wine
Which, ere I sipped it, gave my eyes delight,
      And drank a toast to our battle line,
      Wishing them courage in the fight.

SOSIA, *aside*

      This final test appears to settle
      The question quite conclusively;
      The man could not have spied on me,
      Unless he was inside the bottle.
                  (*Aloud:*)
After these proofs you've given, I can't deny
That you are Sosia; to that I'll say amen.
But if you're he, tell me who *I* am, then—
Because I must be someone, mustn't I?

MERCURY

      When I am Sosia no more,
      You may be he; I think that's fair.
But while I'm he, I'll kill you if you dare
      To pose as my competitor.

SOSIA

All this confusion leaves me stupefied;
My reason and my senses are at war.
I've never been so very tired before.
If you'll excuse me, I shall go inside.

MERCURY

Ha! So you wish once more to taste my cane?

SOSIA, *beaten by Mercury*

Oh, no! These heavy blows aren't done in sport;
My back will have to bear a month of pain.
I'll flee this devil, and go back to the port.
Dear gods! My mission was indeed in vain.

MERCURY, *alone*

At last I've driven him off, and made him pay
In drubbings for his many past misdeeds.
But now great Jupiter, who gently leads
The amorous Alcmena, comes this way.

SCENE THREE

Jupiter (under the form of Amphitryon),
Alcmena, Cleanthis, Mercury

JUPITER

Have the torches, dear Alcmena, remain inside;
I prize their light, which lets me see you clear,
Yet they might give away my presence here,
      Which it is best to hide.

My love, long thwarted through the noble cares
To which I have been bound by martial duty,
Has stolen a little time from such affairs
      And given it to your beauty.

This offering to your charms, this theft of time,
Might well seem guilty in the public view,
And the sole witness I desire is you,
      Who think the deed no crime.

ALCMENA

I take the greatest pride, Amphitryon,
In the glory you have gained through your successes;
    The brilliant victory you've won
Has warmed my spirit's innermost recesses;
But when I ponder how this just renown
    Keeps me from him I chose to marry,
My love for you can make me so contrary
    That I view your honors with a frown,
And quarrel with that edict of the crown
Which made you general of our military.
After a victory, it is sweet to find
That one we love has scaled the heights of glory;
But with such fame, such perils are combined
That soon we dread to hear a sadder story.
How many fears one's soul must undergo

When news of any fray or clash is told!
Nor can one think, when chilled and harrowed so,
    Of any way to be consoled
      For the horror of the threatened blow.
Whatever wreath the hero's brow may wear,
Whatever share one has in that high honor,
Is it worth the pains a loving wife must bear
When fears for him at all times weigh upon her?

JUPITER

There's nothing in you that I don't adore;
To deepest love your least look testifies;
And, I must own, it makes my spirit soar
To see such ardor in my dear one's eyes.
But in the affection I receive from you
There's one small thing that troubles me a bit;
It would be even sweeter if I knew
That duty did not enter into it;
That the soft looks and favors that you show me
Stemmed from your passion and my self alone,
And were not tributes to a husband, shown
    Because they're something that you owe me.

ALCMENA

It's because you are my spouse that my devotion
    Has any right to be expressed;
I don't quite understand this sudden notion
    That's making trouble in your breast.

JUPITER

The love I feel for you—the tenderness—
    No husband could be capable of;
And in our rapturous moments you cannot guess
    The delicacy of my love.
You can't know how a sensitive heart like mine
Dwells upon trifles with devout excess,
    And studies ever to refine
    The manner of its happiness.

    Alcmena dearest, in me you see
A husband, and a lover; and the latter's
The only one, I think, who really matters.
The husband merely cramps and hinders me.
The lover, fiercely jealous of your heart,
Would be the only one for whom you care,
    And will not settle for some part
    Of what the husband deigns to share.
He would obtain your love at its pure source,
And not by way of nuptial bonds and rights,
Or duty, which compels the heart by force
And so corrupts all loving intercourse
    And spoils all amorous delights.
In this small matter which perturbs him so,
He asks that, in your thinking, you divide
Him from that other self he can't abide;
That the husband be for virtue and for show
Alone; and that your gracious heart bestow
All love, all passion, on the lover's side.

ALCMENA
    Really, Amphitryon,
You must be jesting in this speech you've made;
If anyone overheard you, I'm afraid
    He'd think your wits were gone.

JUPITER
    There's much more sense in what I say
    Than you suppose, Alcmena dear.
But I must not prolong my secret stay,
And my departure for the port draws near.
Farewell. Harsh duty says our tryst is over,
    And tears me from you for a space.
Fair one, when next you see your husband's face,
    Think too, I pray you, of the lover.

ALCMENA

What the gods have joined, I shall not separate;
For husband and lover both, my love is great.

CLEANTHIS, *aside*

Oh, my! How sweet is the caress
Of a spouse on whom one's heart can dote!
And my wretched husband—how remote
He is from all such tenderness!

MERCURY, *aside*

I shall go tell the goddess Night
That it's time she furled her shades and fled;
The sun must rise now from his bed,
And sweep the litter of the stars from sight.

SCENE FOUR

Cleanthis, Mercury

CLEANTHIS, *halting Mercury, who was departing*
How can you leave me in that way?

MERCURY
What ails you, woman? I propose
    To do my duty as valet,
And follow where my lord Amphitryon goes.

CLEANTHIS
But must you part from me, you lout,
    In a manner so abrupt and rough?

MERCURY
That's a strange thing to complain about.
God knows we'll be together long enough!

CLEANTHIS
So! You take leave of me in brutal style,
Without one loving word or tender smile!

MERCURY
How in the devil should I still know
    What pretty words to please you by?
In fifteen years of marriage, talk runs dry.
We've said our say to each other, long ago.

CLEANTHIS
Look at Amphitryon, you beast;
See how his ardor for his wife is shown;
And blush then, since you fail to make the least
    Display of feeling toward your own.

MERCURY

Heavens, Cleanthis, they're at the amorous age;
    After a time, all that will pass;
What now becomes them, at this early stage,
Would, in old married folk like us, seem crass;
How would it be to see us two engage
    In sugary talk, like lad and lass?

CLEANTHIS

Wretch! Do you mean that I'm no longer fair,
    And could not hope to inspire a sigh?

MERCURY

    Oh no, I'd not say that, not I;
But I'm too old for sighing—I wouldn't dare,
    And I'd be laughed at should I try.

CLEANTHIS

Do you deserve—you, with your squalid life—
To have a virtuous woman as your wife?

MERCURY

    Great gods! You're virtuous to excess,
    And your goodness does me little good.
    Stop playing Spotless Womanhood
    And badger me a little less.

CLEANTHIS

You talk as if my virtue were a sin!

MERCURY

Sweetness is woman's most endearing trait;
    Your virtue makes a ceaseless din,
    And keeps me in a frazzled state.

CLEANTHIS

Would you prefer the feigning tenderness
Of the sort of wife who, full of pretty talents,

Smothers her spouse with kiss and warm caress,
To make him overlook her many gallants?

CENTER
MERCURY

Do you want a frank reply from me?
What's cuckoldry? Only fools are troubled by it.
From now on, let my motto be
"Less honor, and more peace and quiet."

CENTER
CLEANTHIS

Do you mean to say that you simply wouldn't care
If I and some gallant had a love affair?

CENTER
MERCURY

Not if it cured you of the need to scold,
And caused your shrewish temper to desert you.
An easygoing vice, I hold,
Is better than an angry virtue.
Farewell, Cleanthis, my duck, my lamb.
I must attend Amphitryon.

CENTER
CLEANTHIS, *alone*

If in my heart there were one dram
Of courage, I'd make him pay for all he's done.
Oh, but I feel a simpleton
To be the honest wife I am!

Act Two

SCENE ONE

———— • • ————

Amphitryon, Sosia

AMPHITRYON

Come here, you knave. Come here, you parasite.
Your words would justify my thrashing you,
And, if I had a stick, I soon would do
    What all these saucy lies invite.

SOSIA

    Sir, if you see things in that light,
    I've nothing more to say; I'm through;
    And you shall be always in the right.

AMPHITRYON

Wretch, would you have me trust in tales that were
Clearly no more than foolish fantasies?

SOSIA

No. I'm the servant and you're the master, Sir;
The truth shall be exactly what you please.

AMPHITRYON

Well, I'll put down my anger. I wish to hear
About your mission, and all its incidents.
    Before I see my wife, a clear
Picture is needed of these late events.
Collect your wits, then; make your thoughts cohere,
And answer me with point and pertinence.

SOSIA

    But, lest I somehow miss my cue,
    Tell me, I pray, before we start,
In what way you would have me answer you.

Shall I speak, Sir, from my conscience and my heart,
Or as the hangers-on of great folk do?
    Shall what I say be simply true,
    Or shall I speak with flattering art?

AMPHITRYON

    No, it's your only obligation
To give an account that's truthful and sincere.

SOSIA

    Good. I'll comply, Sir, never fear.
    Proceed with your interrogation.

AMPHITRYON

When I gave you a certain order yesterday? . . .

SOSIA

I set out under skies both black and bleak,
Cursing you as I made my painful way,
And railing at the order of which you speak.

AMPHITRYON

What, rascal!

SOSIA

    Sir, if it's not the truth you seek,
Just bid me lie, and I'll obey.

AMPHITRYON

Behold with what goodwill our lackeys serve us!
No matter. And on the journey, what occurred?

SOSIA

    I was made gibberingly nervous
By the least thing that peeped or stirred.

AMPHITRYON

You coward!

SOSIA
Nature, in forming us, contrives
To give us temperaments which greatly vary;
Some revel in finding ways to risk their lives:
    I, in avoiding all that's scary.

AMPHITRYON
When you reached the house? . . .

SOSIA
    I thought that for a while
I might rehearse my lines, outside the door,
    Deciding in what tone and style
To speak my glorious tidings of the war.

AMPHITRYON
And then?

SOSIA
    Then someone came and cut me short.

AMPHITRYON
Who?

SOSIA
    Sosia; another me; a man who was
Dispatched by you to Alcmena from the port,
And who knows our secrets, of whatever sort,
    As well as the me now speaking does.

AMPHITRYON
What rubbish!

SOSIA
    Those are the facts, Sir, of the case.
That me was at the house ahead of me;
    For I had got there, don't you see,
    Before I ever reached the place.

AMPHITRYON

Pray, where in the devil did you find
Such nonsense? Have you lost your mind?
To what else could this be assigned—
To drink, or dreams, or both combined?
Or humor of a sickly kind?

SOSIA

No, Sir, it's simply what occurred;
    There's nothing frivolous about it.
I'm a man of honor, and you have my word;
    I tell you, though you're free to doubt it,
That, thinking myself one Sosia, I drew near
    Our gate, and found that I was two;
That, of the rival me's who parleyed here,
One's now in the house, while the other talks with you;
That the me you see, road-weary and half dead,
Found the other chipper, fresh, and wide awake,
    Without a worry in his head
    Save how to find some bones to break.

AMPHITRYON

My nature must be, I surmise,
Patient, and calm, and gentle to the core,
If I let a lackey feed me all these lies!

SOSIA

Careful; don't lose your temper, or
I shall not tell you any more.
We so agreed, you realize.

AMPHITRYON

Well, I'll restrain myself and hear you out,
As promised. But tell me honestly, if you would:
Does this weird mystery you've told about
    Have the least shadow of likelihood?

SOSIA

No, you're quite right. What I've described must seem
    Beyond belief, I must confess.
    What it all means, one cannot guess.
It's a stupid tale, ridiculous and extreme,
    Which shocks one's reason like a dream;
    But it's a fact, Sir, nonetheless.

AMPHITRYON

What must one do to believe it—go insane?

SOSIA

I too was doubtful, and inclined to take
My doubleness as a sign of mental strain;
I thought my other self a fraud, a fake;
But at last he made me see that I was twain;
I saw that he was I, and no mistake;
From head to foot he's like me—handsome, clever,
Well-made, with charms no lady could withstand;
    In short, two drops of milk were never
    So much alike as we are, and,
But for a certain heaviness in his hand,
    I'd see no difference whatever.

AMPHITRYON

Oh, this takes patience and self-discipline!
But tell me, now; did you not go inside?

SOSIA

    Ha! Go inside, despite my twin?
Am I so reckless? Am I a suicide?
Did I not bar myself from going in?

AMPHITRYON

    How?

SOSIA

With a stick, which thumped my hide
So fiercely, that my back still hurts like sin.

AMPHITRYON

You were beaten?

SOSIA

Indeed.

AMPHITRYON

By whom?

SOSIA

By me.

AMPHITRYON

By you?

SOSIA

Yes; not the me you're talking to,
But the one inside, who wields a wicked paddle.

AMPHITRYON

May Heaven confound you for this fiddle-faddle!

SOSIA

My words were serious and correct.
The me whom I have met of late
Excels the me you see, in one respect;
His arm is strong, his courage great;
Of these I've felt the full effect;
The me to whom I owe my battered state
Is a fiend whose furies are unchecked.

AMPHITRYON

Well, on with it. You've seen my wife?

SOSIA

No.

AMPHITRYON

Why?

SOSIA

For reasons that I've given before.

AMPHITRYON

Explain, you scoundrel. What were you hindered by?

SOSIA

Must I say the same thing twenty times and more?
It was that me who's more robust than I;
That me who wouldn't let me in the door;
     That me who fed me humble pie;
     Who wants to be the only me,
     And looks on me with jealous eye;
     That me whose rage could terrify
     My craven self, and make me flee;
     That me who's in our house nearby;
     That me who smote me hip and thigh
     Till I confessed his mastery.

AMPHITRYON

He drank too much last night, I judge, and must
     Be still quite muddled in the head.

SOSIA

If I drank a thing but water, strike me dead!
     I give my oath, which you should trust.

AMPHITRYON

It must be, then, that sleep benumbed your sense,
And that a dream, all full of strange confusions,
     Caused you to have these wild delusions
     Which you describe as real events.

SOSIA

That's not true either. I didn't sleep last night,
    Which I still don't feel inclined to do.
    I'm wide awake as I talk to you;
This morning I was wide awake, all right,
And the other Sosia was conscious, too,
    As he battered me with all his might.

AMPHITRYON

    Follow me, now, and do be still.
    My mind's been wearied quite enough.
I am an ass to let a servant fill
My patient ear with all this foolish stuff.

SOSIA, *aside*

    All speech is foolish if it's framed
    By someone of obscure estate:
    But the same words, uttered by the great,
    Would be applauded and acclaimed.

AMPHITRYON

    Let's enter, without more delays.
But look, my fair Alcmena is coming out;
She doesn't expect me yet, and so, no doubt,
    She'll be surprised to see my face.

SCENE TWO

———— • • ————

*Alcmena, Amphitryon,
Cleanthis, Sosia*

ALCMENA, *not seeing Amphitryon*
Cleanthis, let us approach the gods, and do
    Them homage in my husband's name,
Thanking them for the victory which through
His valorous deeds, the Theban state can claim.
                    (*Seeing Amphitryon:*)
Oh!

AMPHITRYON
    May victorious Amphitryon
Be welcomed by his loving wife anew!
May Heaven, which restores you to my view,
Restore as well the peerless heart I won,
        And may that heart look fondly on
        Your spouse, as he now looks on you!

ALCMENA
What! Back so soon?

AMPHITRYON
                    Those words, I'm forced to say,
Don't welcome me in very ardent fashion.
    On such occasions as today,
To say "What! Back so soon?" is not the way
    To manifest a burning passion.
    I dared suppose that in this case
You'd feared for me, and missed me; was I wrong?
Yearning for someone, when desire is strong,
Makes every moment move at sluggish pace,
    And the absence of a cherished face,
However brief, is always far too long.

ALCMENA

I don't see . . .

AMPHITRYON

No, Alcmena; when thoughts are on
An absent love, the minutes seem to crawl;
But you've reckoned the time that I've been gone
Like one who doesn't love at all.
When we are truly amorous,
The briefest parting is an agony,
And the one whom we delight to see
Cannot come back too soon for us.
My fervent feelings, I confess,
Were disappointed by your words of greeting;
I thought your heart, at such a meeting,
Would melt, instead, with joy and tenderness.

ALCMENA

I can't imagine what could be
The basis of that speech just uttered by you;
And if you have complaints of me
I don't know, in all honesty,
What I could do to satisfy you.
Last night, when you so happily returned,
I was, I think, most joyous and most tender,
Answering the love with which you burned
With all the love a woman's heart could render.

AMPHITRYON

What? What?

ALCMENA

Did I not plainly manifest
My rapturous delight? Did I not clearly
Convey to you how glad I felt, how blest,
To see once more a spouse I loved so dearly?

AMPHITRYON

What are you saying?

ALCMENA

               That you showed no lack
Of joy, yourself, when I thus rhapsodized;
And that, since you departed at the crack
Of dawn, and then so suddenly came back,
    I had some right to be surprised.

AMPHITRYON

Perhaps, Alcmena, you anticipated,
Last night, in visions of your sleeping mind,
    The glad return I contemplated,
And having, in this dream your mind created,
      Repaid my eager love in kind,
      Feel that your heart is vindicated?

ALCMENA

Perhaps, Amphitryon, you are aberrated,
    And vapors so becloud your mind
That memories of last night are dissipated,
And you can question all that I have stated,
      And my true love, by your unkind
      Mistrust, be slandered and negated?

AMPHITRYON

    Those vapors that you've given me seem,
    To say the least, a little strange.

ALCMENA

    I think that they're a fair exchange
    For that imaginary dream.

AMPHITRYON

Unless you had a dream, there is no way
The things you've said to me can be excused.

ALCMENA

Unless those vapors make your head confused,
One cannot justify the things you say.

AMPHITRYON

Enough of vapors, Alcmena; you've had your sport.

ALCMENA

Enough too of that dream, Amphitryon.

AMPHITRYON

A joke can soon be overdone,
When it concerns a matter of this sort.

ALCMENA

Yes; and to lend those words support,
I feel a slight impatience coming on.

AMPHITRYON

Is this how you will make it up to me
For the cold welcome of which I have complained?

ALCMENA

Is this amnesia that you've feigned
Amusing you sufficiently?

AMPHITRYON

Oh, Heavens, Alcmena, let's stop right where we are,
And talk a little sense.

ALCMENA

Amphitryon, don't go on with this pretense;
You've carried the joke too far.

AMPHITRYON

Come, will you tell me to my face that I
Was here before this present hour, pray?

ALCMENA

Come, shall you have the boldness to deny
That you came here, just at twilight, yesterday?

AMPHITRYON

I came here yesterday?

ALCMENA

Yes; and left once more
When the first fires of sunrise blazed.

AMPHITRYON, *aside*

Was such a squabble ever heard before?
And would not any hearer be amazed?
Eh, Sosia?

SOSIA

She needs six grains of hellebore;
I fear, Sir, that her wits are crazed.

AMPHITRYON

Alcmena, by all the gods on high,
Wild talk can have dire consequences!
Before you speak again, do try
To think, and to regain your senses.

ALCMENA

I'm quite sane, and quite serious;
And my whole staff knows you slept beneath this roof.
I don't know why you are behaving thus,
But if there truly were a need for proof
Of what your memory could not restore,
From whom could I have gained, unless from you,
The news that you had won the war,
And the five diamonds that Pterelas bore
Until your sword consigned him to
The shades below for evermore?
How could one ask for surer proofs than those?

AMPHITRYON
I've already given you, you declare,
The cluster of bright diamonds that I chose,
    And which I meant that you should wear?

ALCMENA
Indeed, yes; and of that I'll give you plain,
Convincing evidence.

AMPHITRYON
How?

ALCMENA, *pointing to the diamond cluster on her girdle*
    Is *this* not clear?

AMPHITRYON
Sosia!

SOSIA, *taking a jewel box from his pocket*
She's joking, Sir, and I have it here.
That trick of hers will be in vain.

AMPHITRYON, *looking at the jewel box*
The seal's unbroken.

ALCMENA, *placing the diamonds in Amphitryon's hand*
    Is this, then, an illusion?
Here. Don't you think that proof is rather strong?

AMPHITRYON
Good gods!

ALCMENA
    Amphitryon, no more feigned confusion;
Your silly prank has gone on much too long,
And all things point, you'll grant, to one conclusion.

AMPHITRYON

Quick, break the seal.

SOSIA, *having opened the jewel box*
                    My word, there's nothing there!
Some witchcraft must have whisked it from its place,
Or else it flew, of its own self, through the air,
Toward her whose beauty it was meant to grace.

AMPHITRYON, *aside*
O Gods, who guide all creatures everywhere,
What does this thing foretell? What do I face
    That my heart will not find hard to bear?

SOSIA, *to Amphitryon*
If she speaks the truth, we have the selfsame fate,
And just like me, Sir, you'll find that you've been doubled.

AMPHITRYON

Hush.

ALCMENA
    Why is your surprise so great,
And why do you seem so greatly troubled?

AMPHITRYON, *aside*
    Oh, what disorder's in my brain!
I see things with no rational foundation,
And my honor cringes from a revelation
    Which common sense cannot explain.

ALCMENA
With such firm evidence in hand, d'you still
Think to deny your visit here last night?

AMPHITRYON
No; but describe what happened, if you will,
    During this visit that you cite.

ALCMENA

Since you ask me to describe it, do you imply
That the person who came last evening wasn't you?

AMPHITRYON

Forgive me; there's a certain reason why
I need to interrogate you as I do.

ALCMENA

Have the great affairs which occupy your mind
Made you forget last night so very fast?

AMPHITRYON

Perhaps; but now, if you will be so kind,
    Tell me the facts, from first to last.

ALCMENA

The tale's not long. I hastened forth to meet you,
    Full of a pleasurable surprise,
    Held out my longing arms to greet you,
And showed my joy by many happy cries.

AMPHITRYON, *aside*

Ah! That sweet welcome galls my jealousy.

ALCMENA

You gave me that rich present, for a start,
Which from the spoils of war you'd picked for me.
    And then with vehemence and art
You told me all the passion of your heart
(Which martial cares had held in slavery),
Your present joy, the pains of being apart,
And how the thought of me had made you smart
    With fierce impatience to be free;
Oh, never had I known you to impart
Your love in such a sweet, impassioned key.

AMPHITRYON, *aside*
Could a man be put to death more painfully?

ALCMENA
All of those transports, all that tenderness,
As you may imagine, gave me no chagrin;
    Indeed, as you may safely guess,
My heart, Amphitryon, found great charm therein.

AMPHITRYON
And then?

ALCMENA
        We talked; and each would interrupt
The other, to leave no fond concern unsaid.
Supper was served and, all alone, we supped;
And after that, we two retired to bed.

AMPHITRYON
Together?

ALCMENA
        Of course. That question is absurd.

AMPHITRYON, *aside*
Ah, there's the cruelest blow of all. It's true!
I shook with jealous dread until I knew.

ALCMENA
What made you blush so deeply at that word?
Did I do wrong in going to bed with you?

AMPHITRYON
To my great grief, Alcmena, it was not I;
And whoever says I came here yesterday
        Tells, of all false things one could say,
        The most abominable lie.

ALCMENA

Amphitryon!

AMPHITRYON

Faithless woman!

ALCMENA

You've lost your head!

AMPHITRYON

No, no, all gentle talk I now disown:
By grief, my self-control is overthrown,
And in this furious hour my heart is dead
    To all but cold revenge alone.

ALCMENA

Revenge on whom? And if you condemn me so,
    What want of faith it shows in you!

AMPHITRYON

It wasn't I, that's all I know;
And in my rage, there's nought I might not do!

ALCMENA

Unworthy husband, my facts speak plain and true,
    But your false claims are cruel and low.
    You have no right to assail me thus,
And charge me with unfaithfulness beside.
If you seek, by making this demented fuss,
An excuse to break the bonds with which I'm tied
    To you in wedlock, as your bride,
    Then all this is superfluous:
    For I'm determined, on my side,
This day to loose the chains uniting us.

AMPHITRYON

After the shameful wrong I've now detected,
That's surely a step for which you must prepare:

It is, indeed, the least that can be expected,
    And things perhaps will not rest there.
Dishonor is certain; that I'm betrayed is plain;
Affection cannot veil that from my eye;
But some details of the matter still remain
Which my just wrath intends to clarify.
Your brother can establish, beyond dispute,
That I didn't leave him till this morning's light;
I'm going to fetch him, so that he may refute
Your false assertion that I was here last night.
And then we'll get to the bottom of this case—
    This strange, unheard-of, dark affair;
And when my righteous anger scents the trace,
    Let him who's done me wrong beware!

SOSIA

Sir . . .

AMPHITRYON

No, you needn't accompany me;
Wait, Sosia, till I come back.

CLEANTHIS, *to Alcmena*

Shall I . . .

ALCMENA

No, there's nothing that I lack;
Don't follow me, Cleanthis. Let me be.

SCENE THREE

Cleanthis, Sosia

CLEANTHIS, *aside*

His brain, it seems, is in a jangled state;
　　But her brother soon will calm his huff
　　And put an end to this debate.

SOSIA, *aside*

For my poor master, this blow was hard enough—
　　A very painful turn of fate.
I may face revelations just as rough,
And I'd better clear things up, now, with my mate.

CLEANTHIS, *aside*

Let's see if he'll dare to speak to me, the lout!
But no, I mustn't let my feelings show.

SOSIA, *aside*

Things can be disagreeable to know,
　　And I tremble at what I might find out.
Perhaps it's safer not to enquire about
　　A matter which might cause me woe?
　　But I must risk it, and be bold,
　　For I just can't keep from wondering.
　　It's an urge that cannot be controlled,
　　One's itch to learn the very thing
　　That one had rather not be told.
Blessings, Cleanthis!

CLEANTHIS

　　　　　　So, you have the gall
To face me again, you scoundrel, you!

SOSIA

Lord, what's the matter? You're always in a stew,
  And you take offense at nothing at all!

CLEANTHIS

What do you mean by "nothing"?

SOSIA

                    What that word
Has always meant in verse, and prose, and such.
  "Nothing," as you have surely heard,
    Means nothing, or at least not much.

CLEANTHIS

  What holds me back I do not know,
    You wretch, from scratching out your eyes,
To show how far a woman's wrath can go.

SOSIA

I say! From what did this wild rage arise?

CLEANTHIS

You call it "nothing," then, the brutish way
  In which you treated me of late?

SOSIA

What?

CLEANTHIS

    Ha! You're playing innocent, eh?
Will you imitate your master, and state
That you truly didn't return here yesterday?

SOSIA

  Oh no, for that would be untrue;
    Let me be altogether frank:
We'd had some wine, of which I freely drank,
And it's made me forget whatever it made me do.

CLEANTHIS

What a sly excuse, to claim that you forget—

SOSIA

No, it's the truth, I swear, I vow.
In my condition, I fear I may have let
    Myself do things I should regret,
    And which I can't remember now.

CLEANTHIS

You don't remember how, in act and word,
You treated me, when you came here from the port?

SOSIA

No, tell me my misdeeds, of every sort.
    I'm a just man, and if I've erred,
I'll stand condemned before my own soul's court.

CLEANTHIS

Well, then. Amphitryon said you soon were due,
And I sat up waiting until you should appear;
You came, but you were chilly and severe,
As if I were not anyone you knew.
    And when I sought a kiss from you,
You turned your head and offered me your ear.

SOSIA

Good!

CLEANTHIS

    Good, you say!

SOSIA

               Oh, Heavens, my dear bride,
    Let me explain that, for I can.
I'd eaten garlic, and like a decent man
I turned my breath a little to one side.

CLEANTHIS

I expressed to you a tender, wifely love,
But to all I said, you were as cold as stone;
    And you never spoke one syllable of
    Affection, in answer to my own.

SOSIA, *aside*

Courage!

CLEANTHIS

    Despite these loving overtures,
My chaste desires were baffled, as I said;
And so extreme was that cold mood of yours,
That you wouldn't even join me in our bed,
As the law of marriage solemnly adjures.

SOSIA

What! I didn't go to bed?

CLEANTHIS
    No.

SOSIA
        Can it be true?

CLEANTHIS

    Yes, traitor, it's a certainty.
You gave me the worst affront a spouse could do.
And this morning, was there any apology?
    No, and you then took leave of me
With words of scorn instead of a fond adieu.

SOSIA

Well done, Sosia!

CLEANTHIS
    So that is your reaction!
You laugh, then, at your gross offense!

SOSIA

I feel profound self-satisfaction.

CLEANTHIS

Is that how you express your penitence?

SOSIA

I never dreamt that I had such good sense.

CLEANTHIS

You don't condemn your cold and faithless action,
But burst, instead, with joyous impudence!

SOSIA

Hold on! If I seem joyous to your eyes,
It's because my heart delights in doing right;
Instinctively, I did what was most wise,
In acting toward you as I did last night.

CLEANTHIS

You scoundrel! Are you making fun?

SOSIA

No, all I say may be believed.
I felt a certain apprehension—one
Which, after you had spoken, was relieved.
I was in terror, fearing that we'd done
A deed for which we later might have grieved.

CLEANTHIS

What dreadful deed did you so wisely shun?

SOSIA

When a man is drunk, the doctors hold,
Lovemaking ought to be eschewed,
Since children so conceived are always rude
And sickly, and the black sheep of the fold.

What if my mood, last night, had not been cold?
Think of what sad results might have ensued!

CLEANTHIS

I wish all doctors were in Hell;
  Their theories are lunatic.
  Let them give orders to the sick,
And not prescribe for people who are well.
  They meddle too much in our affairs,
Giving our chaste desires harsh rules to follow;
  And when the dog days come, their wares
Are just the same—those grim decrees of theirs,
  And a lot of old wives' tales to swallow.

SOSIA

Gently, now.

CLEANTHIS

   No, such folly I won't approve;
'Twas crackbrained people who conceived those rules.
No wine or weather can blight the doing of
Those duties which belong to married love.
  Your doctors are a pack of fools.

SOSIA

I wish your rage at them would moderate;
They're decent men, whatever the world may say.

CLEANTHIS

In vain you try to appease and palliate:
Your lame excuse won't do, in any way;
And, sooner or later, I'll retaliate
For the cold contempt you show me every day.
I've not forgotten what you said of late,
And I mean to profit, my perfidious mate,
From your most kind permission to go astray.

SOSIA

What?

CLEANTHIS

Wretch, you told me that you wouldn't mind
If I took a lover, that I was free—

SOSIA

Oh, no! On second thoughts, I find
That I'd rather you didn't. It would reflect on me.
I urge you to do nothing of the kind.

CLEANTHIS

Still, if I find I can persuade
Myself to do as you suggest . . .

SOSIA

We must break off now, I'm afraid.
Here comes Amphitryon, looking self-possessed.

SCENE FOUR

———————•◆•———————

Jupiter, Cleanthis, Sosia

JUPITER, *aside*

I'll take this opportunity to appease
Alcmena, and to banish her vexation,
And in so doing taste the ecstasies
            Of happy reconciliation.
                        (*To Cleanthis:*)
      Alcmena is upstairs, I presume?

CLEANTHIS

      Yes, in her agitated mood
      She feels a wish for solitude,
And bade me not to follow her to her room.

JUPITER

      Whomever else she may have banished,
      Her words do not apply to me.

CLEANTHIS

      His grief, so far as I can see,
      Has, in a matter of minutes, vanished.

SCENE FIVE

Cleanthis, Sosia

SOSIA
What do you think of my master's cheerful mien,
    Cleanthis, after that dreadful brawl?

CLEANTHIS
    Women, I think, should vent their spleen
By sending men to the Devil, one and all;
    The best of them's not worth a bean.

SOSIA
    That's what your anger makes you say;
But women are too attached to men for that;
You'd find existence very drab and flat
    If the Devil took us all away.

CLEANTHIS
You think so, do you?

            SOSIA
            Hush; it's they.

SCENE SIX

————— •• —————

Jupiter, Alcmena, Cleanthis, Sosia

JUPITER

Fairest Alcmena, do not go!
My heart could not survive that pain.

ALCMENA

No, I can't possibly remain
With you, the author of my woe.

JUPITER

I beg you . . .

ALCMENA

Leave me.

JUPITER
What!

ALCMENA
I tell you, leave me.

JUPITER, *sotto voce, aside*

Her young tears touch my heart; her sufferings grieve me.
(*Aloud:*)
Let me at least . . .

ALCMENA
No, no, don't follow me.

JUPITER

Where do you mean to go?

ALCMENA
Where you won't be.

JUPITER

That will be very hard to do.
I am so bound to you, who are so fair,
That not for a moment shall we part, I swear.
    Wherever you go, I'll follow you.

ALCMENA

And I shall flee you everywhere.

JUPITER

I must indeed be terrifying!

ALCMENA

You *are* so; more than can be said.
Yes, I behold in you a petrifying
    Monster, a monster dire and dread,
    A monster whose approaching tread
    Frightens its victim into flying.
At the sight of you, my heart is turned to lead;
    I agonize, and feel like dying;
    All of the horrors that bespread
    The earth, and must be feared and fled,
Are less malign than you, less horrifying.

JUPITER

To hear you talk, you hate me rather a lot.

ALCMENA

My heart has still more rage on call,
And it annoys my heart that it cannot
    Find words in which to express it all.

JUPITER

Alcmena, how do I deserve
To be called a monster, and to be chided thus?

ALCMENA

What a thing to ask! How disingenuous!
You madden me with your outrageous nerve.

JUPITER

Relent, and let me speak, I pray . . .

ALCMENA

No, never again shall I see or hear you. Never.

JUPITER

Have you the heart to treat me in this way?
    Is this the love that would last forever,
Of which you sweetly spoke just yesterday?

ALCMENA

No, it is not: your brutish nature clashes
    With all that's sweet, and makes it tart.
That tender, passionate love is now but ashes.
You've wantonly destroyed it in my heart
    By a hundred cruel cuts and slashes.
Now, in its place, is a wrath that won't abate,
A bitter scorn that will not dissipate,
A desperate heart, incensed by your affronts,
Which now shall view you with dislike as great
As the love with which it looked upon you once—
    That is to say, with boundless hate.

JUPITER

Your love for me was very weak, perforce,
If by so small a thing it was undone!
Should a little joke occasion a divorce,
And should one bridle at what was meant in fun?

ALCMENA

    Ah, that's what gives me such distress,
        And seems unpardonable to me:
The transports of an honest jealousy

Would trouble me far less.
Jealousy is a violent notion
Which, like a storm at sea, can rock the soul;
And the wisest spirit, tossed on such an ocean,
Can find it difficult to control
The helm of its emotion.
The anger of a heart thus blindly driven
Is someway pardoned, even as it gives offense,
And can, for all its violence,
Recall the love that gave it birth, and hence
Make claim to be forgiven.
Yes, he who offends us by a jealous fit
Can always plead its origin in love,
Which no man is the master of,
And therefore be absolved of it.
But, oh, to pass from what was merely
A bit of teasing to a sudden rage;
Without the shadow of a cause, to wage
War on a heart that loved you dearly,
And wound my honor so severely;
That was a heartless onslaught which, I fear me,
Nothing will ever soften or assuage.

JUPITER

You're right, Alcmena, as I must concede.
'Twas an odious crime, and I no longer claim
That there's the least excuse to plead:
But let me exonerate my heart, and name
The person whom you ought to blame
For that unconscionable deed.
Hear me, Alcmena, for this is true:
Only the husband is at fault,
And he should be the culprit, in your view.
The lover had no part in that assault,
And his heart's not capable of slandering you.
That heart, which worships you with humble sighs,
Would never dream of acting so;
And it would wish, should it in any wise

Wound you, or cause you any woe,
To be stabbed a hundred times before your eyes.
But the husband's failed to respect you, to maintain
    That deference which you should be shown;
Those harsh words that you heard were his alone,
For he thinks a husband's temper has free rein.
Yes, yes, it's he, the husband, who has transgressed;
It's he who has maltreated you, that's clear.
    He's yours to hate, and to detest;
    I yield him up to you, my dear.
But spare the lover, Alcmena, that severe
    Resentment which is in your breast.
    In this offense, he has no share;
    Detach him from the guilty one,
    And, so as to be just and fair,
Don't punish him for what he hasn't done.

                    ALCMENA
The fine distinction that you've made
    Is of a very frivolous kind;
    Such airy nonsense, I'm afraid,
Is not appealing to an angry mind.
In vain you play that silly verbal game.
I'll spare no part of him who does me wrong;
It's the whole man at whom my rage takes aim,
    And to my anger, just and strong,
The husband and the lover look the same.
Both of them, in my thoughts, combine and fuse;
And both are painted in the same dark hues
    By the heart which they have violated;
Both have insulted me; both I accuse,
    And both, by me, are fiercely hated.

                    JUPITER
Well then, I'm guilty, as you say,
    So far as this great crime's concerned,
And there is justice in the fiery way
You treat me like some traitor who should be burned.

It's wholly proper that your heart has turned
Against me, and the wrath that you display
Is a harsh torment that I've fully earned.
It's right indeed that you should shun my face,
    And that you threaten ever to
    Elude my steps, if I give chase.
    I must seem wholly vile to you,
And worthy to be skewered through and through.
No deed could be more horrible and base
    Than bringing tears to eyes so blue;
It's a crime against mankind, and Heaven, too;
And I deserve that you should close my case
    By mustering all your hate apace
    To do the worst that it can do.
    Yet I appeal to you for grace,
And go down on my knees to beg it of you,
Pleading with you for mercy in the name
    Of the tenderest and brightest flame
    With which an ardent soul could love you.
    Fairest Alcmena, if you deny
The pardon that I ask, that I implore,
    By one quick thrust, then, shall I die,
    And be delivered from a sore
    And bitter agony which I
    Have not the strength to suffer more.
    Yes, I am in a desperate state,
    Alcmena, and I hope you know
That I, who love your heavenly beauty so,
Could not, for a single day, survive your hate.
Already I feel these minutes, cruel and slow,
    Draining the life of my sad heart,
    Each tick or tock a mortal blow;
A thousand vultures, tearing me apart,
Would hurt far less than what I undergo.
If I've no right to hope for clemency,
Tell me as much, Alcmena, and you shall see
This sword of mine plunge swiftly, to the hilt,

Into a wretched heart that owns its guilt,
A heart that, wronging you, has proven to be
Richly deserving that its blood be spilt.
Yet I'll rejoice in Hades' dark domains
If, by my death, I can appease your ire,
And clear your spirit, as this sad day wanes,
  Of any tinge of hate that stains
   Your memory of my love's pure fire.
That is the one great boon I dare desire.

ALCMENA

Oh, cruel husband!

JUPITER

  Speak, speak, and end my pains.

ALCMENA

Am I to show you kindness, if you please,
After such insults and indignities?

JUPITER

However much one may abhor his crimes,
Can one reject a lover who repents?

ALCMENA

A proper lover would die a thousand times
Before he gave his loved one any offense.

JUPITER

The more we love, the more we tolerate . . .

ALCMENA

No, speak no further; you deserve my hate.

JUPITER

You hate me, then?

ALCMENA

I do my best; I try;
But all your insults, to my great vexation,
Have not produced the vengeful detestation
　　I feel I should be driven by.

JUPITER

Why all this struggling and frustration,
When, to avenge you, I'm prepared to die?
Just sentence me to death, and I'll obey you.

ALCMENA

If I can't hate you, how can I wish to slay you?

JUPITER

I cannot live unless the angry feeling
　　With which you scald my soul is ended,
And that most gracious pardon is extended
　　For which I beg, thus humbly kneeling.
　　　　　(*Sosia and Cleanthis also kneel.*)
Choose, now: I wait in dread to hear
Whether you'll punish, or forgive.

ALCMENA

Alas, the one alternative
　　That I can choose is all too clear.
My heart's betrayed me utterly, and I'm
　　Unable to remain irate:
　　If I tell you that I cannot hate,
　　Are you not pardoned for your crime?

JUPITER

Ah! Lovely Alcmena, I am overjoyed . . .

ALCMENA

Enough; my weakness makes me much annoyed.

JUPITER

Go, Sosia; make haste and see,
While this sweet rapture makes my heart expand,
What officers of the army are at hand,
    And bid them come and dine with me.
            (*Sotto voce, aside:*)
    While he is absent for a space,
    Good Mercury shall take his place.

SCENE SEVEN

Cleanthis, Sosia

SOSIA

Our betters know the art of mending fences.
Come, shall we copy them in this,
And have ourselves a little armistice
In which to solve our differences?

CLEANTHIS

You think we can chat our way to wedded bliss?

SOSIA

Then you won't talk?

CLEANTHIS

No.

SOSIA

Oh, well; I don't much care.
The loss is yours.

CLEANTHIS

Come back, you idiot.

SOSIA

No, by the Devil, I shall not,
And it's my turn now to let my temper flare.

CLEANTHIS

Good riddance, then, you beast! So there!
(*Alone:*)
A virtuous woman has a weary lot.

Act Three

SCENE ONE

Amphitryon

AMPHITRYON

I cannot find her brother anywhere;
My search is vain, my weariness complete.
What could be harsher than the lot I bear?
The man I seek eludes me, yet as my feet
  Lead me distracted here and there,
I meet a throng I have no wish to meet.
A thousand folk I've scarcely seen before,
Unwitting pests, extol our deeds of war,
And madden me with their congratulations.
Tormented as I am by private cares,
I suffer under this applause of theirs,
And their embraces sharpen my impatience.
  Vainly I seek to dodge their dread
  Acclaim, for everywhere I fly,
Their kindly persecution stops me dead;
And as they gush at me, and I reply
  With shrugs and noddings of the head,
I mutter curses at them on the sly.
Ah, me! How little praise and honor mean,
And all else that a brilliant victory brings,
When the soul is overcome with grief so keen!
How gladly one would barter all such things
  If the heart could once more be serene!
  Incessantly, my jealous brain
  Dwells on my dark vicissitudes,
  And yet, the more it mulls and broods,
The less it can untangle or explain.
The theft of the diamonds I can understand;
A seal will not deter a clever thief;
But her claim that they were given her by my hand,

Last night, is baffling and beyond belief.
'Twixt men, there can be similarities
Whereby impostors manage to deceive;
But that some crafty rascal could with ease
Impersonate a husband, I can't conceive;
There'd be innumerable disparities
Which any wife would readily perceive.

    As for Thessalian sorcery,
Those famous tales that everybody tells
Of ladies fair seduced through magic spells
Have always seemed preposterous to me;
And it would be a jest of Fate if I,

      Returning from the war in glory,
      Must play the butt of such a story,
      And see my honor lost thereby.
I mean to question her again, and see
If what she said was not a fantasy
Caused by some transient fever of the brain.

    Just Heaven! For my peace of mind,
    Let that be proven; let me find
That she was temporarily insane!

SCENE TWO

———————————— ◆◆ ————————————

Mercury, Amphitryon

MERCURY, *on the balcony of Amphitryon's house,*
unseen and unheard by Amphitryon
Since, here, I've no amours to give me pleasure,
I shall devise some other sport instead,
And put some life into my tedious leisure
By driving poor Amphitryon out of his head.
In a god, that sounds uncharitable and callous,
But it's not my nature to behave benignly;
    My planet's attributes incline me
    To deal in mischief and in malice.

AMPHITRYON
Why has this door been locked so very early?

MERCURY
Ho! Easy there! Who's knocking?

AMPHITRYON, *not seeing Mercury*
                I.

MERCURY
                Who's I?

AMPHITRYON, *perceiving Mercury,*
whom he takes to be Sosia
Ah! Open up.

MERCURY
        For you? Who *are* you? Why
Must you make so great a noise, and sound so surly?

AMPHITRYON
What! Don't you know me?

MERCURY
No, my lad,
And you're no one I would care to know.

AMPHITRYON, *aside*

Has everyone, today, gone raving mad?
Is folly catching? Sosia! Sosia! Hullo!

MERCURY

Sosia's the name I've always had;
It's good of you to remind me, though.

AMPHITRYON

Do you see me clearly?

MERCURY
Yes. What makes you wreak
Such battery on the door? My word!
What do you want, eh? What do you seek?

AMPHITRYON

What do I want, you gallows-bird?

MERCURY

What do you *not* want, then? Come, speak,
If you want your wishes to be heard.

AMPHITRYON

Just wait, you wretch! I'll come up there
With a stick, and make my feelings plain,
And teach you what it costs, in pain,
To address me with that saucy air.

MERCURY

Take care! If you lay one knuckle on that door,
I'll send you missives of a hurtful type.

AMPHITRYON

Gods! Was such insolence ever heard before?
And from a lackey, too! A guttersnipe!

MERCURY

Well, have you sized me up, and looked your fill?
Have you pierced me with that gaze so fierce and grim?
Look at the great big glaring eyes on him!
    My, my! Already, if looks could kill,
    He would have stared me limb from limb.

AMPHITRYON

I shudder to see you work your own undoing
    By all these rash remarks you make.
Above your head, a terrible storm is brewing!
What a shower of blows your back is going to take!

MERCURY

My friend, unless you say a prompt good-bye,
I'll play a tune upon your skeleton.

AMPHITRYON

If you did, you blackguard, I'd show you what is done
To men who attack their masters. Best not try.

MERCURY

Ha! You, my master!

AMPHITRYON

    Knave, that you can't deny.

MERCURY

I have no master save Amphitryon.

AMPHITRYON

And who is this Amphitryon, if not I?

MERCURY

Amphitryon—you!

AMPHITRYON

Of course.

MERCURY

You're addled, son.
Tell me, in what fine pothouse, or what inn,
Has drinking turned your wits askew?

AMPHITRYON

More gibes!

MERCURY

Was the wine of noble origin?

AMPHITRYON

Good gods!

MERCURY

Was the vintage old, or new?

AMPHITRYON

What gall!

MERCURY

New wine can cause the head to spin,
Unless you add some water, too.

AMPHITRYON

I'm going to tear your tongue out, do you hear?

MERCURY

Now, now, good friend, you'd best move on;
You might disturb someone, I fear.
Wine is a powerful thing. Be off, begone,
And leave Amphitryon to enjoy his dear.

AMPHITRYON

What! Is Amphitryon within?

MERCURY

                    Oh, yes:
Crowned with victorious laurels, and with his bride,
        The fair Alcmena, at his side,
He shares an hour of dulcet happiness.
After a curious sort of lovers' tiff,
They're now recovering their amorous poise.
Take care: don't interrupt their secret joys,
        Unless you'd have him give you a stiff
        Beating for that unwelcome noise.

SCENE THREE

—•—•—

Amphitryon

AMPHITRYON

Oh, but he's dealt my soul a staggering blow,
And given my poor mind a brutal jar!
If things are as the rascal says they are,
Look how my love and honor are brought low!
Whether to hush things up, or to proclaim
    This outrage, reason must decide.
Should I speak out in anger, or should I hide
    This blot upon my house and name?
But need I *think*, when the wrong is so extreme?
What matter if I publish or conceal?
    Let bitter hate be all I feel,
    And vengeance be my only theme.

SCENE FOUR

———— •• ————

Amphitryon and *Sosia; Naucrates* and *Polidas*
at the back of the stage

SOSIA, *to Amphitryon*
Sir, I've done my best, but the best that I could do
Was to bring you those two gentlemen whom you see.

AMPHITRYON
So you're here, eh?

SOSIA
Sir.

AMPHITRYON
You insolent vermin, you!

SOSIA
What's this?

AMPHITRYON
I'll teach you to make game of me.

SOSIA
What's the matter?

AMPHITRYON, *drawing his sword*
"What's the matter," eh? You cur!

SOSIA, *to Naucrates and Polidas*
Please help me, gentlemen! Quickly! Come!

NAUCRATES, *to Amphitryon*
I pray you, hold.

SOSIA

Of what am I guilty, Sir?

AMPHITRYON

No need to tell you that, you scum!
(*To Naucrates, who is restraining him:*)
My just wrath has a right to be expressed.

SOSIA

When they hang a fellow, at least they tell him why.

NAUCRATES, *to Amphitryon*

Do tell us in what way this man's transgressed.

SOSIA

Yes, gentlemen, press him to reply.

AMPHITRYON

Just now he had the cheek—d'you hear?—
To shut my own door in my face;
And then, with many a threat and jeer,
He sought to run me off the place.
(*Seeking to strike Sosia:*)
You scoundrel, you!

SOSIA, *dropping to his knees*
I'm dead.

NAUCRATES, *to Amphitryon*
Be calm, I pray.

SOSIA

Gentlemen!

POLIDAS, *to Sosia*
Yes?

SOSIA
Have I been beaten yet?

AMPHITRYON, *to Naucrates*
No, I insist that he must pay
For his impudent words, and that's a heavy debt.

SOSIA
How could I do the things you say,
When I was gathering guests for your little fête?
These gentlemen right here could tell you how
I've just invited them to dine with you.

NAUCRATES
Yes, yes, he brought your message to us just now,
And he never left us. It's all quite true.

AMPHITRYON
Who bade you invite them?

SOSIA
You did, Sir.

AMPHITRYON
When?

SOSIA
After your reconciliation—
When, having soothed Alcmena's deep vexation,
You rejoiced at being one again with her.
(*Sosia stands up again.*)

AMPHITRYON
Great Heavens! At every step I take,
New sufferings are added to my throes,
And all's so muddled and opaque,
I don't know what to say or to suppose.

NAUCRATES

The happenings at your house, of which he's told,
Transcend the natural, and ere
You do some deed that's daft or overbold,
You must find out the truth of this affair.

AMPHITRYON

Then let's find out together, you and I;
The Heavens have sent you here most apropos.
Let's see what fortune this day will bestow,
What fate behind these mysteries may lie.
It is a thing I burn to know,
And fear more than I fear to die.
(*Amphitryon knocks at the door of his house.*)

SCENE FIVE

Jupiter, Amphitryon, Naucrates, Polidas, Sosia

JUPITER

Who makes me come downstairs? Who knocks
As if he were the master here?

AMPHITRYON

Gods! What do I see?

NAUCRATES

Oh, what a paradox
That two Amphitryons should at once appear!

AMPHITRYON, *aside*

My heart is utterly congealed:
Alas, I am undone; my quest is ended.
My destiny is now revealed;
One glance, and all is comprehended.

NAUCRATES

The more I scan and scrutinize these two,
The more each man is like the other one.

SOSIA, *crossing to the side of Jupiter*

Sirs, this is the real Amphitryon;
The other's an impostor, through and through.

POLIDAS

Despite minute comparison,
I cannot tell you who is who.

AMPHITRYON

You've all been hoodwinked by a charlatan;
This sword will break the spell that's binding you.

NAUCRATES, *to Amphitryon, who has drawn his sword*
Stop!

AMPHITRYON

No!

NAUCRATES
What dreadful deed would you perform?

AMPHITRYON
I'd punish that impostor's vile deceit.

JUPITER
Gently, now: there's no need to rage and storm;
Men judge, when someone's temper is overwarm,
That an honest cause would not require such heat.

SOSIA
Yes, he's a sorcerer who can take the form
Of any head of household he may meet.

AMPHITRYON, *to Sosia*
For those outrageous words, you knave,
I vow that I shall give you many a stroke.

SOSIA
My master's heart is kind and brave,
And he won't let people beat his serving-folk.

AMPHITRYON
Now let me sate my anger, and in the gore
Of a rank villain wash my shame away.

NAUCRATES, *stopping Amphitryon*
No, we shall not permit so strange a fray—
Amphitryon and himself at war!

AMPHITRYON

What! Will my friends forsake my honor so,
And come to the defense of that low sneak?
Gods! Far from furthering the revenge I seek,
They stand between my just wrath and my foe!

NAUCRATES

But how, with any confidence,
Can we make up our minds, and act,
When two Amphitryons, in fact,
Keep all our loyal feelings in suspense?
We'd be afraid, if we supported you,
That we'd mistaken your identity.
We see in you the great Amphitryon, he
To whom the thanks of rescued Thebes are due;
But we see the same thing in your rival, too,
And we can't tell who the genuine you might be.
      What we must do is obvious:
By our hands, the impostor must be slain.
But the likeness of you two now baffles us,
      And it would be too hazardous
      To strike before the truth's made plain.
      Let us employ our wits and eyes
To find out who's the impostor, you or he;
Once we have solved that puzzle, there will be
No need to tell us where our duty lies.

JUPITER

Well said. Our strange resemblance justifies
Your having doubts of both of us—him, and me.
I'm far too reasonable to criticize
Your hesitation and uncertainty.
Since the eye can't tell us two apart, it's wise
Not to act rashly. Sirs, we quite agree.
You don't see me becoming fierce and hot,
      You see no drawn sword in my hand;
That's a poor way to unsnarl this Gordian knot,

And I have means more certain and more bland.
     One of us is Amphitryon;
But which is he, you've no idea on earth.
I'll soon clear up that mystery, and have done.
Yes, who I am shall be so well set forth
That even he will grant my name and worth,
And the high lineage that gave me birth,
And have no further wrongs to brood upon.
When I bare the truth to you, my words must fall
Upon the listening ears of Thebes entire;
This matter's of such weight as to require
     Wide audience, and I desire
     To explain things in the sight of all.
Alcmena asks of me that explanation.
Her virtue, sullied by this confrontation,
Asks to be proven pure, and that's my aim.
My love for her makes that an obligation;
And I've invited here a delegation
Of noblest chiefs, to hear me clear her name.
While we await those worthies, come and share
     The pleasures of that board whereto
     Good Sosia invited you,
     And honor me by your presence there.

SOSIA

Gentlemen, I was right; behold the winner.
     Behold the true Amphitryon.
     The true Amphitryon's the one
     Who asks us in and gives us dinner.

AMPHITRYON

What worse humiliation could Fate afford?
I'm forced to listen to the things this base
Deceiver has been saying to my face,
And though his discourse makes my hot blood race,
     My friends won't let me draw my sword!

NAUCRATES, *to Amphitryon*

Do have a little patience. Let's wait and hear
    His statement, which should make it clear
    If any wrath is justified.
    Is he a charlatan? I don't know,
    But, I must say, he sounds as though
    He had some reason on his side.

AMPHITRYON

Go, lukewarm friends, go hear him, and applaud:
I've other friends who have more resolution;
They'll share my detestation of this fraud,
And back me as I seek just retribution.

JUPITER

Well, I'll await their coming, and they can be
    Enlightened by my statement, too.

AMPHITRYON

Mere talk, you wretch, won't make you safe from me;
I'll be avenged, whatever you say or do.

JUPITER

    To all these insults I have heard
    I shall not stoop now to reply;
    But wait, and I shall by and by
    Confound your anger with a word.

AMPHITRYON

Not Heaven itself could give you sanctuary;
And I'll pursue you to the depths of Hell.

JUPITER

    That really won't be necessary;
I shan't flee, as you'll soon see very well.

AMPHITRYON, *aside*

While he's at table, I must quickly go
And find some fighting friends who'll share my wrath,
    Then hasten on the homeward path
    And slaughter him with thrust and blow.

JUPITER

    Don't stand on ceremony, now;
    Come, enter, if you'll be so kind.

NAUCRATES

    This whole affair, I must avow,
    Staggers the senses and the mind.

SOSIA

Enough amazement, sirs; go take your seats,
And feast till dawn in pure beatitude.
        (*Alone:*)
Now I shall gorge, and get into the mood
    To swap brave tales of martial feats!
    I itch for soups and wines and meats;
    I've never had such a lust for food.

SCENE SIX

Mercury, Sosia

MERCURY

Halt! So, you poke your nose in at my door,
  You sniffer-out of food and wine!

SOSIA

Ouch! Not so rough, please!

MERCURY

                    So, you're back for more!
  You want me to massage your spine.

SOSIA

  Spare me, O brave and generous me;
  Do practice more restraint and measure;
  Good Sosia, let poor Sosia be,
And do not beat yourself with so much pleasure.

MERCURY

  From whom did you receive permission
  To use that thrice-forbidden name?
Did I not promise to lambaste your frame
If you ignored my stringent prohibition?

SOSIA

Since we serve one master, it's a name that we
  May both, without confusion, share.
I am addressed as Sosia everywhere;
    I gladly allow you to be he;
    Grant me the same; it's only fair.
    Let's let the two Amphitryons
    Have jealous quarrels that never cease,
    And be their own fierce partisans,
While the two Sosias live in perfect peace.

MERCURY

No, one of them's enough; I'll let no other
    Divide my self and name in two.

SOSIA

I'll gladly yield the precedence to you;
I'll be the younger, and you the older brother.

MERCURY

No, a brother is an annoyance I'll forgo;
    I want to be an only son.

SOSIA

    O cruel heart! O tyrannous one!
Permit me at least to be your shadow.

MERCURY

                No.

SOSIA

Oh, come; be human; show me some compassion!
Let me, in that dim rôle, be at your side:
I'll shadow you in such obsequious fashion
    That you'll be pleased and gratified.

MERCURY

    No quarter; your appeal's denied.
If you dare set foot again on this estate,
    You'll get the usual thousand blows.

SOSIA

    Alas, poor Sosia! Your fate
Is very cruel, Heaven knows.

MERCURY

    What! Do you still presume to give
Yourself a name I've told you to resign?

SOSIA

The name I mentioned wasn't mine;
That Sosia was a relative
Somewhere in my paternal line,
Whom someone harsh and primitive
Drove off once, just when it was time to dine.

MERCURY

Well, as for names, if you desire to live,
Learn to distinguish between Mine and Thine.

SOSIA, *aside*

How I'd thrash you, if my courage weren't so weak,
You son of a strumpet, all puffed up with pride!

MERCURY

What?

SOSIA

Nothing.

MERCURY

It seems to me I heard you speak.

SOSIA

Ask anyone; I merely sighed.

MERCURY

Yet someone muttered something about
"Son of a strumpet" in my hearing;
I'm sure of it.

SOSIA

It was, no doubt,
Some parrot, thrilled to see the weather clearing.

MERCURY

Farewell. Remember, if your back should itch,
   That this is the place in which I dwell.

SOSIA, *alone*

   Ah! Dinnertime's an hour at which
To be excluded is to be in Hell.
But let's accept what the grim Fates have spun;
Let's do what their blind whim would have me do,
   And, in a fitting liaison,
   Let's join the unfortunate Sosia to
   Unfortunate Amphitryon—
Who now, with reinforcements, comes in view.

SCENE SEVEN

———— • • ————

Amphitryon, Argatiphontidas, Posicles, and *Sosia*—
the last in a corner of the stage, unseen

AMPHITRYON, *to several other officers who accompany him*
Stop there, gentlemen; keep to my rear a bit,
    And don't advance, I beg of you,
    Until there is a need for it.

POSICLES
I know that this great blow must grieve you sadly.

AMPHITRYON
Yes, all my being is most sorely tried,
    And I suffer in my love as badly
    As in my honor and my pride.

POSICLES
If the likeness is as great as you report,
    Alcmena might not be to blame . . .

AMPHITRYON
    Ah, in a matter of this sort,
Error, though pure, is guilty all the same,
And innocence gets no mercy from the court.
Such errors, in whatever light one views them,
    Are bound to touch us where we live,
And though our reason often may excuse them,
Our honor and our love will not forgive.

ARGATIPHONTIDAS
I don't let such ideas confuse my thought;
But I scorn your other friends for their delay;
Such hanging back, I say, is good for nought;
A brave man never would behave that way.
When a friend enlists us in his cause, we ought

To plunge headfirst into the fray.
Argatiphontidas hates compromise.
For men of honor, it's wrong to listen to
A comrade's foe, and meekly hear his view,
When the voice of vengeance calls for his demise.
    Negotiation I despise:
In a case like this, the first thing one should do
    Is hack the bloody swine in two,
    Rather than talk and temporize.
    Yes, come what may, as you shall see,
Argatiphontidas will perform his task;
    And when we meet your enemy,
    Promise me, Sir—it's all I ask—
That the scoundrel may be killed by me.

AMPHITRYON

Come, then!

SOSIA, *to Amphitryon, clasping his knees*
    I kneel, Sir, and await your dread
Chastisement of my impudence and nerve.
Bludgeon me, Sir; rain blows upon my head,
    Or in your fury strike me dead:
    'Twill be no more than I deserve,
And not one word of protest shall be said.

AMPHITRYON

Get up. What's happening?

SOSIA

    I've been evicted, too.
I thought to join the rest in festive eating,
    But found that I was there anew
    To offer me a brutal greeting.
Yes, the other me, who serves the other you,
    Has given me another beating.
    Sir, we are similarly fated,
    And similarly victimized.

Just as I've been dis-Sosiated,
You have been de-Amphitryonized.

AMPHITRYON

Follow me.

SOSIA

Someone's coming; it's best we waited.

SCENE EIGHT

Cleanthis, Amphitryon, Argatiphontidas,
Polidas, Naucrates, Posicles, Sosia

CLEANTHIS

Oh, mercy!

AMPHITRYON
Why this cry of fear?
Why do you look so terrified?

CLEANTHIS
Alas, you're up there, and I see you here!

NAUCRATES, *to Amphitryon*
No hurry; he shortly will appear
And speak, and all this will be clarified.
If one may credit what we heard inside,
Your grief will soon give way to better cheer.

SCENE NINE

Mercury, Amphitryon, Argatiphontidas,
Polidas, Naucrates, Cleanthis, Sosia

MERCURY

Yes, all shall hear him. Prepare to see the great
    Master of all the gods on high,
Who, in the likeness of her cherished mate,
Descended to Alcmena from the sky.
    And as for me, I'm Mercury,
Who gave this rogue, for pastime, many a whack,
    And borrowed his identity;
But now he need not think his fate so black,
    For it's an honor to have one's back
    Lambasted by a deity.

SOSIA

My goodness, Mister God, I thank Your Grace;
But I could have done without your gracious favor.

MERCURY

Let him be Sosia now; he has my waiver;
I'm tired of wearing a mug so commonplace,
And up in Heaven, at my ambrosial laver,
    I'll wash those features off my face.
        (*Mercury flies up to Heaven.*)

SOSIA

May Heaven keep you away from me forever!
Your malice is implacable and evil.
    Truly, in all my life I've never
    Met any god so like a devil.

SCENE TEN

Jupiter, Amphitryon, Naucrates, Argatiphontidas,
Polidas, Posicles, Cleanthis, Sosia

JUPITER, *announced by the sound of thunder,*
armed with his thunderbolt, in a cloud, on his eagle
Behold, Amphitryon, your impostor; see
How Jove looks when his features are his own.
By these my symbols I am readily known,
And I am sure that this epiphany
  Will free your heart from rage and moan,
And fill your house once more with harmony.
My name, which the world adores at every minute,
Will stifle any scandal that might occur:
  To share a love with Jupiter
  Has surely no dishonor in it;
And surely it must seem a glorious thing
To be the rival of Olympus' king.
You have, I think, no shame or wrong to bear,
  And it is I, in this affair,
Who, god though I am, must utter jealous sighs.
Alcmena's wholly yours, whatever one does,
And it should warm your heart to realize
That the only way for one to please her was
  To assume her cherished husband's guise;
That Jove, revealed in his immortal splendor,
Could not have tempted her to be untrue,
  And that her gifts to him of tender
Love were truly given only to you.

SOSIA
Lord Jove knows how to sugarcoat the pill.

JUPITER
Then overcome your dark resentment, please,
And bid your agitated heart be still.

A child shall be born to you, whose fame shall fill
The universe; you shall call him Hercules.
Your future days, replete with all good things,
Will show the world that you are in my care,
    And lesser mortals everywhere
    Will envy what my favor brings.
    You may feel confident about
    The promised joys I adumbrate,
    And which it were a crime to doubt:
    For when the voice of Jove rings out,
    His words are the decrees of Fate.
            (*He vanishes into the clouds.*)

NAUCRATES

These gracious gifts are cause for jubilation . . .

SOSIA

Will you allow me, sirs, a small request?
    Do not embark with too much zest
    On speeches of congratulation:
    Such compliments, let me suggest,
Would seem, to all, embarrassing at best
    In so complex a situation.
We have been honored by the Gods' great King,
Who offers us unparalleled largesse;
Our future is replete with each good thing,
And we shall have, to crown our happiness,
A son with whose renown the world shall ring;
    And all that's very fine, I guess;
    But let us cut our speeches short,
And quietly retire now, if you will.
    Regarding matters of this sort,
    It's wisest always to be still.

Tartuffe

COMEDY IN FIVE ACTS, 1669

For my brother Lawrence

Introduction

There may be people who deny comedy the right to be serious, and think it improper for any but trivial themes to consort with laughter. It would take people of that kind to find in *Tartuffe* anything offensive to religion. The warped characters of the play express an obviously warped religious attitude, which is corrected by the reasonable orthodoxy of Cléante, the wholesomeness of Dorine, and the entire testimony of the action. The play is not a satire on religion, as those held who kept it off the boards for five years. Is it, then, a satire on religious hypocrisy, as Molière claimed in his polemical preface of 1669?

The play speaks often of religious hypocrisy, displays it in action, and sometimes seems to be gesturing toward its practitioners in seventeenth-century French society. Tartuffe is made to recommend, more than once, those Jesuitical techniques for easing the conscience which Pascal attacked in the *Provincial Letters*. Cléante makes a long speech against people who feign piety for the sake of preferment or political advantage. And yet no one in the play can be said to be a religious hypocrite in any representative sense. Tartuffe may at times suggest or symbolize the slippery casuist, or the sort of hypocrite denounced by Cléante, but he is not himself such a person. He is a versatile parasite or confidence man, with a very long criminal record, and to pose as a holy man is not his only *modus operandi*: we see him, in the last act, shifting easily from the role of saint to that of hundred-percenter. As for the other major characters who might qualify, Madame Pernelle is simply a nasty bigot, while the religious attitudes of her son Orgon are, for all their underlying corruption, quite sincere.

Tartuffe is only incidentally satiric; what we experience in reading or seeing it, as several modern critics have argued, is not a satire but a "deep" comedy in which (1) a knave tries to control life by cold chicanery, (2) a fool tries to oppress life by unconscious misuse of the highest values, and (3) life, happily, will not have it.

Orgon, the central character of the play, is a rich bourgeois of middle age, with two grown children by his first wife. His second wife, Elmire, is attractive, young, and socially clever. We gather from the maid Dorine that Orgon has until lately seemed a good and sensible man, but the Orgon whom we meet in Act One, Scene Four has become a fool. What has happened to him? It appears that he, like many another middle-aged man, has been alarmed by a sense of failing powers and failing authority, and that he has compensated by adopting an extreme religious severity. In this he is comparable to the aging coquette described by Dorine, who "quits a world which fast is quitting her," and saves face by becoming a censorious prude.

Orgon's resort to bigotry has coincided with his discovery of Tartuffe, a wily opportunist who imposes upon him by a pretense of sanctity, and is soon established in Orgon's house as honored guest, spiritual guide, and moral censor. Tartuffe's attitude toward Orgon is perfectly simple: he regards his benefactor as a dupe, and proposes to swindle him as badly as he can. Orgon's attitude toward Tartuffe is more complex and far less conscious. It consists, in part, of an unnatural fondness or "crush" about which the clear-sighted Dorine is explicit:

> He pets and pampers him with love more tender
> Than any pretty mistress could engender. . . .

It also involves, in the strict sense of the word, idolatry: Orgon's febrile religious emotions are all related to Tartuffe and appear to terminate in him. Finally, and least consciously, Orgon cherishes Tartuffe because, with the sanction of the latter's austere precepts, he can tyrannize over his family and punish them for possessing what he feels himself to be losing: youth, gaiety, strong natural desires. This punitive motive comes to the surface, looking like plain sadism, when Orgon orders his daughter to

Marry Tartuffe, and mortify your flesh!

Orgon is thus both Tartuffe's victim and his unconscious exploiter; once we apprehend this, we can better understand Orgon's stubborn refusal to see Tartuffe for the fraud that he is.

When Orgon says to Cléante,

My mother, children, brother and wife could die,
And I'd not feel a single moment's pain,

he is parodying or perverting a Christian idea which derives from the Gospels and rings out purely in Luther's "A Mighty Fortress is Our God":

Let goods and kindred go,
This mortal life also. . . .

The trouble with Orgon's high spirituality is that one cannot obey the first commandment without obeying the second also. Orgon has withdrawn all proper feeling from those about him, and his vicious fatuity creates an atmosphere which is the comic equivalent of *King Lear*'s. All natural bonds of love and trust are strained or broken; evil is taken for good; truth must to kennel. Cléante's reasonings, the rebellious protests of Damis, the entreaties of Mariane, and the mockeries of Dorine are ineffectual against Orgon's folly; he must see Tartuffe paw at his wife, and hear Tartuffe speak contemptuously of him, before he is willing to part with the sponsor of his spiteful piety. How little "religion" there has been in Orgon's behavior, how much it has arisen from infatuation and bitterness, we may judge by his indiscriminate outburst in the fifth act:

> *Enough, by God! I'm through with pious men!*
> *Henceforth I'll hate the whole false brotherhood,*
> *And persecute them worse than Satan could.*

By the time Orgon is made to see Tartuffe's duplicity, the latter has accomplished his swindle, and is in a position to bring about Orgon's material ruin. It takes Louis XIV himself to save the day, in a conclusion which may seem both forced and flattering, but which serves to contrast a judicious, humane and forgiving ruler with the domestic tyrant Orgon. The King's moral insight is Tartuffe's final undoing; nevertheless there is an earlier scene in which we are given better assurance of the invincibility of the natural and sane. I refer to Tartuffe's first conversation with Elmire, in which passion compels the hypocrite recklessly to abandon his role. What comes out of Tartuffe in that scene is an expression of helpless lust, couched in an appalling mixture of the languages of gallantry and devotion. It is not attractive; and yet one is profoundly satisfied to discover that, as W. G. Moore puts it, "Tartuffe's human nature escapes his calculation." To be flawlessly monstrous is, thank heaven, not easy.

In translating *Tartuffe* I have tried, as with *The Misanthrope* some years ago, to reproduce with all possible fidelity both Molière's words and his poetic form. The necessity of keeping verse and rhyme, in such plays as these, was argued at some length in an introduction to the earlier translation, and I shall not repeat all those arguments here. It is true that *Tartuffe* presents an upper-bourgeois rather than a courtly milieu; there is less deliberate wit and elegance than in the dialogue of *The Misanthrope*, and consequently there is less call for the couplet as a conveyor of epigrammatic effects. Yet there are such effects in *Tartuffe*, and rhyme and verse are required here for other good reasons: to pay out the long speeches with clarifying emphasis, and at an assimilable rate; to couple farcical sequences to passages of greater weight and resonance; and to give a purely formal pleasure, as when balancing verse-patterns support the "ballet" movement of the close of Act Two. My convictions being what they are, I am happy to report what a number of productions of the *Misanthrope* translation have shown: that contemporary audiences are quite willing to put up with rhymed verse on the stage.

I thank Messrs. Jacques Barzun and Eric Bentley for encouraging me to undertake this translation; Messrs. Harry Levin, Frederic Musser and Edward Williamson for suggesting improvements in the text; and the Ford and Philadelphia Community Foundations for their support of the project.

Richard Wilbur
Portland, Connecticut
February, 1963

CHARACTERS

MME PERNELLE, Orgon's mother

ORGON, Elmire's husband

ELMIRE, Orgon's wife

DAMIS, Orgon's son, Elmire's stepson

MARIANE, Orgon's daughter, Elmire's stepdaughter,
   in love with Valère

VALÈRE, in love with Mariane

CLÉANTE, Orgon's brother-in-law

TARTUFFE, a hypocrite

DORINE, Mariane's lady's-maid

M. LOYAL, a bailiff

A POLICE OFFICER

FLIPOTE, Mme Pernelle's maid

PLACE
The scene throughout: Orgon's house in Paris

Act One
SCENE ONE

———◆◆———

Madame Pernelle and *Flipote,* her maid, *Elmire,*
Mariane, Dorine, Damis, Cléante

MADAME PERNELLE
Come, come, Flipote; it's time I left this place.

ELMIRE
I can't keep up, you walk at such a pace.

MADAME PERNELLE
Don't trouble, child; no need to show me out.
It's not your manners I'm concerned about.

ELMIRE
We merely pay you the respect we owe.
But, Mother, why this hurry? Must you go?

MADAME PERNELLE
I must. This house appals me. No one in it
Will pay attention for a single minute.
Children, I take my leave much vexed in spirit.
I offer good advice, but you won't hear it.
You all break in and chatter on and on.
It's like a madhouse with the keeper gone.

DORINE
If . . .

MADAME PERNELLE
Girl, you talk too much, and I'm afraid
You're far too saucy for a lady's-maid.
You push in everywhere and have your say.

DAMIS

But . . .

MADAME PERNELLE

You, boy, grow more foolish every day.
To think my grandson should be such a dunce!
I've said a hundred times, if I've said it once,
That if you keep the course on which you've started,
You'll leave your worthy father broken-hearted.

MARIANE

I think . . .

MADAME PERNELLE

And you, his sister, seem so pure,
So shy, so innocent, and so demure.
But you know what they say about still waters.
I pity parents with secretive daughters.

ELMIRE

Now, Mother . . .

MADAME PERNELLE

And as for you, child, let me add
That your behavior is extremely bad,
And a poor example for these children, too.
Their dear, dead mother did far better than you.
You're much too free with money, and I'm distressed
To see you so elaborately dressed.
When it's one's husband that one aims to please,
One has no need of costly fripperies.

CLÉANTE

Oh, Madam, really . . .

MADAME PERNELLE

You are her brother, Sir,
And I respect and love you; yet if I were

My son, this lady's good and pious spouse,
I wouldn't make you welcome in my house.
You're full of worldly counsels which, I fear,
Aren't suitable for decent folk to hear.
I've spoken bluntly, Sir; but it behooves us
Not to mince words when righteous fervor moves us.

DAMIS

Your man Tartuffe is full of holy speeches . . .

MADAME PERNELLE

And practises precisely what he preaches.
He's a fine man, and should be listened to.
I will not hear him mocked by fools like you.

DAMIS

Good God! Do you expect me to submit
To the tyranny of that carping hypocrite?
Must we forgo all joys and satisfactions
Because that bigot censures all our actions?

DORINE

To hear him talk—and he talks all the time—
There's nothing one can do that's not a crime.
He rails at everything, your dear Tartuffe.

MADAME PERNELLE

Whatever he reproves deserves reproof.
He's out to save your souls, and all of you
Must love him, as my son would have you do.

DAMIS

Ah no, Grandmother, I could never take
To such a rascal, even for my father's sake.
That's how I feel, and I shall not dissemble.
His every action makes me seethe and tremble
With helpless anger, and I have no doubt
That he and I will shortly have it out.

DORINE

Surely it is a shame and a disgrace
To see this man usurp the master's place—
To see this beggar who, when first he came,
Had not a shoe or shoestring to his name
So far forget himself that he behaves
As if the house were his, and we his slaves.

MADAME PERNELLE

Well, mark my words, your souls would fare far better
If you obeyed his precepts to the letter.

DORINE

You see him as a saint. I'm far less awed;
In fact, I see right through him. He's a fraud.

MADAME PERNELLE

Nonsense!

DORINE

His man Laurent's the same, or worse;
I'd not trust either with a penny purse.

MADAME PERNELLE

I can't say what his servant's morals may be;
His own great goodness I can guarantee.
You all regard him with distaste and fear
Because he tells you what you're loath to hear,
Condemns your sins, points out your moral flaws,
And humbly strives to further Heaven's cause.

DORINE

If sin is all that bothers him, why is it
He's so upset when folk drop in to visit?
Is Heaven so outraged by a social call
That he must prophesy against us all?
I'll tell you what I think: if you ask me,
He's jealous of my mistress' company.

MADAME PERNELLE

Rubbish! (*To Elmire:*) He's not alone, child, in complaining
Of all of your promiscuous entertaining.
Why, the whole neighborhood's upset, I know,
By all these carriages that come and go,
With crowds of guests parading in and out
And noisy servants loitering about.
In all of this, I'm sure there's nothing vicious;
But why give people cause to be suspicious?

CLÉANTE

They need no cause; they'll talk in any case.
Madam, this world would be a joyless place
If, fearing what malicious tongues might say,
We locked our doors and turned our friends away.
And even if one did so dreary a thing,
D'you think those tongues would cease their chattering?
One can't fight slander; it's a losing battle;
Let us instead ignore their tittle-tattle.
Let's strive to live by conscience' clear decrees,
And let the gossips gossip as they please.

DORINE

If there is talk against us, I know the source:
It's Daphne and her little husband, of course.
Those who have greatest cause for guilt and shame
Are quickest to besmirch a neighbor's name.
When there's a chance for libel, they never miss it;
When something can be made to seem illicit
They're off at once to spread the joyous news,
Adding to fact what fantasies they choose.
By talking up their neighbor's indiscretions
They seek to camouflage their own transgressions,
Hoping that others' innocent affairs
Will lend a hue of innocence to theirs,
Or that their own black guilt will come to seem
Part of a general shady color-scheme.

MADAME PERNELLE

All that is quite irrelevant. I doubt
That anyone's more virtuous and devout
Than dear Orante; and I'm informed that she
Condemns your mode of life most vehemently.

DORINE

Oh, yes, she's strict, devout, and has no taint
Of worldliness; in short, she seems a saint.
But it was time which taught her that disguise;
She's thus because she can't be otherwise.
So long as her attractions could enthrall,
She flounced and flirted and enjoyed it all,
But now that they're no longer what they were
She quits a world which fast is quitting her,
And wears a veil of virtue to conceal
Her bankrupt beauty and her lost appeal.
That's what becomes of old coquettes today:
Distressed when all their lovers fall away,
They see no recourse but to play the prude,
And so confer a style on solitude.
Thereafter, they're severe with everyone,
Condemning all our actions, pardoning none,
And claiming to be pure, austere, and zealous
When, if the truth were known, they're merely jealous,
And cannot bear to see another know
The pleasures time has forced them to forgo.

MADAME PERNELLE (*Initially to Elmire:*)

That sort of talk is what you like to hear;
Therefore you'd have us all keep still, my dear,
While Madam rattles on the livelong day.
Nevertheless, I mean to have my say.
I tell you that you're blest to have Tartuffe
Dwelling, as my son's guest, beneath this roof;
That Heaven has sent him to forestall its wrath
By leading you, once more, to the true path;
That all he reprehends is reprehensible,

And that you'd better heed him, and be sensible.
These visits, balls, and parties in which you revel
Are nothing but inventions of the Devil.
One never hears a word that's edifying:
Nothing but chaff and foolishness and lying,
As well as vicious gossip in which one's neighbor
Is cut to bits with epee, foil, and saber.
People of sense are driven half-insane
At such affairs, where noise and folly reign
And reputations perish thick and fast.
As a wise preacher said on Sunday last,
Parties are Towers of Babylon, because
The guests all babble on with never a pause;
And then he told a story which, I think . . .
                    (*To Cléante:*)
I heard that laugh, Sir, and I saw that wink!
Go find your silly friends and laugh some more!
Enough; I'm going; don't show me to the door.
I leave this household much dismayed and vexed;
I cannot say when I shall see you next.
                    (*Slapping Flipote:*)
Wake up, don't stand there gaping into space!
I'll slap some sense into that stupid face.
Move, move, you slut.

SCENE TWO

Cléante, Dorine

CLÉANTE
I think I'll stay behind;
I want no further pieces of her mind.
How that old lady . . .

DORINE
Oh, what wouldn't she say
If she could hear you speak of her that way!
She'd thank you for the *lady*, but I'm sure
She'd find the *old* a little premature.

CLÉANTE
My, what a scene she made, and what a din!
And how this man Tartuffe has taken her in!

DORINE
Yes, but her son is even worse deceived;
His folly must be seen to be believed.
In the late troubles, he played an able part
And served his king with wise and loyal heart,
But he's quite lost his senses since he fell
Beneath Tartuffe's infatuating spell.
He calls him brother, and loves him as his life,
Preferring him to mother, child, or wife.
In him and him alone will he confide;
He's made him his confessor and his guide;
He pets and pampers him with love more tender
Than any pretty mistress could engender,
Gives him the place of honor when they dine,
Delights to see him gorging like a swine,
Stuffs him with dainties till his guts distend,
And when he belches, cries "God bless you, friend!"
In short, he's mad; he worships him; he dotes;

His deeds he marvels at, his words he quotes,
Thinking each act a miracle, each word
Oracular as those that Moses heard.
Tartuffe, much pleased to find so easy a victim,
Has in a hundred ways beguiled and tricked him,
Milked him of money, and with his permission
Established here a sort of Inquisition.
Even Laurent, his lackey, dares to give
Us arrogant advice on how to live;
He sermonizes us in thundering tones
And confiscates our ribbons and colognes.
Last week he tore a kerchief into pieces
Because he found it pressed in a *Life of Jesus*:
He said it was a sin to juxtapose
Unholy vanities and holy prose.

SCENE THREE

———— •• ————

Elmire, Mariane, Damis, Cléante, Dorine

ELMIRE (*To Cléante:*)
You did well not to follow; she stood in the door
And said *verbatim* all she'd said before.
I saw my husband coming. I think I'd best
Go upstairs now, and take a little rest.

CLÉANTE
I'll wait and greet him here; then I must go.
I've really only time to say hello.

DAMIS
Sound him about my sister's wedding, please.
I think Tartuffe's against it, and that he's
Been urging Father to withdraw his blessing.
As you well know, I'd find that most distressing.
Unless my sister and Valère can marry,
My hopes to wed *his* sister will miscarry,
And I'm determined . . .

DORINE
He's coming.

SCENE FOUR

———————●●———————

Orgon, Cléante, Dorine

ORGON

Ah, Brother, good-day.

CLÉANTE

Well, welcome back. I'm sorry I can't stay.
How was the country? Blooming, I trust, and green?

ORGON

Excuse me, Brother; just one moment.
(*To Dorine:*)

Dorine . . .
(*To Cléante:*)
To put my mind at rest, I always learn
The household news the moment I return.
(*To Dorine:*)
Has all been well, these two days I've been gone?
How are the family? What's been going on?

DORINE

Your wife, two days ago, had a bad fever,
And a fierce headache which refused to leave her.

ORGON

Ah. And Tartuffe?

DORINE

Tartuffe? Why, he's round and red,
Bursting with health, and excellently fed.

ORGON

Poor fellow!

DORINE

That night, the mistress was unable
To take a single bite at the dinner-table.
Her headache-pains, she said, were simply hellish.

ORGON

Ah. And Tartuffe?

DORINE

He ate his meal with relish,
And zealously devoured in her presence
A leg of mutton and a brace of pheasants.

ORGON

Poor fellow!

DORINE

Well, the pains continued strong,
And so she tossed and tossed the whole night long,
Now icy-cold, now burning like a flame.
We sat beside her bed till morning came.

ORGON

Ah. And Tartuffe?

DORINE

Why, having eaten, he rose
And sought his room, already in a doze,
Got into his warm bed, and snored away
In perfect peace until the break of day.

ORGON

Poor fellow!

DORINE

After much ado, we talked her
Into dispatching someone for the doctor.
He bled her, and the fever quickly fell.

ORGON
Ah. And Tartuffe?

DORINE
He bore it very well.
To keep his cheerfulness at any cost,
And make up for the blood *Madame* had lost,
He drank, at lunch, four beakers full of port.

ORGON
Poor fellow!

DORINE
Both are doing well, in short.
I'll go and tell *Madame* that you've expressed
Keen sympathy and anxious interest.

SCENE FIVE

Orgon, Cléante

CLÉANTE

That girl was laughing in your face, and though
I've no wish to offend you, even so
I'm bound to say that she had some excuse.
How can you possibly be such a goose?
Are you so dazed by this man's hocus-pocus
That all the world, save him, is out of focus?
You've given him clothing, shelter, food, and care;
Why must you also . . .

ORGON

               Brother, stop right there.
You do not know the man of whom you speak.

CLÉANTE

I grant you that. But my judgment's not so weak
That I can't tell, by his effect on others . . .

ORGON

Ah, when you meet him, you two will be like brothers!
There's been no loftier soul since time began.
He is a man who . . . a man who . . . an excellent man.
To keep his precepts is to be reborn,
And view this dunghill of a world with scorn.
Yes, thanks to him I'm a changed man indeed.
Under his tutelage my soul's been freed
From earthly loves, and every human tie:
My mother, children, brother, and wife could die,
And I'd not feel a single moment's pain.

CLÉANTE

That's a fine sentiment, Brother; most humane.

ORGON

Oh, had you seen Tartuffe as I first knew him,
Your heart, like mine, would have surrendered to him.
He used to come into our church each day
And humbly kneel nearby, and start to pray.
He'd draw the eyes of everybody there
By the deep fervor of his heartfelt prayer;
He'd sigh and weep, and sometimes with a sound
Of rapture he would bend and kiss the ground;
And when I rose to go, he'd run before
To offer me holy-water at the door.
His serving-man, no less devout than he,
Informed me of his master's poverty;
I gave him gifts, but in his humbleness
He'd beg me every time to give him less.
"Oh, that's too much," he'd cry, "too much by twice!
I don't deserve it. The half, Sir, would suffice."
And when I wouldn't take it back, he'd share
Half of it with the poor, right then and there.
At length, Heaven prompted me to take him in
To dwell with us, and free our souls from sin.
He guides our lives, and to protect my honor
Stays by my wife, and keeps an eye upon her;
He tells me whom she sees, and all she does,
And seems more jealous than I ever was!
And how austere he is! Why, he can detect
A mortal sin where you would least suspect;
In smallest trifles, he's extremely strict.
Last week, his conscience was severely pricked
Because, while praying, he had caught a flea
And killed it, so he felt, too wrathfully.

CLÉANTE

Good God, man! Have you lost your common sense—
Or is this all some joke at my expense?
How can you stand there and in all sobriety . . .

ORGON

Brother, your language savors of impiety.
Too much free-thinking's made your faith unsteady,
And as I've warned you many times already,
'Twill get you into trouble before you're through.

CLÉANTE

So I've been told before by dupes like you:
Being blind, you'd have all others blind as well,
The clear-eyed man you call an infidel,
And he who sees through humbug and pretense
Is charged, by you, with want of reverence.
Spare me your warnings, Brother; I have no fear
Of speaking out, for you and Heaven to hear,
Against affected zeal and pious knavery.
There's true and false in piety, as in bravery,
And just as those whose courage shines the most
In battle, are the least inclined to boast,
So those whose hearts are truly pure and lowly
Don't make a flashy show of being holy.
There's a vast difference, so it seems to me,
Between true piety and hypocrisy:
How do you fail to see it, may I ask?
Is not a face quite different from a mask?
Cannot sincerity and cunning art,
Reality and semblance, be told apart?
Are scarecrows just like men, and do you hold
That a false coin is just as good as gold?
Ah, Brother, man's a strangely fashioned creature
Who seldom is content to follow Nature,
But recklessly pursues his inclination
Beyond the narrow bounds of moderation,
And often, by transgressing Reason's laws,
Perverts a lofty aim or noble cause.
A passing observation, but it applies.

ORGON

I see, dear Brother, that you're profoundly wise;
You harbor all the insight of the age.
You are our one clear mind, our only sage,
The era's oracle, its Cato too,
And all mankind are fools compared to you.

CLÉANTE

Brother, I don't pretend to be a sage,
Nor have I all the wisdom of the age.
There's just one insight I would dare to claim:
I know that true and false are not the same;
And just as there is nothing I more revere
Than a soul whose faith is steadfast and sincere,
Nothing that I more cherish and admire
Than honest zeal and true religious fire,
So there is nothing that I find more base
Than specious piety's dishonest face—
Than these bold mountebanks, these histrios
Whose impious mummeries and hollow shows
Exploit our love of Heaven, and make a jest
Of all that men think holiest and best;
These calculating souls who offer prayers
Not to their Maker, but as public wares,
And seek to buy respect and reputation
With lifted eyes and sighs of exaltation;
These charlatans, I say, whose pilgrim souls
Proceed, by way of Heaven, toward earthly goals,
Who weep and pray and swindle and extort,
Who preach the monkish life, but haunt the court,
Who make their zeal the partner of their vice—
Such men are vengeful, sly, and cold as ice,
And when there is an enemy to defame
They cloak their spite in fair religion's name,
Their private spleen and malice being made
To seem a high and virtuous crusade,
Until, to mankind's reverent applause,
They crucify their foe in Heaven's cause.

Such knaves are all too common; yet, for the wise,
True piety isn't hard to recognize,
And, happily, these present times provide us
With bright examples to instruct and guide us.
Consider Ariston and Périandre;
Look at Oronte, Alcidamas, Clitandre;
Their virtue is acknowledged; who could doubt it?
But you won't hear them beat the drum about it.
They're never ostentatious, never vain,
And their religion's moderate and humane;
It's not their way to criticize and chide:
They think censoriousness a mark of pride,
And therefore, letting others preach and rave,
They show, by deeds, how Christians should behave.
They think no evil of their fellow man,
But judge of him as kindly as they can.
They don't intrigue and wangle and conspire;
To lead a good life is their one desire;
The sinner wakes no rancorous hate in them;
It is the sin alone which they condemn;
Nor do they try to show a fiercer zeal
For Heaven's cause than Heaven itself could feel.
These men I honor, these men I advocate
As models for us all to emulate.
Your man is not their sort at all, I fear:
And, while your praise of him is quite sincere,
I think that you've been dreadfully deluded.

ORGON

Now then, dear Brother, is your speech concluded?

CLÉANTE

Why, yes.

ORGON

Your servant, Sir. (*He turns to go.*)

CLÉANTE
                              No, Brother; wait.
There's one more matter. You agreed of late
That young Valère might have your daughter's hand.

ORGON
I did.

CLÉANTE
And set the date, I understand.

ORGON
Quite so.

CLÉANTE
You've now postponed it; is that true?

ORGON
No doubt.

CLÉANTE
The match no longer pleases you?

ORGON
Who knows?

CLÉANTE
D'you mean to go back on your word?

ORGON
I won't say that.

CLÉANTE
Has anything occurred
Which might entitle you to break your pledge?

ORGON
Perhaps.

CLÉANTE
Why must you hem, and haw, and hedge?
The boy asked me to sound you in this affair . . .

ORGON
It's been a pleasure.

CLÉANTE
But what shall I tell Valère?

ORGON
Whatever you like.

CLÉANTE
But what have you decided?
What are your plans?

ORGON
I plan, Sir, to be guided
By Heaven's will.

CLÉANTE
Come, Brother, don't talk rot.
You've given Valère your word; will you keep it, or not?

ORGON
Good day.

CLÉANTE
This looks like poor Valère's undoing;
I'll go and warn him that there's trouble brewing.

Act Two

SCENE ONE

───────◆◆───────

Orgon, Mariane

ORGON

Mariane.

MARIANE

Yes, Father?

ORGON

A word with you; come here.

MARIANE

What are you looking for?

ORGON (*Peering into a small closet:*)
Eavesdroppers, dear.
I'm making sure we shan't be overheard.
Someone in there could catch our every word.
Ah, good, we're safe. Now, Mariane, my child,
You're a sweet girl who's tractable and mild,
Whom I hold dear, and think most highly of.

MARIANE

I'm deeply grateful, Father, for your love.

ORGON

That's well said, Daughter; and you can repay me
If, in all things, you'll cheerfully obey me.

MARIANE

To please you, Sir, is what delights me best.

ORGON

Good, good. Now, what d'you think of Tartuffe, our guest?

MARIANE

I, Sir?

ORGON

Yes. Weigh your answer; think it through.

MARIANE

Oh, dear. I'll say whatever you wish me to.

ORGON

That's wisely said, my Daughter. Say of him, then,
That he's the very worthiest of men,
And that you're fond of him, and would rejoice
In being his wife, if that should be my choice.
Well?

MARIANE

What?

ORGON

What's that?

MARIANE

I . . .

ORGON

Well?

MARIANE

Forgive me, pray.

ORGON

Did you not hear me?

MARIANE

Of *whom*, Sir, must I say
That I am fond of him, and would rejoice
In being his wife, if that should be your choice?

ORGON

Why, of Tartuffe.

MARIANE

But, Father, that's false, you know.
Why would you have me say what isn't so?

ORGON

Because I am resolved it shall be true.
That it's my wish should be enough for you.

MARIANE

You can't mean, Father . . .

ORGON

Yes, Tartuffe shall be
Allied by marriage to this family,
And he's to be your husband, is that clear?
It's a father's privilege . . .

SCENE TWO

Dorine, Orgon, Mariane

ORGON (*To Dorine:*)
     What are you doing in here?
Is curiosity so fierce a passion
With you, that you must eavesdrop in this fashion?

DORINE

There's lately been a rumor going about—
Based on some hunch or chance remark, no doubt—
That you mean Mariane to wed Tartuffe.
I've laughed it off, of course, as just a spoof.

ORGON

You find it so incredible?

DORINE

     Yes, I do.
I won't accept that story, even from you.

ORGON

Well, you'll believe it when the thing is done.

DORINE

Yes, yes, of course. Go on and have your fun.

ORGON

I've never been more serious in my life.

DORINE

Ha!

ORGON

Daughter, I mean it; you're to be his wife.

DORINE

No, don't believe your father; it's all a hoax.

ORGON

See here, young woman . . .

DORINE

Come, Sir, no more jokes;
You can't fool us.

ORGON

How dare you talk that way?

DORINE

All right, then: we believe you, sad to say.
But how a man like you, who looks so wise
And wears a moustache of such splendid size,
Can be so foolish as to . . .

ORGON

Silence, please!
My girl, you take too many liberties.
I'm master here, as you must not forget.

DORINE

Do let's discuss this calmly; don't be upset.
You can't be serious, Sir, about this plan.
What should that bigot want with Mariane?
Praying and fasting ought to keep him busy.
And then, in terms of wealth and rank, what is he?
Why should a man of property like you
Pick out a beggar son-in-law?

ORGON

That will do.
Speak of his poverty with reverence.
His is a pure and saintly indigence
Which far transcends all worldly pride and pelf.

He lost his fortune, as he says himself,
Because he cared for Heaven alone, and so
Was careless of his interests here below.
I mean to get him out of his present straits
And help him to recover his estates—
Which, in his part of the world, have no small fame.
Poor though he is, he's a gentleman just the same.

DORINE

Yes, so he tells us; and, Sir, it seems to me
Such pride goes very ill with piety.
A man whose spirit spurns this dungy earth
Ought not to brag of lands and noble birth;
Such worldly arrogance will hardly square
With meek devotion and the life of prayer.
. . . But this approach, I see, has drawn a blank;
Let's speak, then, of his person, not his rank.
Doesn't it seem to you a trifle grim
To give a girl like her to a man like him?
When two are so ill-suited, can't you see
What the sad consequence is bound to be?
A young girl's virtue is imperilled, Sir,
When such a marriage is imposed on her;
For if one's bridegroom isn't to one's taste,
It's hardly an inducement to be chaste,
And many a man with horns upon his brow
Has made his wife the thing that she is now.
It's hard to be a faithful wife, in short,
To certain husbands of a certain sort,
And he who gives his daughter to a man she hates
Must answer for her sins at Heaven's gates.
Think, Sir, before you play so risky a role.

ORGON

This servant-girl presumes to save my soul!

DORINE

You would do well to ponder what I've said.

ORGON

Daughter, we'll disregard this dunderhead.
Just trust your father's judgment. Oh, I'm aware
That I once promised you to young Valère;
But now I hear he gambles, which greatly shocks me;
What's more, I've doubts about his orthodoxy.
His visits to church, I note, are very few.

DORINE

Would you have him go at the same hours as you,
And kneel nearby, to be sure of being seen?

ORGON

I can dispense with such remarks, Dorine.
(*To Mariane:*)
Tartuffe, however, is sure of Heaven's blessing,
And that's the only treasure worth possessing.
This match will bring you joys beyond all measure;
Your cup will overflow with every pleasure;
You two will interchange your faithful loves
Like two sweet cherubs, or two turtle-doves.
No harsh word shall be heard, no frown be seen,
And he shall make you happy as a queen.

DORINE

And she'll make him a cuckold, just wait and see.

ORGON

What language!

DORINE

Oh, he's a man of destiny;
He's *made* for horns, and what the stars demand
Your daughter's virtue surely can't withstand.

ORGON

Don't interrupt me further. Why can't you learn
That certain things are none of your concern?

DORINE

It's for your own sake that I interfere.
(*She repeatedly interrupts Orgon just as he is turning
to speak to his daughter:*)

ORGON

Most kind of you. Now, hold your tongue, d'you hear?

DORINE

If I didn't love you . . .

ORGON
      Spare me your affection.

DORINE

I'll love you, Sir, in spite of your objection.

ORGON

Blast!

DORINE

      I can't bear, Sir, for your honor's sake,
To let you make this ludicrous mistake.

ORGON

You mean to go on talking?

DORINE

         If I didn't protest
This sinful marriage, my conscience couldn't rest.

ORGON

If you don't hold your tongue, you little shrew . . .

DORINE

What, lost your temper? A pious man like you?

ORGON

Yes! Yes! You talk and talk. I'm maddened by it.
Once and for all, I tell you to be quiet.

DORINE

Well, I'll be quiet. But I'll be thinking hard.

ORGON

Think all you like, but you had better guard
That saucy tongue of yours, or I'll . . .
                              (*Turning back to Mariane:*)
                                             Now, child,
I've weighed this matter fully.

DORINE (*Aside:*)
                              It drives me wild
That I can't speak.
              (*Orgon turns his head, and she is silent.*)

ORGON
              Tartuffe is no young dandy,
But, still, his person . . .

DORINE (*Aside:*)
              Is as sweet as candy.

ORGON

Is such that, even if you shouldn't care
For his other merits . . .
              (*He turns and stands facing Dorine, arms crossed.*)

DORINE (*Aside:*)
              They'll make a lovely pair.
If I were she, no man would marry me
Against my inclination, and go scot-free.
He'd learn, before the wedding-day was over,
How readily a wife can find a lover.

ORGON (*To Dorine:*)
It seems you treat my orders as a joke.

DORINE

Why, what's the matter? 'Twas not to you I spoke.

ORGON

What *were* you doing?

DORINE
Talking to myself, that's all.

ORGON

Ah! (*Aside:*) One more bit of impudence and gall,
And I shall give her a good slap in the face.
(*He puts himself in position to slap her; Dorine,
whenever he glances at her, stands immobile
and silent:*)
Daughter, you shall accept, and with good grace,
The husband I've selected . . . Your wedding-day . . .
(*To Dorine:*)
Why don't you talk to yourself?

DORINE
I've nothing to say.

ORGON

Come, just one word.

DORINE
No thank you, Sir. I pass.

ORGON

Come, speak; I'm waiting.

DORINE
I'd not be such an ass.

ORGON (*Turning to Mariane:*)
In short, dear Daughter, I mean to be obeyed,
And you must bow to the sound choice I've made.

DORINE (*Moving away:*)
I'd not wed such a monster, even in jest.
                    (*Orgon attempts to slap her, but misses.*)

ORGON
Daughter, that maid of yours is a thorough pest;
She makes me sinfully annoyed and nettled.
I can't speak further; my nerves are too unsettled.
She's so upset me by her insolent talk,
I'll calm myself by going for a walk.

SCENE THREE

————— • • —————

Dorine, Mariane

DORINE (*Returning:*)
Well, have you lost your tongue, girl? Must I play
Your part, and say the lines you ought to say?
Faced with a fate so hideous and absurd,
Can you not utter one dissenting word?

MARIANE
What good would it do? A father's power is great.

DORINE
Resist him now, or it will be too late.

MARIANE
But . . .

DORINE
          Tell him one cannot love at a father's whim;
That you shall marry for yourself, not him;
That since it's you who are to be the bride,
It's you, not he, who must be satisfied;
And that if his Tartuffe is so sublime,
He's free to marry him at any time.

MARIANE
I've bowed so long to Father's strict control,
I couldn't oppose him now, to save my soul.

DORINE
Come, come, Mariane. Do listen to reason, won't you?
Valère has asked your hand. Do you love him, or don't you?

MARIANE

Oh, how unjust of you! What can you mean
By asking such a question, dear Dorine?
You know the depth of my affection for him;
I've told you a hundred times how I adore him.

DORINE

I don't believe in everything I hear;
Who knows if your professions were sincere?

MARIANE

They were, Dorine, and you do me wrong to doubt it;
Heaven knows that I've been all too frank about it.

DORINE

You love him, then?

MARIANE

Oh, more than I can express.

DORINE

And he, I take it, cares for you no less?

MARIANE

I think so.

DORINE

And you both, with equal fire,
Burn to be married?

MARIANE

That is our one desire.

DORINE

What of Tartuffe, then? What of your father's plan?

MARIANE

I'll kill myself, if I'm forced to wed that man.

DORINE

I hadn't thought of that recourse. How splendid!
Just die, and all your troubles will be ended!
A fine solution. Oh, it maddens me
To hear you talk in that self-pitying key.

MARIANE

Dorine, how harsh you are! It's most unfair.
You have no sympathy for my despair.

DORINE

I've none at all for people who talk drivel
And, faced with difficulties, whine and snivel.

MARIANE

No doubt I'm timid, but it would be wrong . . .

DORINE

True love requires a heart that's firm and strong.

MARIANE

I'm strong in my affection for Valère,
But coping with my father is his affair.

DORINE

But if your father's brain has grown so cracked
Over his dear Tartuffe that he can retract
His blessing, though your wedding-day was named,
It's surely not Valère who's to be blamed.

MARIANE

If I defied my father, as you suggest,
Would it not seem unmaidenly, at best?
Shall I defend my love at the expense
Of brazenness and disobedience?
Shall I parade my heart's desires, and flaunt . . .

DORINE

No, I ask nothing of you. Clearly you want
To be Madame Tartuffe, and I feel bound
Not to oppose a wish so very sound.
What right have I to criticize the match?
Indeed, my dear, the man's a brilliant catch.
Monsieur Tartuffe! Now, there's a man of weight!
Yes, yes, Monsieur Tartuffe, I'm bound to state,
Is quite a person; that's not to be denied;
'Twill be no little thing to be his bride.
The world already rings with his renown;
He's a great noble—in his native town;
His ears are red, he has a pink complexion,
And all in all, he'll suit you to perfection.

MARIANE

Dear God!

DORINE

Oh, how triumphant you will feel
At having caught a husband so ideal!

MARIANE

Oh, do stop teasing, and use your cleverness
To get me out of this appalling mess.
Advise me, and I'll do whatever you say.

DORINE

Ah no, a dutiful daughter must obey
Her father, even if he weds her to an ape.
You've a bright future; why struggle to escape?
Tartuffe will take you back where his family lives,
To a small town aswarm with relatives—
Uncles and cousins whom you'll be charmed to meet.
You'll be received at once by the elite,
Calling upon the bailiff's wife, no less—
Even, perhaps, upon the mayoress,

Who'll sit you down in the *best* kitchen chair.
Then, once a year, you'll dance at the village fair
To the drone of bagpipes—two of them, in fact—
And see a puppet-show, or an animal act.
Your husband . . .

                    MARIANE
                Oh, you turn my blood to ice!
Stop torturing me, and give me your advice.

            DORINE (*Threatening to go:*)
Your servant, Madam.

                    MARIANE
                Dorine, I beg of you . . .

                    DORINE
No, you deserve it; this marriage must go through.

                    MARIANE

Dorine!

                    DORINE

        No.

                    MARIANE
            Not Tartuffe! You know I think him . . .

                    DORINE
Tartuffe's your cup of tea, and you shall drink him.

                    MARIANE
I've always told you everything, and relied . . .

                    DORINE
No. You deserve to be tartuffified.

MARIANE

Well, since you mock me and refuse to care,
I'll henceforth seek my solace in despair:
Despair shall be my counsellor and friend,
And help me bring my sorrows to an end.
(*She starts to leave.*)

DORINE

There now, come back; my anger has subsided.
You do deserve some pity, I've decided.

MARIANE

Dorine, if Father makes me undergo
This dreadful martyrdom, I'll die, I know.

DORINE

Don't fret; it won't be difficult to discover
Some plan of action . . . But here's Valère, your lover.

SCENE FOUR

Valère, Mariane, Dorine

VALÈRE

Madam, I've just received some wondrous news
Regarding which I'd like to hear your views.

MARIANE

What news?

VALÈRE

You're marrying Tartuffe.

MARIANE

               I find
That Father does have such a match in mind.

VALÈRE

Your father, Madam . . .

MARIANE

            . . . has just this minute said
That it's Tartuffe he wishes me to wed.

VALÈRE

Can he be serious?

MARIANE

          Oh, indeed he can;
He's clearly set his heart upon the plan.

VALÈRE

And what position do you propose to take,
Madam?

MARIANE

Why—I don't know.

VALÈRE

For heaven's sake—

You don't know?

MARIANE

No.

VALÈRE

Well, well!

MARIANE

Advise me, do.

VALÈRE

Marry the man. That's my advice to you.

MARIANE

That's your advice?

VALÈRE

Yes.

MARIANE

Truly?

VALÈRE

Oh, absolutely.

You couldn't choose more wisely, more astutely.

MARIANE

Thanks for this counsel; I'll follow it, of course.

VALÈRE

Do, do; I'm sure 'twill cost you no remorse.

MARIANE

To give it didn't cause your heart to break.

VALÈRE

I gave it, Madam, only for your sake.

MARIANE

And it's for your sake that I take it, Sir.

DORINE (*Withdrawing to the rear of the stage:*)
Let's see which fool will prove the stubborner.

VALÈRE

So! I am nothing to you, and it was flat
Deception when you . . .

MARIANE

Please, enough of that.
You've told me plainly that I should agree
To wed the man my father's chosen for me,
And since you've deigned to counsel me so wisely,
I promise, Sir, to do as you advise me.

VALÈRE

Ah, no, 'twas not by me that you were swayed.
No, your decision was already made;
Though now, to save appearances, you protest
That you're betraying me at my behest.

MARIANE

Just as you say.

VALÈRE

Quite so. And I now see
That you were never truly in love with me.

MARIANE

Alas, you're free to think so if you choose.

VALÈRE

I choose to think so, and here's a bit of news:
You've spurned my hand, but I know where to turn
For kinder treatment, as you shall quickly learn.

MARIANE

I'm sure you do. Your noble qualities
Inspire affection . . .

VALÈRE

                    Forget my qualities, please.
They don't inspire you overmuch, I find.
But there's another lady I have in mind
Whose sweet and generous nature will not scorn
To compensate me for the loss I've borne.

MARIANE

I'm no great loss, and I'm sure that you'll transfer
Your heart quite painlessly from me to her.

VALÈRE

I'll do my best to take it in my stride.
The pain I feel at being cast aside
Time and forgetfulness may put an end to.
Or if I can't forget, I shall pretend to.
No self-respecting person is expected
To go on loving once he's been rejected.

MARIANE

Now, that's a fine, high-minded sentiment.

VALÈRE

One to which any sane man would assent.
Would you prefer it if I pined away
In hopeless passion till my dying day?
Am I to yield you to a rival's arms
And not console myself with other charms?

MARIANE

Go then: console yourself; don't hesitate.
I wish you to; indeed, I cannot wait.

VALÈRE

You wish me to?

MARIANE

Yes.

VALÈRE

That's the final straw.
Madam, farewell. Your wish shall be my law.
(*He starts to leave, and then returns: this repeatedly:*)

MARIANE

Splendid.

VALÈRE (*Coming back again:*)
This breach, remember, is of your making;
It's you who've driven me to the step I'm taking.

MARIANE

Of course.

VALÈRE (*Coming back again:*)
Remember, too, that I am merely
Following your example.

MARIANE

I see that clearly.

VALÈRE

Enough. I'll go and do your bidding, then.

MARIANE

Good.

VALÈRE (*Coming back again:*)
You shall never see my face again.

MARIANE

Excellent.

VALÈRE (*Walking to the door, then turning about:*)
Yes?

MARIANE

What?

VALÈRE
What's that? What did you say?

MARIANE

Nothing. You're dreaming.

VALÈRE
Ah. Well, I'm on my way.
Farewell, *Madame.*
(*He moves slowly away.*)

MARIANE
Farewell.

DORINE (*To Mariane:*)
If you ask me,
Both of you are as mad as mad can be.
Do stop this nonsense, now. I've only let you
Squabble so long to see where it would get you.
Whoa there, Monsieur Valère!
(*She goes and seizes Valère by the arm; he makes a great
show of resistance.*)

VALÈRE
What's this, Dorine?

DORINE

Come here.

VALÈRE

No, no, my heart's too full of spleen.
Don't hold me back; her wish must be obeyed.

DORINE

Stop!

VALÈRE

It's too late now; my decision's made.

DORINE

Oh, pooh!

MARIANE (*Aside:*)

He hates the sight of me, that's plain.
I'll go, and so deliver him from pain.

DORINE (*Leaving Valère, running after Mariane:*)
And now *you* run away! Come back.

MARIANE

No, no.
Nothing you say will keep me here. Let go!

VALÈRE (*Aside:*)
She cannot bear my presence, I perceive.
To spare her further torment, I shall leave.

DORINE (*Leaving Mariane, running after Valère:*)
Again! You'll not escape, Sir; don't you try it.
Come here, you two. Stop fussing, and be quiet.
    (*She takes Valère by the hand, then Mariane,
    and draws them together.*)

VALÈRE (*To Dorine:*)
What do you want of me?

MARIANE (*To Dorine:*)
What is the point of this?

DORINE
We're going to have a little armistice.
(*To Valère:*)
Now, weren't you silly to get so overheated?

VALÈRE
Didn't you see how badly I was treated?

DORINE (*To Mariane:*)
Aren't you a simpleton, to have lost your head?

MARIANE
Didn't you hear the hateful things he said?

DORINE (*To Valère:*)
You're both great fools. Her sole desire, Valère,
Is to be yours in marriage. To that I'll swear.
(*To Mariane:*)
He loves you only, and he wants no wife
But you, Mariane. On that I'll stake my life.

MARIANE (*To Valère:*)
Then why you advised me so, I cannot see.

VALÈRE (*To Mariane:*)
On such a question, why ask advice of *me*?

DORINE
Oh, you're impossible. Give me your hands, you two.
(*To Valère:*)
Yours first.

VALÈRE (*Giving Dorine his hand:*)
But why?

DORINE (*To Mariane:*)
And now a hand from you.

MARIANE (*Also giving Dorine her hand:*)
What are you doing?

DORINE
There: a perfect fit.
You suit each other better than you'll admit.
    (*Valère and Mariane hold hands for some time without
    looking at each other.*)

VALÈRE (*Turning toward Mariane:*)
Ah, come, don't be so haughty. Give a man
A look of kindness, won't you, Mariane?
    (*Mariane turns toward Valère and smiles.*)

DORINE
I tell you, lovers are completely mad!

VALÈRE (*To Mariane:*)
Now come, confess that you were very bad
To hurt my feelings as you did just now.
I have a just complaint, you must allow.

MARIANE
You must allow that you were most unpleasant . . .

DORINE
Let's table that discussion for the present;
Your father has a plan which must be stopped.

MARIANE
Advise us, then; what means must we adopt?

DORINE

We'll use all manner of means, and all at once.
(*To Mariane:*)
Your father's addled; he's acting like a dunce.
Therefore you'd better humor the old fossil.
Pretend to yield to him, be sweet and docile,
And then postpone, as often as necessary,
The day on which you have agreed to marry.
You'll thus gain time, and time will turn the trick.
Sometimes, for instance, you'll be taken sick,
And that will seem good reason for delay;
Or some bad omen will make you change the day—
You'll dream of muddy water, or you'll pass
A dead man's hearse, or break a looking-glass.
If all else fails, no man can marry you
Unless you take his ring and say "I do."
But now, let's separate. If they should find
Us talking here, our plot might be divined.
(*To Valère:*)
Go to your friends, and tell them what's occurred,
And have them urge her father to keep his word.
Meanwhile, we'll stir her brother into action,
And get Elmire, as well, to join our faction.
Good-bye.

VALÈRE (*To Mariane:*)
Though each of us will do his best,
It's your true heart on which my hopes shall rest.

MARIANE (*To Valère:*)
Regardless of what Father may decide,
None but Valère shall claim me as his bride.

VALÈRE
Oh, how those words content me! Come what will . . .

DORINE

Oh, lovers, lovers! Their tongues are never still.
Be off, now.

VALÈRE (*Turning to go, then turning back:*)
One last word . . .

DORINE

No time to chat:
You leave by this door; and *you* leave by that.
(*Dorine pushes them, by the shoulders, toward opposing
doors.*)

Act Three

SCENE ONE

———— ◆ ————

Damis, Dorine

DAMIS

May lightning strike me even as I speak,
May all men call me cowardly and weak,
If any fear or scruple holds me back
From settling things, at once, with that great quack!

DORINE

Now, don't give way to violent emotion.
Your father's merely talked about this notion,
And words and deeds are far from being one.
Much that is talked about is left undone.

DAMIS

No, I must stop that scoundrel's machinations;
I'll go and tell him off; I'm out of patience.

DORINE

Do calm down and be practical. I had rather
My mistress dealt with him—and with your father.
She has some influence with Tartuffe, I've noted.
He hangs upon her words, seems most devoted,
And may, indeed, be smitten by her charm.
Pray Heaven it's true! 'Twould do our cause no harm.
She sent for him, just now, to sound him out
On this affair you're so incensed about;
She'll find out where he stands, and tell him, too,
What dreadful strife and trouble will ensue
If he lends countenance to your father's plan.
I couldn't get in to see him, but his man
Says that he's almost finished with his prayers.
Go, now. I'll catch him when he comes downstairs.

DAMIS

I want to hear this conference, and I will.

DORINE

No, they must be alone.

DAMIS

Oh, I'll keep still.

DORINE

Not you. I know your temper. You'd start a brawl,
And shout and stamp your foot and spoil it all.
Go on.

DAMIS

I won't; I have a perfect right . . .

DORINE

Lord, you're a nuisance! He's coming; get out of sight.
(*Damis conceals himself in a closet at the rear of the stage.*)

SCENE TWO

———— •◦• ————

Tartuffe, Dorine

TARTUFFE (*Observing Dorine, and calling to his
manservant offstage:*)
Hang up my hair-shirt, put my scourge in place,
And pray, Laurent, for Heaven's perpetual grace.
I'm going to the prison now, to share
My last few coins with the poor wretches there.

DORINE (*Aside:*)
Dear God, what affectation! What a fake!

TARTUFFE
You wished to see me?

DORINE
Yes . . .

TARTUFFE (*Taking a handkerchief from his pocket:*)
For mercy's sake,
Please take this handkerchief, before you speak.

DORINE
What?

TARTUFFE
Cover that bosom, girl. The flesh is weak,
And unclean thoughts are difficult to control.
Such sights as that can undermine the soul.

DORINE
Your soul, it seems, has very poor defenses,
And flesh makes quite an impact on your senses.
It's strange that you're so easily excited;
My own desires are not so soon ignited,

And if I saw you naked as a beast,
Not all your hide would tempt me in the least.

TARTUFFE

Girl, speak more modestly; unless you do,
I shall be forced to take my leave of you.

DORINE

Oh, no, it's I who must be on my way;
I've just one little message to convey.
Madame is coming down, and begs you, Sir,
To wait and have a word or two with her.

TARTUFFE

Gladly.

DORINE (*Aside:*)
That had a softening effect!
I think my guess about him was correct.

TARTUFFE

Will she be long?

DORINE
No: that's her step I hear.
Ah, here she is, and I shall disappear.

SCENE THREE

———•●•———

Elmire, Tartuffe

TARTUFFE

May Heaven, whose infinite goodness we adore,
Preserve your body and soul forevermore,
And bless your days, and answer thus the plea
Of one who is its humblest votary.

ELMIRE

I thank you for that pious wish. But please,
Do take a chair and let's be more at ease.
                    (*They sit down.*)

TARTUFFE

I trust that you are once more well and strong?

ELMIRE

Oh, yes: the fever didn't last for long.

TARTUFFE

My prayers are too unworthy, I am sure,
To have gained from Heaven this most gracious cure;
But lately, Madam, my every supplication
Has had for object your recuperation.

ELMIRE

You shouldn't have troubled so. I don't deserve it.

TARTUFFE

Your health is priceless, Madam, and to preserve it
I'd gladly give my own, in all sincerity.

ELMIRE

Sir, you outdo us all in Christian charity.
You've been most kind. I count myself your debtor.

TARTUFFE

'Twas nothing, Madam. I long to serve you better.

ELMIRE

There's a private matter I'm anxious to discuss.
I'm glad there's no one here to hinder us.

TARTUFFE

I too am glad; it floods my heart with bliss
To find myself alone with you like this.
For just this chance I've prayed with all my power—
But prayed in vain, until this happy hour.

ELMIRE

This won't take long, Sir, and I hope you'll be
Entirely frank and unconstrained with me.

TARTUFFE

Indeed, there's nothing I had rather do
Than bare my inmost heart and soul to you.
First, let me say that what remarks I've made
About the constant visits you are paid
Were prompted not by any mean emotion,
But rather by a pure and deep devotion,
A fervent zeal . . .

ELMIRE

No need for explanation.
Your sole concern, I'm sure, was my salvation.

TARTUFFE (*Taking Elmire's hand and pressing
her fingertips:*)
Quite so; and such great fervor do I feel . . .

ELMIRE

Ooh! Please! You're pinching!

TARTUFFE
'Twas from excess of zeal.
I never meant to cause you pain, I swear.
I'd rather . . .
(*He places his hand on Elmire's knee.*)

ELMIRE
What can your hand be doing there?

TARTUFFE
Feeling your gown; what soft, fine-woven stuff!

ELMIRE
Please, I'm extremely ticklish. That's enough.
(*She draws her chair away; Tartuffe pulls his after her.*)

TARTUFFE (*Fondling the lace collar of her gown:*)
My, my, what lovely lacework on your dress!
The workmanship's miraculous, no less.
I've not seen anything to equal it.

ELMIRE
Yes, quite. But let's talk business for a bit.
They say my husband means to break his word
And give his daughter to you, Sir. Had you heard?

TARTUFFE
He did once mention it. But I confess
I dream of quite a different happiness.
It's elsewhere, Madam, that my eyes discern
The promise of that bliss for which I yearn.

ELMIRE
I see: you care for nothing here below.

TARTUFFE
Ah, well—my heart's not made of stone, you know.

ELMIRE

All your desires mount heavenward, I'm sure,
In scorn of all that's earthly and impure.

TARTUFFE

A love of heavenly beauty does not preclude
A proper love for earthly pulchritude;
Our senses are quite rightly captivated
By perfect works our Maker has created.
Some glory clings to all that Heaven has made;
In you, all Heaven's marvels are displayed.
On that fair face, such beauties have been lavished,
The eyes are dazzled and the heart is ravished;
How could I look on you, O flawless creature,
And not adore the Author of all Nature,
Feeling a love both passionate and pure
For you, his triumph of self-portraiture?
At first, I trembled lest that love should be
A subtle snare that Hell had laid for me;
I vowed to flee the sight of you, eschewing
A rapture that might prove my soul's undoing;
But soon, fair being, I became aware
That my deep passion could be made to square
With rectitude, and with my bounden duty.
I thereupon surrendered to your beauty.
It is, I know, presumptuous on my part
To bring you this poor offering of my heart,
And it is not my merit, Heaven knows,
But your compassion on which my hopes repose.
You are my peace, my solace, my salvation;
On you depends my bliss—or desolation;
I bide your judgment and, as you think best,
I shall be either miserable or blest.

ELMIRE

Your declaration is most gallant, Sir,
But don't you think it's out of character?

You'd have done better to restrain your passion
And think before you spoke in such a fashion.
It ill becomes a pious man like you . . .

TARTUFFE

I may be pious, but I'm human too:
With your celestial charms before his eyes,
A man has not the power to be wise.
I know such words sound strangely, coming from me,
But I'm no angel, nor was meant to be,
And if you blame my passion, you must needs
Reproach as well the charms on which it feeds.
Your loveliness I had no sooner seen
Than you became my soul's unrivalled queen;
Before your seraph glance, divinely sweet,
My heart's defenses crumbled in defeat,
And nothing fasting, prayer, or tears might do
Could stay my spirit from adoring you.
My eyes, my sighs have told you in the past
What now my lips make bold to say at last,
And if, in your great goodness, you will deign
To look upon your slave, and ease his pain,—
If, in compassion for my soul's distress,
You'll stoop to comfort my unworthiness,
I'll raise to you, in thanks for that sweet manna,
An endless hymn, an infinite hosanna.
With me, of course, there need be no anxiety,
No fear of scandal or of notoriety.
These young court gallants, whom all the ladies fancy,
Are vain in speech, in action rash and chancy;
When they succeed in love, the world soon knows it;
No favor's granted them but they disclose it
And by the looseness of their tongues profane
The very altar where their hearts have lain.
Men of my sort, however, love discreetly,
And one may trust our reticence completely.
My keen concern for my good name insures

The absolute security of yours;
In short, I offer you, my dear Elmire,
Love without scandal, pleasure without fear.

ELMIRE

I've heard your well-turned speeches to the end,
And what you urge I clearly apprehend.
Aren't you afraid that I may take a notion
To tell my husband of your warm devotion,
And that, supposing he were duly told,
His feelings toward you might grow rather cold?

TARTUFFE

I know, dear lady, that your exceeding charity
Will lead your heart to pardon my temerity;
That you'll excuse my violent affection
As human weakness, human imperfection;
And that—O fairest!—you will bear in mind
That I'm but flesh and blood, and am not blind.

ELMIRE

Some women might do otherwise, perhaps,
But I shall be discreet about your lapse;
I'll tell my husband nothing of what's occurred
If, in return, you'll give your solemn word
To advocate as forcefully as you can
The marriage of Valère and Mariane,
Renouncing all desire to dispossess
Another of his rightful happiness,
And . . .

SCENE FOUR

———— • • ————

Damis, Elmire, Tartuffe

DAMIS (*Emerging from the closet where he has
been hiding:*)
    No! We'll not hush up this vile affair;
I heard it all inside that closet there,
Where Heaven, in order to confound the pride
Of this great rascal, prompted me to hide.
Ah, now I have my long-awaited chance
To punish his deceit and arrogance,
And give my father clear and shocking proof
Of the black character of his dear Tartuffe.

ELMIRE

Ah no, Damis; I'll be content if he
Will study to deserve my leniency.
I've promised silence—don't make me break my word;
To make a scandal would be too absurd.
Good wives laugh off such trifles, and forget them;
Why should they tell their husbands, and upset them?

DAMIS

You have your reasons for taking such a course,
And I have reasons, too, of equal force.
To spare him now would be insanely wrong.
I've swallowed my just wrath for far too long
And watched this insolent bigot bringing strife
And bitterness into our family life.
Too long he's meddled in my father's affairs,
Thwarting my marriage-hopes, and poor Valère's.
It's high time that my father was undeceived,
And now I've proof that can't be disbelieved—
Proof that was furnished me by Heaven above.
It's too good not to take advantage of.

This is my chance, and I deserve to lose it
If, for one moment, I hesitate to use it.

ELMIRE

Damis . . .

DAMIS

          No, I must do what I think right.
Madam, my heart is bursting with delight,
And, say whatever you will, I'll not consent
To lose the sweet revenge on which I'm bent.
I'll settle matters without more ado;
And here, most opportunely, is my cue.

SCENE FIVE

———— •◆• ————

Orgon, Damis, Tartuffe, Elmire

DAMIS

Father, I'm glad you've joined us. Let us advise you
Of some fresh news which doubtless will surprise you.
You've just now been repaid with interest
For all your loving-kindness to our guest.
He's proved his warm and grateful feelings toward you;
It's with a pair of horns he would reward you.
Yes, I surprised him with your wife, and heard
His whole adulterous offer, every word.
She, with her all too gentle disposition,
Would not have told you of his proposition;
But I shall not make terms with brazen lechery,
And feel that not to tell you would be treachery.

ELMIRE

And I hold that one's husband's peace of mind
Should not be spoilt by tattle of this kind.
One's honor doesn't require it: to be proficient
In keeping men at bay is quite sufficient.
These are my sentiments, and I wish, Damis,
That you had heeded me and held your peace.

SCENE SIX

Orgon, Damis, Tartuffe

ORGON

Can it be true, this dreadful thing I hear?

TARTUFFE

Yes, Brother, I'm a wicked man, I fear:
A wretched sinner, all depraved and twisted,
The greatest villain that has ever existed.
My life's one heap of crimes, which grows each minute;
There's naught but foulness and corruption in it;
And I perceive that Heaven, outraged by me,
Has chosen this occasion to mortify me.
Charge me with any deed you wish to name;
I'll not defend myself, but take the blame.
Believe what you are told, and drive Tartuffe
Like some base criminal from beneath your roof;
Yes, drive me hence, and with a parting curse:
I shan't protest, for I deserve far worse.

ORGON (*To Damis:*)

Ah, you deceitful boy, how dare you try
To stain his purity with so foul a lie?

DAMIS

What! Are you taken in by such a bluff?
Did you not hear . . . ?

ORGON

Enough, you rogue, enough!

TARTUFFE

Ah, Brother, let him speak: you're being unjust.
Believe his story; the boy deserves your trust.
Why, after all, should you have faith in me?

How can you know what I might do, or be?
Is it on my good actions that you base
Your favor? Do you trust my pious face?
Ah, no, don't be deceived by hollow shows;
I'm far, alas, from being what men suppose;
Though the world takes me for a man of worth,
I'm truly the most worthless man on earth.
                    (*To Damis:*)
Yes, my dear son, speak out now: call me the chief
Of sinners, a wretch, a murderer, a thief;
Load me with all the names men most abhor;
I'll not complain; I've earned them all, and more;
I'll kneel here while you pour them on my head
As a just punishment for the life I've led.

                    ORGON (*To Tartuffe:*)
This is too much, dear Brother.
                    (*To Damis:*)
                              Have you no heart?

                    DAMIS
Are you so hoodwinked by this rascal's art . . . ?

                    ORGON
Be still, you monster.
                    (*To Tartuffe:*)
                    Brother, I pray you, rise.
                    (*To Damis:*)
Villain!

                    DAMIS
        But . . .

                    ORGON
          Silence!

                    DAMIS
          Can't you realize . . . ?

ORGON

Just one word more, and I'll tear you limb from limb.

TARTUFFE

In God's name, Brother, don't be harsh with him.
I'd rather far be tortured at the stake
Than see him bear one scratch for my poor sake.

ORGON (*To Damis:*)

Ingrate!

TARTUFFE

    If I must beg you, on bended knee,
To pardon him . . .

ORGON (*Falling to his knees, addressing Tartuffe:*)
        Such goodness cannot be!
        (*To Damis:*)

Now, *there's* true charity!

DAMIS
What, you . . . ?

ORGON
                  Villain, be still!
I know your motives; I know you wish him ill:
Yes, all of you—wife, children, servants, all—
Conspire against him and desire his fall,
Employing every shameful trick you can
To alienate me from this saintly man.
Ah, but the more you seek to drive him away,
The more I'll do to keep him. Without delay,
I'll spite this household and confound its pride
By giving him my daughter as his bride.

DAMIS
You're going to force her to accept his hand?

ORGON

Yes, and this very night, d'you understand?
I shall defy you all, and make it clear
That I'm the one who gives the orders here.
Come, wretch, kneel down and clasp his blessed feet,
And ask his pardon for your black deceit.

DAMIS

I ask that swindler's pardon? Why, I'd rather . . .

ORGON

So! You insult him, and defy your father!
A stick! A stick! (*To Tartuffe:*) No, no—release me, do.
(*To Damis:*)
Out of my house this minute! Be off with you,
And never dare set foot in it again.

DAMIS

Well, I shall go, but . . .

ORGON

Well, go quickly, then.
I disinherit you; an empty purse
Is all you'll get from me—except my curse!

SCENE SEVEN

Orgon, Tartuffe

ORGON

How he blasphemed your goodness! What a son!

TARTUFFE

Forgive him, Lord, as I've already done.
(*To Orgon:*)
You can't know how it hurts when someone tries
To blacken me in my dear Brother's eyes.

ORGON

Ahh!

TARTUFFE

The mere thought of such ingratitude
Plunges my soul into so dark a mood . . .
Such horror grips my heart . . . I gasp for breath,
And cannot speak, and feel myself near death.

ORGON

(*He runs, in tears, to the door through which he has
just driven his son.*)
You blackguard! Why did I spare you? Why did I not
Break you in little pieces on the spot?
Compose yourself, and don't be hurt, dear friend.

TARTUFFE

These scenes, these dreadful quarrels, have got to end.
I've much upset your household, and I perceive
That the best thing will be for me to leave.

ORGON

What are you saying!

TARTUFFE
They're all against me here:
They'd have you think me false and insincere.

ORGON
Ah, what of that? Have I ceased believing in you?

TARTUFFE
Their adverse talk will certainly continue,
And charges which you now repudiate
You may find credible at a later date.

ORGON
No, Brother, never.

TARTUFFE
Brother, a wife can sway
Her husband's mind in many a subtle way.

ORGON
No, no.

TARTUFFE
To leave at once is the solution;
Thus only can I end their persecution.

ORGON
No, no, I'll not allow it; you shall remain.

TARTUFFE
Ah, well; 'twill mean much martyrdom and pain,
But if you wish it . . .

ORGON
Ah!

TARTUFFE
Enough; so be it.

But one thing must be settled, as I see it.
For your dear honor, and for our friendship's sake,
There's one precaution I feel bound to take.
I shall avoid your wife, and keep away . . .

ORGON

No, you shall not, whatever they may say.
It pleases me to vex them, and for spite
I'd have them see you with her day and night.
What's more, I'm going to drive them to despair
By making you my only son and heir;
This very day, I'll give to you alone
Clear deed and title to everything I own.
A dear, good friend and son-in-law-to-be
Is more than wife, or child, or kin to me.
Will you accept my offer, dearest son?

TARTUFFE

In all things, let the will of Heaven be done.

ORGON

Poor fellow! Come, we'll go draw up the deed.
Then let them burst with disappointed greed!

Act Four

SCENE ONE

Cléante, Tartuffe

CLÉANTE

Yes, all the town's discussing it, and truly,
Their comments do not flatter you unduly.
I'm glad we've met, Sir, and I'll give my view
Of this sad matter in a word or two.
As for who's guilty, that I shan't discuss;
Let's say it was Damis who caused the fuss;
Assuming, then, that you have been ill-used
By young Damis, and groundlessly accused,
Ought not a Christian to forgive, and ought
He not to stifle every vengeful thought?
Should you stand by and watch a father make
His only son an exile for your sake?
Again I tell you frankly, be advised:
The whole town, high and low, is scandalized;
This quarrel must be mended, and my advice is
Not to push matters to a further crisis.
No, sacrifice your wrath to God above,
And help Damis regain his father's love.

TARTUFFE

Alas, for my part I should take great joy
In doing so. I've nothing against the boy.
I pardon all, I harbor no resentment;
To serve him would afford me much contentment.
But Heaven's interest will not have it so:
If he comes back, then I shall have to go.
After his conduct—so extreme, so vicious—
Our further intercourse would look suspicious.
God knows what people would think! Why, they'd describe
My goodness to him as a sort of bribe;

They'd say that out of guilt I made pretense
Of loving-kindness and benevolence—
That, fearing my accuser's tongue, I strove
To buy his silence with a show of love.

CLÉANTE

Your reasoning is badly warped and stretched,
And these excuses, Sir, are most far-fetched.
Why put yourself in charge of Heaven's cause?
Does Heaven need our help to enforce its laws?
Leave vengeance to the Lord, Sir; while we live,
Our duty's not to punish, but forgive;
And what the Lord commands, we should obey
Without regard to what the world may say.
What! Shall the fear of being misunderstood
Prevent our doing what is right and good?
No, no; let's simply do what Heaven ordains,
And let no other thoughts perplex our brains.

TARTUFFE

Again, Sir, let me say that I've forgiven
Damis, and thus obeyed the laws of Heaven;
But I am not commanded by the Bible
To live with one who smears my name with libel.

CLÉANTE

Were you commanded, Sir, to indulge the whim
Of poor Orgon, and to encourage him
In suddenly transferring to your name
A large estate to which you have no claim?

TARTUFFE

'Twould never occur to those who know me best
To think I acted from self-interest.
The treasures of this world I quite despise;
Their specious glitter does not charm my eyes;
And if I have resigned myself to taking
The gift which my dear Brother insists on making,

I do so only, as he well understands,
Lest so much wealth fall into wicked hands,
Lest those to whom it might descend in time
Turn it to purposes of sin and crime,
And not, as I shall do, make use of it
For Heaven's glory and mankind's benefit.

CLÉANTE

Forget these trumped-up fears. Your argument
Is one the rightful heir might well resent;
It *is* a moral burden to inherit
Such wealth, but give Damis a chance to bear it.
And would it not be worse to be accused
Of swindling, than to see that wealth misused?
I'm shocked that you allowed Orgon to broach
This matter, and that you feel no self-reproach;
Does true religion teach that lawful heirs
May freely be deprived of what is theirs?
And if the Lord has told you in your heart
That you and young Damis must dwell apart,
Would it not be the decent thing to beat
A generous and honorable retreat,
Rather than let the son of the house be sent,
For your convenience, into banishment?
Sir, if you wish to prove the honesty
Of your intentions . . .

TARTUFFE

            Sir, it is half-past three.
I've certain pious duties to attend to,
And hope my prompt departure won't offend you.

CLÉANTE (*Alone:*)

Damn.

SCENE TWO

———— ◦ ————

Elmire, Mariane, Cléante, Dorine

DORINE
    Stay, Sir, and help Mariane, for Heaven's sake!
She's suffering so, I fear her heart will break.
Her father's plan to marry her off tonight
Has put the poor child in a desperate plight.
I hear him coming. Let's stand together, now,
And see if we can't change his mind, somehow,
About this match we all deplore and fear.

SCENE THREE

Orgon, Elmire, Mariane, Cléante, Dorine

ORGON
Hah! Glad to find you all assembled here.
(*To Mariane:*)
This contract, child, contains your happiness,
And what it says I think your heart can guess.

MARIANE (*Falling to her knees:*)
Sir, by that Heaven which sees me here distressed,
And by whatever else can move your breast,
Do not employ a father's power, I pray you,
To crush my heart and force it to obey you,
Nor by your harsh commands oppress me so
That I'll begrudge the duty which I owe—
And do not so embitter and enslave me
That I shall hate the very life you gave me.
If my sweet hopes must perish, if you refuse
To give me to the one I've dared to choose,
Spare me at least—I beg you, I implore—
The pain of wedding one whom I abhor;
And do not, by a heartless use of force,
Drive me to contemplate some desperate course.

ORGON (*Feeling himself touched by her:*)
Be firm, my soul. No human weakness, now.

MARIANE
I don't resent your love for him. Allow
Your heart free rein, Sir; give him your property,
And if that's not enough, take mine from me;
He's welcome to my money; take it, do,
But don't, I pray, include my person too.
Spare me, I beg you; and let me end the tale
Of my sad days behind a convent veil.

ORGON

A convent! Hah! When crossed in their amours,
All lovesick girls have the same thought as yours.
Get up! The more you loathe the man, and dread him,
The more ennobling it will be to wed him.
Marry Tartuffe, and mortify your flesh!
Enough; don't start that whimpering afresh.

DORINE

But why . . . ?

ORGON

      Be still, there. Speak when you're spoken to.
Not one more bit of impudence out of you.

CLÉANTE

If I may offer a word of counsel here . . .

ORGON

Brother, in counseling you have no peer;
All your advice is forceful, sound, and clever;
I don't propose to follow it, however.

ELMIRE (*To Orgon:*)

I am amazed, and don't know what to say;
Your blindness simply takes my breath away.
You are indeed bewitched, to take no warning
From our account of what occurred this morning.

ORGON

Madam, I know a few plain facts, and one
Is that you're partial to my rascal son;
Hence, when he sought to make Tartuffe the victim
Of a base lie, you dared not contradict him.
Ah, but you underplayed your part, my pet;
You should have looked more angry, more upset.

ELMIRE

When men make overtures, must we reply
With righteous anger and a battle-cry?
Must we turn back their amorous advances
With sharp reproaches and with fiery glances?
Myself, I find such offers merely amusing,
And make no scenes and fusses in refusing;
My taste is for good-natured rectitude,
And I dislike the savage sort of prude
Who guards her virtue with her teeth and claws,
And tears men's eyes out for the slightest cause:
The Lord preserve me from such honor as that,
Which bites and scratches like an alley-cat!
I've found that a polite and cool rebuff
Discourages a lover quite enough.

ORGON

I know the facts, and I shall not be shaken.

ELMIRE

I marvel at your power to be mistaken.
Would it, I wonder, carry weight with you
If I could *show* you that our tale was true?

ORGON

Show me?

ELMIRE

Yes.

ORGON

Rot.

ELMIRE

Come, what if I found a way
To make you see the facts as plain as day?

ORGON

Nonsense.

ELMIRE

Do answer me; don't be absurd.
I'm not now asking you to trust our word.
Suppose that from some hiding-place in here
You learned the whole sad truth by eye and ear—
What would you say of your good friend, after that?

ORGON

Why, I'd say . . . nothing, by Jehoshaphat!
It can't be true.

ELMIRE

You've been too long deceived,
And I'm quite tired of being disbelieved.
Come now: let's put my statements to the test,
And you shall see the truth made manifest.

ORGON

I'll take that challenge. Now do your uttermost.
We'll see how you make good your empty boast.

ELMIRE (*To Dorine:*)

Send him to me.

DORINE

He's crafty; it may be hard
To catch the cunning scoundrel off his guard.

ELMIRE

No, amorous men are gullible. Their conceit
So blinds them that they're never hard to cheat.
Have him come down. (*To Cléante & Mariane:*) Please leave
us, for a bit.

SCENE FOUR

———•—•———

Elmire, Orgon

ELMIRE

Pull up this table, and get under it.

ORGON

What?

ELMIRE

It's essential that you be well-hidden.

ORGON

Why there?

ELMIRE

Oh, Heavens! Just do as you are bidden.
I have my plans; we'll soon see how they fare.
Under the table, now; and once you're there,
Take care that you are neither seen nor heard.

ORGON

Well, I'll indulge you, since I gave my word
To see you through this infantile charade.

ELMIRE

Once it is over, you'll be glad we played.
        (*To her husband, who is now under the table:*)
I'm going to act quite strangely, now, and you
Must not be shocked at anything I do.
Whatever I may say, you must excuse
As part of that deceit I'm forced to use.
I shall employ sweet speeches in the task
Of making that imposter drop his mask;
I'll give encouragement to his bold desires,
And furnish fuel to his amorous fires.

Since it's for your sake, and for his destruction,
That I shall seem to yield to his seduction,
I'll gladly stop whenever you decide
That all your doubts are fully satisfied.
I'll count on you, as soon as you have seen
What sort of man he is, to intervene,
And not expose me to his odious lust
One moment longer than you feel you must.
Remember: you're to save me from my plight
Whenever . . . He's coming! Hush! Keep out of sight!

SCENE FIVE

———— • • ————

Tartuffe, Elmire, Orgon

TARTUFFE
You wish to have a word with me, I'm told.

ELMIRE
Yes. I've a little secret to unfold.
Before I speak, however, it would be wise
To close that door, and look about for spies.
      (*Tartuffe goes to the door, closes it, and returns.*)
The very last thing that must happen now
Is a repetition of this morning's row.
I've never been so badly caught off guard.
Oh, how I feared for you! You saw how hard
I tried to make that troublesome Damis
Control his dreadful temper, and hold his peace.
In my confusion, I didn't have the sense
Simply to contradict his evidence;
But as it happened, that was for the best,
And all has worked out in our interest.
This storm has only bettered your position;
My husband doesn't have the least suspicion,
And now, in mockery of those who do,
He bids me be continually with you.
And that is why, quite fearless of reproof,
I now can be alone with my Tartuffe,
And why my heart—perhaps too quick to yield—
Feels free to let its passion be revealed.

TARTUFFE
Madam, your words confuse me. Not long ago,
You spoke in quite a different style, you know.

ELMIRE
Ah, Sir, if that refusal made you smart,

It's little that you know of woman's heart,
Or what that heart is trying to convey
When it resists in such a feeble way!
Always, at first, our modesty prevents
The frank avowal of tender sentiments;
However high the passion which inflames us,
Still, to confess its power somehow shames us.
Thus we reluct, at first, yet in a tone
Which tells you that our heart is overthrown,
That what our lips deny, our pulse confesses,
And that, in time, all noes will turn to yesses.
I fear my words are all too frank and free,
And a poor proof of woman's modesty;
But since I'm started, tell me, if you will—
Would I have tried to make Damis be still,
Would I have listened, calm and unoffended,
Until your lengthy offer of love was ended,
And been so very mild in my reaction,
Had your sweet words not given me satisfaction?
And when I tried to force you to undo
The marriage-plans my husband has in view,
What did my urgent pleading signify
If not that I admired you, and that I
Deplored the thought that someone else might own
Part of a heart I wished for mine alone?

TARTUFFE

Madam, no happiness is so complete
As when, from lips we love, come words so sweet;
Their nectar floods my every sense, and drains
In honeyed rivulets through all my veins.
To please you is my joy, my only goal;
Your love is the restorer of my soul;
And yet I must beg leave, now, to confess
Some lingering doubts as to my happiness.
Might this not be a trick? Might not the catch
Be that you wish me to break off the match

With Mariane, and so have feigned to love me?
I shan't quite trust your fond opinion of me
Until the feelings you've expressed so sweetly
Are demonstrated somewhat more concretely,
And you have shown, by certain kind concessions,
That I may put my faith in your professions.

ELMIRE (*She coughs, to warn her husband.*)
Why be in such a hurry? Must my heart
Exhaust its bounty at the very start?
To make that sweet admission cost me dear,
But you'll not be content, it would appear,
Unless my store of favors is disbursed
To the last farthing, and at the very first.

TARTUFFE
The less we merit, the less we dare to hope,
And with our doubts, mere words can never cope.
We trust no promised bliss till we receive it;
Not till a joy is ours can we believe it.
I, who so little merit your esteem,
Can't credit this fulfillment of my dream,
And shan't believe it, Madam, until I savor
Some palpable assurance of your favor.

ELMIRE
My, how tyrannical your love can be,
And how it flusters and perplexes me!
How furiously you take one's heart in hand,
And make your every wish a fierce command!
Come, must you hound and harry me to death?
Will you not give me time to catch my breath?
Can it be right to press me with such force,
Give me no quarter, show me no remorse,
And take advantage, by your stern insistence,
Of the fond feelings which weaken my resistance?

TARTUFFE

Well, if you look with favor upon my love,
Why, then, begrudge me some clear proof thereof?

ELMIRE

But how can I consent without offense
To Heaven, toward which you feel such reverence?

TARTUFFE

If Heaven is all that holds you back, don't worry.
I can remove that hindrance in a hurry.
Nothing of that sort need obstruct our path.

ELMIRE

Must one not be afraid of Heaven's wrath?

TARTUFFE

Madam, forget such fears, and be my pupil,
And I shall teach you how to conquer scruple.
Some joys, it's true, are wrong in Heaven's eyes;
Yet Heaven is not averse to compromise;
There is a science, lately formulated,
Whereby one's conscience may be liberated,
And any wrongful act you care to mention
May be redeemed by purity of intention.
I'll teach you, Madam, the secrets of that science;
Meanwhile, just place on me your full reliance.
Assuage my keen desires, and feel no dread:
The sin, if any, shall be on my head.
          (*Elmire coughs, this time more loudly.*)
You've a bad cough.

ELMIRE

Yes, yes. It's bad indeed.

TARTUFFE (*Producing a little paper bag:*)
A bit of licorice may be what you need.

ELMIRE

No, I've a stubborn cold, it seems. I'm sure it
Will take much more than licorice to cure it.

TARTUFFE

How aggravating.

ELMIRE

Oh, more than I can say.

TARTUFFE

If you're still troubled, think of things this way:
No one shall know our joys, save us alone,
And there's no evil till the act is known;
It's scandal, Madam, which makes it an offense,
And it's no sin to sin in confidence.

ELMIRE (*Having coughed once more:*)

Well, clearly I must do as you require,
And yield to your importunate desire.
It is apparent, now, that nothing less
Will satisfy you, and so I acquiesce.
To go so far is much against my will;
I'm vexed that it should come to this; but still,
Since you are so determined on it, since you
Will not allow mere language to convince you,
And since you ask for concrete evidence, I
See nothing for it, now, but to comply.
If this is sinful, if I'm wrong to do it,
So much the worse for him who drove me to it.
The fault can surely not be charged to me.

TARTUFFE

Madam, the fault is mine, if fault there be,
And . . .

ELMIRE

Open the door a little, and peek out;
I wouldn't want my husband poking about.

TARTUFFE

Why worry about the man? Each day he grows
More gullible; one can lead him by the nose.
To find us here would fill him with delight,
And if he saw the worst, he'd doubt his sight.

ELMIRE

Nevertheless, do step out for a minute
Into the hall, and see that no one's in it.

SCENE SIX

Orgon, Elmire

ORGON (*Coming out from under the table:*)
That man's a perfect monster, I must admit!
I'm simply stunned. I can't get over it.

ELMIRE
What, coming out so soon? How premature!
Get back in hiding, and wait until you're sure.
Stay till the end, and be convinced completely;
We mustn't stop till things are proved concretely.

ORGON
Hell never harbored anything so vicious!

ELMIRE
Tut, don't be hasty. Try to be judicious.
Wait, and be certain that there's no mistake.
No jumping to conclusions, for Heaven's sake!
    (*She places Orgon behind her, as Tartuffe re-enters.*)

SCENE SEVEN

Tartuffe, Elmire, Orgon

TARTUFFE (*Not seeing Orgon:*)
Madam, all things have worked out to perfection;
I've given the neighboring rooms a full inspection;
No one's about; and now I may at last . . .

ORGON (*Intercepting him:*)
Hold on, my passionate fellow, not so fast!
I should advise a little more restraint.
Well, so you thought you'd fool me, my dear saint!
How soon you wearied of the saintly life—
Wedding my daughter, and coveting my wife!
I've long suspected you, and had a feeling
That soon I'd catch you at your double-dealing.
Just now, you've given me evidence galore;
It's quite enough; I have no wish for more.

ELMIRE (*To Tartuffe:*)
I'm sorry to have treated you so slyly,
But circumstances forced me to be wily.

TARTUFFE
Brother, you can't think . . .

ORGON
                No more talk from you;
Just leave this household, without more ado.

TARTUFFE
What I intended . . .

ORGON
                That seems fairly clear.
Spare me your falsehoods and get out of here.

TARTUFFE

No, I'm the master, and you're the one to go!
This house belongs to me, I'll have you know,
And I shall show you that you can't hurt *me*
By this contemptible conspiracy,
That those who cross me know not what they do,
And that I've means to expose and punish you,
Avenge offended Heaven, and make you grieve
That ever you dared order me to leave.

SCENE EIGHT

Elmire, Orgon

ELMIRE

What was the point of all that angry chatter?

ORGON

Dear God, I'm worried. This is no laughing matter.

ELMIRE

How so?

ORGON

I fear I understood his drift.
I'm much disturbed about that deed of gift.

ELMIRE

You gave him . . . ?

ORGON

Yes, it's all been drawn and signed.
But one thing more is weighing on my mind.

ELMIRE

What's that?

ORGON

I'll tell you; but first let's see if there's
A certain strong-box in his room upstairs.

Act Five

SCENE ONE

———— • • ————

Orgon, Cléante

CLÉANTE

Where are you going so fast?

ORGON

God knows!

CLÉANTE

Then wait;

Let's have a conference, and deliberate
On how this situation's to be met.

ORGON

That strong-box has me utterly upset;
This is the worst of many, many shocks.

CLÉANTE

Is there some fearful mystery in that box?

ORGON

My poor friend Argas brought that box to me
With his own hands, in utmost secrecy;
'Twas on the very morning of his flight.
It's full of papers which, if they came to light,
Would ruin him—or such is my impression.

CLÉANTE

Then why did you let it out of your possession?

ORGON

Those papers vexed my conscience, and it seemed best
To ask the counsel of my pious guest.

The cunning scoundrel got me to agree
To leave the strong-box in his custody,
So that, in case of an investigation,
I could employ a slight equivocation
And swear I didn't have it, and thereby,
At no expense to conscience, tell a lie.

CLÉANTE

It looks to me as if you're out on a limb.
Trusting him with that box, and offering him
That deed of gift, were actions of a kind
Which scarcely indicate a prudent mind.
With two such weapons, he has the upper hand,
And since you're vulnerable, as matters stand,
You erred once more in bringing him to bay.
You should have acted in some subtler way.

ORGON

Just think of it: behind that fervent face,
A heart so wicked, and a soul so base!
I took him in, a hungry beggar, and then . . .
Enough, by God! I'm through with pious men:
Henceforth I'll hate the whole false brotherhood,
And persecute them worse than Satan could.

CLÉANTE

Ah, there you go—extravagant as ever!
Why can you not be rational? You never
Manage to take the middle course, it seems,
But jump, instead, between absurd extremes.
You've recognized your recent grave mistake
In falling victim to a pious fake;
Now, to correct that error, must you embrace
An even greater error in its place,
And judge our worthy neighbors as a whole
By what you've learned of one corrupted soul?
Come, just because one rascal made you swallow
A show of zeal which turned out to be hollow,

Shall you conclude that all men are deceivers,
And that, today, there are no true believers?
Let atheists make that foolish inference;
Learn to distinguish virtue from pretense,
Be cautious in bestowing admiration,
And cultivate a sober moderation.
Don't humor fraud, but also don't asperse
True piety; the latter fault is worse,
And it is best to err, if err one must,
As you have done, upon the side of trust.

SCENE TWO

Damis, Orgon, Cléante

DAMIS

Father, I hear that scoundrel's uttered threats
Against you; that he pridefully forgets
How, in his need, he was befriended by you,
And means to use your gifts to crucify you.

ORGON

It's true, my boy. I'm too distressed for tears.

DAMIS

Leave it to me, Sir; let me trim his ears.
Faced with such insolence, we must not waver.
I shall rejoice in doing you the favor
Of cutting short his life, and your distress.

CLÉANTE

What a display of young hotheadedness!
Do learn to moderate your fits of rage.
In this just kingdom, this enlightened age,
One does not settle things by violence.

SCENE THREE

———————•●•———————

Madame Pernelle, Mariane, Elmire, Dorine, Damis,
Orgon, Cléante

MADAME PERNELLE

I hear strange tales of very strange events.

ORGON

Yes, strange events which these two eyes beheld.
The man's ingratitude is unparalleled.
I save a wretched pauper from starvation,
House him, and treat him like a blood relation,
Shower him every day with my largesse,
Give him my daughter, and all that I possess;
And meanwhile the unconscionable knave
Tries to induce my wife to misbehave;
And not content with such extreme rascality,
Now threatens me with my own liberality,
And aims, by taking base advantage of
The gifts I gave him out of Christian love,
To drive me from my house, a ruined man,
And make me end a pauper, as he began.

DORINE

Poor fellow!

MADAME PERNELLE

No, my son, I'll never bring
Myself to think him guilty of such a thing.

ORGON

How's that?

MADAME PERNELLE

The righteous always were maligned.

ORGON

Speak clearly, Mother. Say what's on your mind.

MADAME PERNELLE

I mean that I can smell a rat, my dear.
You know how everybody hates him, here.

ORGON

That has no bearing on the case at all.

MADAME PERNELLE

I told you a hundred times, when you were small,
That virtue in this world is hated ever;
Malicious men may die, but malice never.

ORGON

No doubt that's true, but how does it apply?

MADAME PERNELLE

They've turned you against him by a clever lie.

ORGON

I've told you, I was there and saw it done.

MADAME PERNELLE

Ah, slanderers will stop at nothing, Son.

ORGON

Mother, I'll lose my temper . . . For the last time,
I tell you I was witness to the crime.

MADAME PERNELLE

The tongues of spite are busy night and noon,
And to their venom no man is immune.

ORGON

You're talking nonsense. Can't you realize
I saw it; saw it; saw it with my eyes?

Saw, do you understand me? Must I shout it
Into your ears before you'll cease to doubt it?

MADAME PERNELLE
Appearances can deceive, my son. Dear me,
We cannot always judge by what we see.

ORGON
Drat! Drat!

MADAME PERNELLE
   One often interprets things awry;
Good can seem evil to a suspicious eye.

ORGON
Was I to see his pawing at Elmire
As an act of charity?

MADAME PERNELLE
    Till his guilt is clear,
A man deserves the benefit of the doubt.
You should have waited, to see how things turned out.

ORGON
Great God in Heaven, what more proof did I need?
Was I to sit there, watching, until he'd . . .
You drive me to the brink of impropriety.

MADAME PERNELLE
No, no, a man of such surpassing piety
Could not do such a thing. You cannot shake me.
I don't believe it, and you shall not make me.

ORGON
You vex me so that, if you weren't my mother,
I'd say to you . . . some dreadful thing or other.

DORINE

It's your turn now, Sir, not to be listened to;
You'd not trust us, and now she won't trust you.

CLÉANTE

My friends, we're wasting time which should be spent
In facing up to our predicament.
I fear that scoundrel's threats weren't made in sport.

DAMIS

Do you think he'd have the nerve to go to court?

ELMIRE

I'm sure he won't: they'd find it all too crude
A case of swindling and ingratitude.

CLÉANTE

Don't be too sure. He won't be at a loss
To give his claims a high and righteous gloss;
And clever rogues with far less valid cause
Have trapped their victims in a web of laws.
I say again that to antagonize
A man so strongly armed was most unwise.

ORGON

I know it; but the man's appalling cheek
Outraged me so, I couldn't control my pique.

CLÉANTE

I wish to Heaven that we could devise
Some truce between you, or some compromise.

ELMIRE

If I had known what cards he held, I'd not
Have roused his anger by my little plot.

ORGON (*To Dorine, as M. Loyal enters:*)
What is that fellow looking for? Who is he?
Go talk to him—and tell him that I'm busy.

SCENE FOUR

Monsieur Loyal, Madame Pernelle, Orgon, Damis,
Mariane, Dorine, Elmire, Cléante

MONSIEUR LOYAL
Good day, dear sister. Kindly let me see
Your master.

DORINE
    He's involved with company,
And cannot be disturbed just now, I fear.

MONSIEUR LOYAL
I hate to intrude; but what has brought me here
Will not disturb your master, in any event.
Indeed, my news will make him most content.

DORINE
Your name?

MONSIEUR LOYAL
    Just say that I bring greetings from
Monsieur Tartuffe, on whose behalf I've come.

DORINE (*To Orgon:*)
Sir, he's a very gracious man, and bears
A message from Tartuffe, which, he declares,
Will make you most content.

CLÉANTE
      Upon my word,
I think this man had best be seen, and heard.

ORGON
Perhaps he has some settlement to suggest.
How shall I treat him? What manner would be best?

CLÉANTE

Control your anger, and if he should mention
Some fair adjustment, give him your full attention.

MONSIEUR LOYAL

Good health to you, good Sir. May Heaven confound
Your enemies, and may your joys abound.

ORGON (*Aside, to Cléante:*)

A gentle salutation: it confirms
My guess that he is here to offer terms.

MONSIEUR LOYAL

I've always held your family most dear;
I served your father, Sir, for many a year.

ORGON

Sir, I must ask your pardon; to my shame,
I cannot now recall your face or name.

MONSIEUR LOYAL

Loyal's my name; I come from Normandy,
And I'm a bailiff, in all modesty.
For forty years, praise God, it's been my boast
To serve with honor in that vital post,
And I am here, Sir, if you will permit
The liberty, to serve you with this writ . . .

ORGON

To—*what?*

MONSIEUR LOYAL

Now, please, Sir, let us have no friction:
It's nothing but an order of eviction.
You are to move your goods and family out
And make way for new occupants, without
Deferment or delay, and give the keys . . .

ORGON

I? Leave this house?

MONSIEUR LOYAL

Why yes, Sir, if you please.
This house, Sir, from the cellar to the roof,
Belongs now to the good Monsieur Tartuffe,
And he is lord and master of your estate
By virtue of a deed of present date,
Drawn in due form, with clearest legal phrasing . . .

DAMIS

Your insolence is utterly amazing!

MONSIEUR LOYAL

Young man, my business here is not with you,
But with your wise and temperate father, who,
Like every worthy citizen, stands in awe
Of justice, and would never obstruct the law.

ORGON

But . . .

MONSIEUR LOYAL

Not for a million, Sir, would you rebel
Against authority; I know that well.
You'll not make trouble, Sir, or interfere
With the execution of my duties here.

DAMIS

Someone may execute a smart tattoo
On that black jacket of yours, before you're through.

MONSIEUR LOYAL

Sir, bid your son be silent. I'd much regret
Having to mention such a nasty threat
Of violence, in writing my report.

DORINE (*Aside:*)
This man Loyal's a most disloyal sort!

MONSIEUR LOYAL
I love all men of upright character,
And when I agreed to serve these papers, Sir,
It was your feelings that I had in mind.
I couldn't bear to see the case assigned
To someone else, who might esteem you less
And so subject you to unpleasantness.

ORGON
What's more unpleasant than telling a man to leave
His house and home?

MONSIEUR LOYAL
          You'd like a short reprieve?
If you desire it, Sir, I shall not press you,
But wait until tomorrow to dispossess you.
Splendid. I'll come and spend the night here, then,
Most quietly, with half a score of men.
For form's sake, you might bring me, just before
You go to bed, the keys to the front door.
My men, I promise, will be on their best
Behavior, and will not disturb your rest.
But bright and early, Sir, you must be quick
And move out all your furniture, every stick:
The men I've chosen are both young and strong,
And with their help it shouldn't take you long.
In short, I'll make things pleasant and convenient,
And since I'm being so extremely lenient,
Please show me, Sir, a like consideration,
And give me your entire cooperation.

ORGON (*Aside:*)
I may be all but bankrupt, but I vow
I'd give a hundred louis, here and now,

Just for the pleasure of landing one good clout
Right on the end of that complacent snout.

CLÉANTE
Careful; don't make things worse.

DAMIS
                                  My bootsole itches
To give that beggar a good kick in the breeches.

DORINE
Monsieur Loyal, I'd love to hear the whack
Of a stout stick across your fine broad back.

MONSIEUR LOYAL
Take care: a woman too may go to jail if
She uses threatening language to a bailiff.

CLÉANTE
Enough, enough, Sir. This must not go on.
Give me that paper, please, and then begone.

MONSIEUR LOYAL
Well, *au revoir*. God give you all good cheer!

ORGON
May God confound you, and him who sent you here!

SCENE FIVE

*Orgon, Cléante, Mariane, Elmire, Madame Pernelle,
Dorine, Damis*

ORGON

Now, Mother, was I right or not? This writ
Should change your notion of Tartuffe a bit.
Do you perceive his villainy at last?

MADAME PERNELLE

I'm thunderstruck. I'm utterly aghast.

DORINE

Oh, come, be fair. You mustn't take offense
At this new proof of his benevolence.
He's acting out of selfless love, I know.
Material things enslave the soul, and so
He kindly has arranged your liberation
From all that might endanger your salvation.

ORGON

Will you not ever hold your tongue, you dunce?

CLÉANTE

Come, you must take some action, and at once.

ELMIRE

Go tell the world of the low trick he's tried.
The deed of gift is surely nullified
By such behavior, and public rage will not
Permit the wretch to carry out his plot.

SCENE SIX

Valère, Orgon, Cléante, Elmire, Mariane,
Madame Pernelle, Damis, Dorine

VALÈRE

Sir, though I hate to bring you more bad news,
Such is the danger that I cannot choose.
A friend who is extremely close to me
And knows my interest in your family
Has, for my sake, presumed to violate
The secrecy that's due to things of state,
And sends me word that you are in a plight
From which your one salvation lies in flight.
That scoundrel who's imposed upon you so
Denounced you to the King an hour ago
And, as supporting evidence, displayed
The strong-box of a certain renegade
Whose secret papers, so he testified,
You had disloyally agreed to hide.
I don't know just what charges may be pressed,
But there's a warrant out for your arrest;
Tartuffe has been instructed, furthermore,
To guide the arresting officer to your door.

CLÉANTE

He's clearly done this to facilitate
His seizure of your house and your estate.

ORGON

That man, I must say, is a vicious beast!

VALÈRE

Quick, Sir; you mustn't tarry in the least.
My carriage is outside, to take you hence;
This thousand louis should cover all expense.
Let's lose no time, or you shall be undone;

The sole defense, in this case, is to run.
I shall go with you all the way, and place you
In a safe refuge to which they'll never trace you.

ORGON

Alas, dear boy, I wish that I could show you
My gratitude for everything I owe you.
But now is not the time; I pray the Lord
That I may live to give you your reward.
Farewell, my dears; be careful . . .

CLÉANTE

                    Brother, hurry.
We shall take care of things; you needn't worry.

SCENE SEVEN

The Officer, Tartuffe, Valère, Orgon, Elmire,
Mariane, Madame Pernelle, Dorine, Cléante, Damis

TARTUFFE

Gently, Sir, gently; stay right where you are.
No need for haste; your lodging isn't far.
You're off to prison, by order of the Prince.

ORGON

This is the crowning blow, you wretch; and since
It means my total ruin and defeat,
Your villainy is now at last complete.

TARTUFFE

You needn't try to provoke me; it's no use.
Those who serve Heaven must expect abuse.

CLÉANTE

You are indeed most patient, sweet, and blameless.

DORINE

How he exploits the name of Heaven! It's shameless.

TARTUFFE

Your taunts and mockeries are all for naught;
To do my duty is my only thought.

MARIANE

Your love of duty is most meritorious,
And what you've done is little short of glorious.

TARTUFFE

All deeds are glorious, Madam, which obey
The sovereign prince who sent me here today.

ORGON

I rescued you when you were destitute;
Have you forgotten that, you thankless brute?

TARTUFFE

No, no, I well remember everything;
But my first duty is to serve my King.
That obligation is so paramount
That other claims, beside it, do not count;
And for it I would sacrifice my wife,
My family, my friend, or my own life.

ELMIRE

Hypocrite!

DORINE

All that we most revere, he uses
To cloak his plots and camouflage his ruses.

CLÉANTE

If it is true that you are animated
By pure and loyal zeal, as you have stated,
Why was this zeal not roused until you'd sought
To make Orgon a cuckold, and been caught?
Why weren't you moved to give your evidence
Until your outraged host had driven you hence?
I shan't say that the gift of all his treasure
Ought to have damped your zeal in any measure;
But if he is a traitor, as you declare,
How could you condescend to be his heir?

TARTUFFE (*To the Officer:*)

Sir, spare me all this clamor; it's growing shrill.
Please carry out your orders, if you will.

OFFICER

Yes, I've delayed too long, Sir. Thank you kindly.
You're just the proper person to remind me.

Come, you are off to join the other boarders
In the King's prison, according to his orders.

TARTUFFE

Who? I, Sir?

OFFICER

      Yes.

TARTUFFE
To prison? This can't be true!

OFFICER

I owe an explanation, but not to you.
(*To Orgon:*)
Sir, all is well; rest easy, and be grateful.
We serve a Prince to whom all sham is hateful,
A Prince who sees into our inmost hearts,
And can't be fooled by any trickster's arts.
His royal soul, though generous and human,
Views all things with discernment and acumen;
His sovereign reason is not lightly swayed,
And all his judgments are discreetly weighed.
He honors righteous men of every kind,
And yet his zeal for virtue is not blind,
Nor does his love of piety numb his wits
And make him tolerant of hypocrites.
'Twas hardly likely that this man could cozen
A King who's foiled such liars by the dozen.
With one keen glance, the King perceived the whole
Perverseness and corruption of his soul,
And thus high Heaven's justice was displayed:
Betraying you, the rogue stood self-betrayed.
The King soon recognized Tartuffe as one
Notorious by another name, who'd done
So many vicious crimes that one could fill
Ten volumes with them, and be writing still.
But to be brief: our sovereign was appalled

By this man's treachery toward you, which he called
The last, worst villainy of a vile career,
And bade me follow the impostor here
To see how gross his impudence could be,
And force him to restore your property.
Your private papers, by the King's command,
I hereby seize and give into your hand.
The King, by royal order, invalidates
The deed which gave this rascal your estates,
And pardons, furthermore, your grave offense
In harboring an exile's documents.
By these decrees, our Prince rewards you for
Your loyal deeds in the late civil war,
And shows how heartfelt is his satisfaction
In recompensing any worthy action,
How much he prizes merit, and how he makes
More of men's virtues than of their mistakes.

DORINE

Heaven be praised!

MADAME PERNELLE

I breathe again, at last.

ELMIRE

We're safe.

MARIANE

I can't believe the danger's past.

ORGON (*To Tartuffe:*)

Well, traitor, now you see . . .

CLÉANTE

          Ah, Brother, please,
Let's not descend to such indignities.
Leave the poor wretch to his unhappy fate,
And don't say anything to aggravate

His present woes; but rather hope that he
Will soon embrace an honest piety,
And mend his ways, and by a true repentance
Move our just King to moderate his sentence.
Meanwhile, go kneel before your sovereign's throne
And thank him for the mercies he has shown.

ORGON

Well said: let's go at once and, gladly kneeling,
Express the gratitude which all are feeling.
Then, when that first great duty has been done,
We'll turn with pleasure to a second one,
And give Valère, whose love has proven so true,
The wedded happiness which is his due.

THE LEARNED LADIES

COMEDY IN FIVE ACTS, 1672

For Gilbert Parker

Introduction

The Learned Ladies resembles *Tartuffe* in that it is the drama of a bourgeois household which has lost its harmony and balance through some recent change. In the case of *Tartuffe*, what has changed is that the head of the house, Orgon, who was formerly a sound and solid man, has succumbed to a sort of specious and menopausal religious frenzy. The whole action of the play follows from this aberration of Orgon's, and the whole familial fabric of affections and responsibilities is shaken before the action is over. In *The Learned Ladies* it is once more—though less obviously—the head of the house to whom the disruption of normal relationships may be traced. Chrysale is a soft, comfort-loving person who speaks too often of "my collars" and "my roast of beef." He considers himself peace-loving and gentle, and his daughter Henriette is so kind as to describe his weakness as good nature; but in fact he is an ineffectual man, given to dreaming of his youth, who has always avoided the unpleasantness of exercising his authority as husband and father. The power vacuum thus created has been fully occupied, not long before the play begins, by Chrysale's wilful wife, Philaminte.

It was an unnatural thing, in the view of Molière's audience, for a wife to assume the husband's dominant role, and this is plainly illustrated by the fact that, in early productions of *Les femmes savantes*, the part of Philaminte was played by a male actor. In usurping the headship of the household, Philaminte has become an unsexed woman or the caricature of a man: instead of quiet authority, she has a vain and impatient coerciveness, and her domestic rule amounts to a reign of terror. Her ambition, and a measure of intelligence, lead her to become a bluestocking and, in emulation of certain great ladies, to turn her house into an academy and salon. She enlists in this program her unmarried sister-in-law, Bélise, and her elder daughter, Armande. The spirited and sensible younger daughter, Henriette, declines to be recruited.

In *Les précieuses ridicules* (1659), Molière had made farcical fun of middle-class young women who aspired to salon life, with its refinements of speech and manner, its witticisms, its "spiritual" gallantries, its madrigals and *bouts-rimés*. As the century grew older, salon habitués became concerned with science and philosophy as well, so that Molière's Learned Ladies of 1672 keep a telescope in the attic and make references to Descartes and Epicurus. The atmosphere, *chez* Philaminte, is above all Platonic. Mind and soul are exalted, the body is scorned, and marriage is viewed with contempt. This ambiance is emotionally convenient for Bélise, who adopts the fantasy that all men are secretly and ethereally in love with her, and who also appeases her balked maternal instinct by schooling the servants in elementary grammar and science. For Armande, membership in her mother's "academy" is a less comfortable fate. Following Philaminte's example, she proclaims a pure devotion to spirit and intellect, and a horror of material and bodily things; but in fact she can neither satisfy herself with intellectual activity nor detach herself from the flesh. She would be a touching figure, as many are who suffer from imperfect idealism, were it not for her pretentiousness and for her jealous spite toward those who enjoy what she has renounced.

The abdication of Chrysale, in other words, has precipitated an abnormal situation in which all of the main characters suffer deformity or strain. Bélise is pacified by her chimeras, but at the cost of a complete divorce from the real feelings of others: when Henriette's suitor, Clitandre, turns to her for help in the play's fourth scene, he might as well be addressing a dead woman. Armande, saddled with an aspiration which is too much for her, is condemned to imposture and envy. Philaminte's bullying insistence on creating an intellectual environment arises not from a true thirst for knowledge but from a desire for personal glory, as well as a rancorous wish (which she shares with Armande) to show men that

> *women may be learnèd if they please,*
> *And found, like men, their own academies.*

Because of the ruthless egoism of her project, and its spirit of revenge, Philaminte suppresses in herself the magnanimity which truly belongs to her nature, and which flashes out briefly in the final scene of the play. Her vanity may also be blamed for the blindness with which she admires the egregious pedant Trissotin, and the heartlessness with which she presses Henriette to marry him against her wishes.

And what of Henriette? Is she, as one French critic has said, a "hateful girl" given to false humility, cutting ironies, and banal conceptions of life? Certainly not. I am of Arthur Tilley's opinion, that "her simplicity, her directness, and above all, her sense of humor, make her the most delightful of Molière's young women." She is far more intelligent and witty than her high-falutin sister, Armande; she is filial without being spiritless; independent without being rebellious; admirable in accepting the fact that she is her lover's second choice; noble in her readiness to release him from what temporarily seems a bad bargain. To find any of her speeches abrasive is to forget her embattled and near-desperate position as a younger daughter under pressure from three variously demented women. We must judge her as we would a noncollaborative citizen of some occupied country. Defending herself against Armande, she banters and teases; with her mother, she sometimes plays dumb or dull; to Clitandre, she gives blunt and practical strategic advice; in her bold confrontation with Trissotin, she proves a cunning debater, and concludes with an understandable asperity. In all of this, she shows her resourcefulness and pluck, but each tactic necessarily entails a temporary distortion of her nature in reaction to circumstances. Of Clitandre, too, it may be supposed that the situation exaggerates some of his attitudes, and turns him into more of a ranter than he would usually be.

The Learned Ladies comes as close to being a satiric play as does anything in Molière's *oeuvre*; yet here as everywhere he subordinates satire to the comic spirit, which is less interested in excoriating human error than in affirming the fullness of life. As always in Molière, there lies in the background of the play a clear and actual France: it is an absolute monarchy with a Catholic culture and a powerful Church; it is characterized by strong class distinctions; in it, all social or familial roles, such as the father's ruling function in any household, are plain matters of natural law; it is a highly centralized state, and life at court or in Paris is very different from life in the provinces. Other basic aspects of Molière's France might be cited; suffice it, however, to add that behind this particular play (as behind *The Misanthrope*) there also lies the Paris of social and literary cliques and salons, an élite world which considered itself more elegant than the court. Our understanding of the characters in *The Learned Ladies* is partially shaped by an awareness of the real France beyond them: we note, for instance, that for the upper-middle-class Philaminte the conducting of a salon is a form of social climbing, and that it gratifies her to hear Trissotin recite under her roof a sonnet which has lately pleased "a certain princess." The life of the characters does *not*, however, consist in the satiric indication of real persons belonging to the salon world of Paris; their vitality and depth result, as I have been trying to suggest, from their intense interplay with each other, and from the way in which an unbalanced family situation has warped, divided, or challenged their personalities. We look *at* and *into* Philaminte or Armande, not *through* them.

To this rule there are a couple of apparent exceptions. The name of Philaminte's salon guest Trissotin was, for the seventeenth-century ear, inevitably suggestive of Molière's contemporary Charles Cotin. A member of the French Academy and a frequenter of the most brilliant salons, the Abbé Cotin was a prolific writer of occasional verse, who had more than once satirically attacked Molière and his friend Boileau. Molière avenged himself by naming an unattractive character Trissotin ("thrice-a-fool"), and also by having that character recite as his own work two vulnerably arch poems of Cotin's composition. In Vadius, with whom Trissotin has a literary spat in Act Three, audiences easily recognized a reference to the distinguished scholar Gilles Ménage, who made verses in French, Italian, Latin, and Greek, and had once, by several accounts, quarreled with Cotin over the merits of one of the latter's poems. Vadius and Trissotin resemble Ménage and Cotin in the above respects, and one might add that Ménage was well known for the peremptoriness of his aesthetic judgments, and Cotin for being vain of his literary productions. But there the resemblances stop. When *Les femmes savantes* was first acted, Cotin was a sixty-eight-year-old man in holy orders, and could not possibly be confused with the fortune-hunting Trissotin of Act Five. No more was Vadius intended as a true portrait of Ménage. Though French audiences of 1672 could enjoy Molière's incidental thrusts as we cannot, the figures of Trissotin and Vadius were finally for them, as for us, two fictional sketches of salon wits. Satire, then, is a secondary and local effect in this play, and the two wits, though less complex than certain other characters, share the same fictional world with them, and serve the same plot and theme.

Plot, in Molière, is best not taken too hard. We should not hold our breaths, toward the close of *Tartuffe*, over the danger that Orgon will lose his property; Molière was not, after all, writing bourgeois melodrama. And neither *The School for Wives* nor *The Learned Ladies* should make us bite our nails for fear that Agnès or Henriette will be forced to marry the wrong man. The use of plot in Molière is, as W. G. Moore has said, "to present an abstract issue in concrete pictures"; the plot is there to shuffle the characters around, providing us with all the confrontations and revelations that are necessary to depict a comic deformity and to define it by contrast to saner behaviors. From this transpires the play's question or theme—which is, in the case of *The Learned Ladies*, the right relation of art and learning to everyday life.

Every major figure in the play, whether male or female, somehow embodies that theme, and the men have their fair share of odiousness and folly. Chrysale, expressing an attitude that many of his original audience would have endorsed, holds that women's "only study and philosophy" should be the rearing of children, the training of servants, the keeping of household accounts, and the making of trousseaus. Nor is he more intellectually ambitious for himself: while there may be nothing scandalous about his indifference to the revolutions of Saturn, he is thoroughly philistine in his scorn of all books save the heavy Plutarch in which he presses his collars. Chrysale's brother, Ariste, is actually more of a catalyst than a character, but one or two of his speeches share Chrysale's distaste for pedantry and for "besotted" intellectuality in women; and the kitchen maid, Martine, vehemently supports her master's aversion to having a bookworm for a son-in-law. None of these persons, of course, speaks for Molière: Ariste's remarks are conditioned by his role as Clitandre's advocate; Chrysale is self-centered and hidebound, and appeals to us only through his wholesome sympathy with young love; Martine has a certain instinctual wisdom, but can scarcely be trusted to appreciate the value that education might have for her betters. And yet we side with this faction, and second what is valid in their speeches, because the "learned ladies" are so ill-motivated and their heroes—Trissotin and Vadius—so appalling. Philaminte, Bélise, and Armande lack, as I have said, any real vocation for the life of the mind, and Act Three demonstrates this in numerous ways. By their continual interruption of Trissotin's verses, the ladies show that they have small interest in poetry proper; by their fatuous praise of Trissotin's verses, they show that they have no taste. The "learning" they display is skimpy and ludicrous, and their dreams of an academy have less to do with knowledge than with self-assertion and celebrity. Finally, the scenes with Trissotin and Vadius are so full of coquetry, so charged with repressed sexuality, as to prove the ladies unfitted to be vestals of science and of the spirit. All this being the case, Philaminte and her associates represent a false and fruitless intellectual pretension which entails neglect of all the normal self-realizations and responsibilities of bourgeois women. As for Trissotin's relation to the theme of this play, he is someone for whom learning, or, rather, a literary career, has become the whole of life. Regarding the

poems which he dedicates to "Irises and Phyllises," he assures
Henriette that

My mind speaks in those verses, not my heart.

But in fact this desiccated man has no heart, and for all his
mixing in society, he is perfectly antisocial in the sense of
being perfectly selfish; all of his attentions and flatteries to
Philaminte's circle, all of his intrigues for dowry or pension,
are for the benefit of a self which consists wholly of literary
vanity and the pursuit of reputation. Literature and thought,
for such a man, are unreal because unrelated to human feeling; in consequence, his life is vicious and his verse is dead.

The healthiest attitudes toward the play's theme are embod-
ied in, and expressed by, Clitandre and Henriette. In respect
of two repeated topics, spirituality and language, they represent an agreeable median position. Philaminte and Armande
urge a life of pure intellect, and Bélise will have nothing to do
with "extended substance"; Chrysale, at the other extreme,
identifies himself with his body (*mon corps est moi-même*); but
in Act Four, Scene Two, Clitandre firmly tells Armande that
he has "both a body and a spirit," and Henriette has already
proven the same of herself in the first scene of the play. In
regard to language, we have at one extreme the pungent,
direct, but limited and ungrammatical speech of Martine; at
the other, we have the stifling or prissy rules of the proposed
academy, the substanceless flatteries and phrase-making of
Trissotin and Vadius, and the absolute dissociation of style
and function in Philaminte's proposal that a French marriage
contract express the dowry "in talent and drachma," and be
dated in "ides and calends." (Since Philaminte twice upbraids
the notary for his barbaric style, it is amusing that she is here
proposing the use of literal barbarisms.) Though Henriette's
speech is at times strategically flat, and though Clitandre,
when aroused, can rattle on for thirty lines like Hotspur, their
discourse is, on the whole, straightforward, pithy, sprightly,
and graceful, and amounts to the best employment of language in the play. The virtues of Clitandre and Henriette are

not all to be discovered in some middle ground, however: for instance, despite all the high-minded talk of others, it is they who, in the final scene, represent the extreme of active unselfishness in *Les femmes savantes*.

It is possible to exaggerate the play's anti-intellectualism. One should remember that the action takes place not in the university, the church, a great salon, or the manor house of Madame de Sévigné, but in an upper-bourgeois milieu, where an ill-founded pursuit of the semblance of culture can pervert all of the norms of life. Molière does not deny that there may be truly learned men and women, or true literati like Boileau, and he has Clitandre speak of persons of genuine wit and brain who are not unwelcome at the court. If the pseudo-intellectuality of the "learned ladies" were not so flamboyant, and Clitandre and Henriette so occupied with resisting it, one would more readily notice that the young lovers are literate people who read poetry (Trissotin's, for example) and judge it with some accuracy. Clitandre, it should be observed, is not unfamiliar with the scholarship of Rasius and Baldus, and is capable of criticizing the Platonic separation of body and soul. He and Henriette are in fact witty, intelligent, tasteful, and independent-minded; yet they do not feel that the cultivation of the mind should estrange one from life's basic fulfillments and duties. Neither, clearly, does Molière.

Clitandre's assertion that "A woman should know something . . . / Of every subject" was a quite liberal sentiment for its day, but we will not now recognize it as such unless *The Learned Ladies* is read (or mounted) quite strictly "in period." Molière is a timeless author in the sense that his art, owing to its clarity and its concern with human fundamentals, is not only readily enjoyed by readers and audiences three centuries after his death, but is often, I think, taken pretty much as it was meant to be taken. This freshness of Molière, his present accessibility, has lately misled some theatrical companies into detaching his art from its temporal background, and giving it the kind of "updating" which involves absurd anachronisms and the loss of meaning through the loss of a credible social frame. Not long ago, I saw a production that aimed to make *Tartuffe* "relevant" by dressing the title character in the sheets and beads of a guru, and having the action take place around a family swimming pool in California. The attempt at topicality was, of course, doomed from the start: it was young people who, in the latter 1960's, were succumbing to the influence of gurus, whereas in Molière's play that is not the situation at all: the children, Damis and Mariane, regard Tartuffe as a fraud, and it is their middle-aged father who is taken in. Not only did the production not mesh with current events, as the director had hoped it would seem to do; it was also miserably confusing, amongst other things, to hear a guru uttering Tartuffe's speeches, which are full of Christian scriptural and liturgical echoes, as well as seventeenth-century Jesuit terminology. More recently, a Boston company based a regrettable "modern-dress" production of *The Misanthrope* on the supposition that Alceste's demand for frankness in social intercourse resembles the demand, lately made by our youth culture, that one "tell it like it is." As a result, the play began with Alceste's entering a twentieth-century American living room in hippie attire, a ten-speed bicycle under his arm. The reader will imagine how implausibly such a figure inhabited the world of the text, where people are addressed as Sir and Madam, where duelling is a serious matter, and where continual reference is made to viscounts, marquesses, and the court of Versailles. I hope that no presenter of this new translation will wish, by means of contemporary costume and set, to attempt a violent conflation of Molière's drama with the current women's movement. And I hope that all readers of this text will envision it in a just historical perspective: Clitandre's liberalism, Henriette's attractively balanced nature, the grotesqueness of the bluestockings, and every nuance of this excellent comedy will then be there to be seen.

Sincere thanks are owed to my colleague Morton Briggs, who urged me to undertake this translation and was so kind as to read it over. I must also thank my wife, and Sonja and William Jay Smith, for their goodness in criticizing both the text and these remarks.

Richard Wilbur

CHARACTERS

CHRYSALE, a well-to-do bourgeois

PHILAMINTE, Chrysale's wife

ARMANDE and } daughters of Chrysale
HENRIETTE   } and Philaminte

ARISTE, Chrysale's brother

BÉLISE, Chrysale's sister

CLITANDRE, Henriette's suitor

TRISSOTIN, a wit

VADIUS, a scholar

MARTINE, kitchen-maid

LÉPINE, a servant

JULIEN, valet to Vadius

A NOTARY

PLACE
The scene: Chrysale's house in Paris

Act One
SCENE ONE

———•———

Armande, Henriette

ARMANDE

What, Sister! Are you truly of a mind
To leave your precious maidenhood behind,
And give yourself in marriage to a man?
Can you be harboring such a vulgar plan?

HENRIETTE

Yes, Sister.

ARMANDE

Yes, you say! When have I heard
So odious and sickening a word?

HENRIETTE

Why does the thought of marriage so repel you?

ARMANDE

Fie, fie! For shame!

HENRIETTE

But what—

ARMANDE

For shame, I tell you!
Can you deny what sordid scenes are brought
To the mind's eye by that distasteful thought,
What coarse, degrading images arise,
What shocking things it makes one visualize?
Do you not shudder, Sister, and grow pale
At what this thought you're thinking would entail?

HENRIETTE

It would entail, as I conceive it, one
Husband, some children, and a house to run;
In all of which, it may as well be said,
I find no cause for loathing or for dread.

ARMANDE

Alas! Such bondage truly appeals to you?

HENRIETTE

At my young age, what better could I do
Than join myself in wedded harmony
To one I love, and who in turn loves me,
And through the deepening bond of man and wife
Enjoy a blameless and contented life?
Does such a union offer no attractions?

ARMANDE

Oh dear, you crave such squalid satisfactions!
How can you choose to play a petty role,
Dull and domestic, and content your soul
With joys no loftier than keeping house
And raising brats, and pampering a spouse?
Let common natures, vulgarly inclined,
Concern themselves with trifles of that kind.
Aspire to nobler objects, seek to attain
To keener joys upon a higher plane,
And, scorning gross material things as naught,
Devote yourself, as we have done, to thought.
We have a mother to whom all pay honor
For erudition; model yourself upon her;
Yes, prove yourself her daughter, as I have done,
Join in the quest for truth that she's begun,
And learn how love of study can impart
A sweet enlargement to the mind and heart.
Why marry, and be the slave of him you wed?
Be married to philosophy instead,

Which lifts us up above mankind, and gives
All power to reason's pure imperatives,
Thus rendering our bestial natures tame
And mastering those lusts which lead to shame.
A love of reason, a passion for the truth,
Should quite suffice one's heart in age or youth,
And I am moved to pity when I note
On what low objects certain women dote.

HENRIETTE

But Heaven, in its wise omnipotence,
Endows us all with differing gifts and bents,
And all souls are not fashioned, I'm afraid,
Of the stuff of which philosophers are made.
If yours was born for soaring to the heights
Of learning, and for speculative flights,
My own weak spirit, Sister, has from birth
Clung to the homelier pleasures of the earth.
Let's not oppose what Heaven has decreed,
But simply follow where our instincts lead.
You, through the towering genius you possess,
Shall dwell in philosophic loftiness,
While my prosaic nature, here below,
Shall taste such joys as marriage can bestow.
Thus, though our lives contrast with one another,
We each shall emulate our worthy mother—
You, in your quest for rational excellence,
I, in the less refined delights of sense;
You, in conceptions lofty and ethereal,
I, in conceptions rather more material.

ARMANDE

Sister, the person whom one emulates
Ought to be followed for her finer traits.
If someone's worthy to be copied, it's
Not for the way in which she coughs and spits.

HENRIETTE

You and your intellect would not be here
If Mother's traits had all been fine, my dear,
And it's most fortunate for you that she
Was not wed solely to philosophy.
Relent, and tolerate in me, I pray,
That urge through which you saw the light of day,
And do not bid me be like you, and scorn
The hopes of some small scholar to be born.

ARMANDE

Your mind, I see, is stupidly contrary,
And won't give up its stubborn wish to marry.
But tell me, do, of this intended match:
Surely it's not Clitandre you aim to catch?

HENRIETTE

Why not? Of what defects could one accuse him?
Would I be vulgar if I were to choose him?

ARMANDE

No. But I don't think much of your design
To lure away a devotee of mine;
Clitandre, as the world well knows, has sighed
And yearned for me, and sought me as his bride.

HENRIETTE

Yes; but such sighs, arising as they do
From base affections, are as naught to you;
Marriage is something you have risen above,
And fair philosophy has all your love.
Since, then, Clitandre isn't necessary
To your well-being, may he and I not marry?

ARMANDE

Though reason bids us shun the baits of sense,
We still may take delight in compliments;

We may refuse a man, yet be desirous
That still he pay us homage, and admire us.

HENRIETTE
I never sought to make him discontinue
His worship of the noble soul that's in you;
But once you had refused him, I felt free
To take the love which he then offered me.

ARMANDE
When a rejected suitor, full of spite,
Claims to adore you, can you trust him quite?
Do you really think he loves you? Are you persuaded
That his intense desire for me has faded?

HENRIETTE
Yes, Sister, I believe it; he's told me so.

ARMANDE
Sister, you're gullible; as you should know,
His talk of leaving me and loving you
Is self-deceptive bluster, and quite untrue.

HENRIETTE
Perhaps; however, Sister, if you'd care
To learn with me the facts of this affair,
I see Clitandre coming; I'm sure, my dear,
That if we ask, he'll make his feelings clear.

SCENE TWO

Clitandre, Armande, Henriette

HENRIETTE

My sister has me in uncertainties
As to your heart's affections. If you please,
Clitandre, tell us where your feelings lie,
And which of us may claim you—she or I.

ARMANDE

No, I'll not join in making you reveal
So publicly the passion which you feel;
You are, I'm sure, reluctant to confess
Your private feelings under such duress.

CLITANDRE (*to Armande*)

Madam, my heart, unused to sly pretense,
Does not reluct to state its sentiments;
I'm not at all embarrassed, and can proclaim
Wholeheartedly, without reserve or shame,
That she whom I most honor, hold most dear,
And whose devoted slave I am . . .
                    (*Gesturing toward Henriette*)
                              is here.
Take no offense; you've nothing to resent:
You've made your choice, and so should be content.
Your charms enthralled me once, as many a sigh
And warm profession served to testify;
I offered you a love which could not fade,
Yet you disdained the conquest you had made.
Beneath your tyrant gaze, my soul has borne
A hundred bitter slights, and every scorn,
Till, wearying at last of whip and chain,
It hungered for a bondage more humane.
Such have I found, *Madame*, in these fair eyes,
          (*Gesturing once more toward Henriette*)

Whose kindness I shall ever love and prize:
They have not spurned the man you cast aside,
And, warmed by their regard, my tears have dried.
Now nothing could persuade me to be free
Of this most amiable captivity,
And I entreat you, Madam, do not strive
To cause my former feelings to revive,
Or sway my heart as once you did, for I
Propose to love this lady till I die.

ARMANDE

Well, Sir! What makes you fancy that one might
Regard you with a jealous appetite?
You're fatuous indeed to harbor such
A thought, and very brash to say as much.

HENRIETTE

Steady now, Sister. Where's that discipline
Of soul which reins one's lower nature in,
And keeps one's temper under firm command?

ARMANDE

And you, dear: are your passions well in hand
When you propose to wed a man without
The leave of those who brought your life about?
You owe your parents a complete submission,
And may not love except by their permission;
Your heart is theirs, and you may not bestow it;
To do so would be wicked, and you know it.

HENRIETTE

I'm very grateful to be thus instructed
In how these matters ought to be conducted.
And just to prove to you that I've imbibed
Your teachings, I shall do as you've prescribed:
Clitandre, I should thank you if you went
And gained from my dear parents their consent,

So that, without the risk of wickedness,
I could return the love which you profess.

CLITANDRE

Now that I have your gracious leave, I'll bend
My every effort towards that happy end.

ARMANDE

You look triumphant, Sister, and appear
To think me vexed by what has happened here.

HENRIETTE

By no means, Sister. I well know how you've checked
Your senses with the reins of intellect,
And how no foolish weakness could disturb
A heart so disciplined by wisdom's curb.
I'm far from thinking you upset; indeed,
I know you'll give me the support I need,
Help win my parents to Clitandre's side,
And speed the day when I may be his bride.
Do lend your influence, Sister, to promote—

ARMANDE

What childish teasing, Sister! And how you gloat
At having made a cast-off heart your prize!

HENRIETTE

Cast-off or not, it's one you don't despise.
Had you the chance to get it back from me,
You'd gladly pick it up on bended knee.

ARMANDE

I shall not stoop to answer that. I deem
This whole discussion silly in the extreme.

HENRIETTE

It is indeed, and you do well to end it.
Your self-control is great, and I commend it.

SCENE THREE

Clitandre, Henriette

HENRIETTE
Your frank avowal left her quite unnerved.

CLITANDRE
Such frankness was no less than she deserved;
Given her haughty airs and foolish pride,
My blunt words were entirely justified.
But now, since you have given me leave, I'll seek
Your father—

HENRIETTE
    It's to Mother you should speak.
My gentle father would say yes, of course,
But his decrees, alas, have little force;
Heaven blessed him with a mild, concessive soul
Which yields in all things to his wife's control.
It's she who rules the house, requiring him
To treat as law her every royal whim.
I wish that you were more disposed to please
My mother, and indulge my Aunt Bélise,
By humoring their fancies, and thereby
Making them view you with a kindly eye.

CLITANDRE
My heart's too frank for that; I could not praise,
Even in your sister, such outlandish ways,
And female sages aren't my cup of tea.
A woman should know something, I agree,
Of every subject, but this proud desire
To pose as erudite I can't admire.
I like a woman who, though she may know
The answers, does not always let it show;
Who keeps her studies secret and, in fine,

Though she's enlightened, feels no need to shine
By means of pompous word and rare quotation
And brilliance on the slightest provocation.
I much respect your mother; nonetheless,
I can't encourage her in foolishness,
Agree with everything she says, and laud
Her intellectual hero—who's a fraud.
I loathe her Monsieur Trissotin; how can
She so esteem so ludicrous a man,
And class with men of genius and of vision
A dunce whose works meet always with derision,
A bore whose dreadful books end, one and all,
As wrapping paper in some market stall?

HENRIETTE

All that he writes or speaks I find a bore;
I could agree with all you say, and more;
But since the creature has my mother's ear,
He's someone you should cultivate, I fear.
A lover seeks the good opinion of
All who surround the object of his love,
And, so that no one will oppose his passion,
Treats even the house-dog in a courtly fashion.

CLITANDRE

You're right; yet Trissotin, I must admit,
So irks me that there's no controlling it.
I can't, to gain his advocacy, stoop
To praise the works of such a nincompoop.
It was those works which introduced me to him;
Before I ever saw the man, I knew him;
From the vile way he wrote, I saw with ease
What, in the flesh, must be his qualities:
The absolute presumption, the complete
And dauntless nature of his self-conceit,
The calm assurance of superior worth
Which renders him the smuggest man on earth,
So that he stands in awe and hugs himself

Before his volumes ranged upon the shelf,
And would not trade his baseless reputation
For that of any general in the nation.

HENRIETTE
If you could see all that, you've got good eyes.

CLITANDRE
I saw still more; for I could visualize,
By studying his dreadful poetry,
Just what the poet's lineaments must be;
I pictured him so truly that, one day,
Seeing a foppish man in the Palais,
I said, "That's Trissotin, by God!"—and found,
Upon enquiry, that my hunch was sound.

HENRIETTE
What a wild story!

CLITANDRE
                      Not at all; it's true.
But here's your aunt. If you'll permit me to,
I'll tell her of our hopes, in hopes that she
Will urge your mother to approve of me.

SCENE FOUR

Clitandre, Bélise

CLITANDRE

Madam, permit a lover's heart to seize
This happy opportunity, if you please,
To tell you of his passion, and reveal—

BÉLISE

Hold, Sir! Don't say too baldly what you feel.
If you belong, Sir, to the ranks of those
Who love me, let your eyes alone disclose
Your sentiments, and do not tell me bluntly
Of coarse desires which only could affront me.
Adore me if you will, but do not show it
In such a way that I'll be forced to know it;
Worship me inwardly, and I shall brook it
If, through your silence, I can overlook it;
But should you dare to speak of it outright,
I'll banish you forever from my sight.

CLITANDRE

My passions, Madam, need cause you no alarms;
It's Henriette who's won me by her charms,
And I entreat your generous soul to aid me
In my design to wed that charming lady.

BÉLISE

Ah, what a subtle dodge; you should be proud;
You're very artful, it must be allowed;
In all the novels that I've read, I've never
Encountered any subterfuge so clever.

CLITANDRE

Madam, I meant no witty indirection;
I've spoken truly of my heart's affection.

By Heaven's will, by ties that cannot part,
I'm bound to Henriette with all my heart;
It's Henriette I cherish, as I've said,
And Henriette whom I aspire to wed.
All that I ask of you is that you lend
Your influence to help me gain that end.

BÉLISE

I well divine the hopes which you have stated,
And how the name you've used should be translated.
A clever substitution, Sir; and I
Shall use the selfsame code in my reply:
"Henriette" disdains to wed, and those who burn
For her must hope for nothing in return.

CLITANDRE

Madam, why make things difficult? Why insist
Upon supposing what does not exist?

BÉLISE

Good heavens, Sir, don't stand on ceremony,
Denying what your looks have often shown me.
Let it suffice, Sir, that I am contented
With this oblique approach you have invented,
And that, beneath such decorous disguise,
Your homage is acceptable in my eyes,
Provided that you make no overture
Which is not noble, rarefied, and pure.

CLITANDRE

But—

BÉLISE

Hush. Farewell. It's time our talk was ended.
I've said, already, more than I intended.

CLITANDRE

You're quite mistaken—

BÉLISE

I'm blushing, can't you see?
All this has overtaxed my modesty.

CLITANDRE

I'm hanged if I love you, Madam! This is absurd.

BÉLISE

No, no, I mustn't hear another word.
(*She exits.*)

CLITANDRE

The devil take her and her addled brain!
What stubborn fancies she can entertain!
Well, I'll turn elsewhere, and shall hope to find
Support from someone with a balanced mind.

Act Two
SCENE ONE

———•————

Ariste

ARISTE (*to Clitandre, who is making his exit*)
Yes, yes, I'll urge and plead as best I can, Sir,
Then hasten back to you and bring his answer.
Lovers! How very much they have to say,
And what extreme impatience they display!
Never—

SCENE TWO

Chrysale, Ariste

ARISTE
Ah! God be with you, Brother dear.

CHRYSALE
And you, dear Brother.

ARISTE
D'you know what brings me here?

CHRYSALE
No, but I'll gladly learn of it; do tell.

ARISTE
I think you know Clitandre rather well?

CHRYSALE
Indeed; he calls here almost every day.

ARISTE
And what is your opinion of him, pray?

CHRYSALE
He's a man of honor, breeding, wit, and spirit;
I know few lads of comparable merit.

ARISTE
Well, I am here at his request; I'm glad
To learn that you think highly of the lad.

CHRYSALE
I knew his father well, during my stay
In Rome.

ARISTE

Ah, good.

CHRYSALE

A fine man.

ARISTE

So they say.

CHRYSALE

We were both young then, twenty-eight or so,
And a pair of dashing gallants, I'll have you know.

ARISTE

I'm sure of it.

CHRYSALE

Oh, those dark-eyed Roman maids!
The whole town talked about our escapades,
And weren't the husbands jealous!

ARISTE

Ho! No doubt!
But let me broach the matter I came about.

SCENE THREE

———— •◦• ————

Bélise (entering quietly and listening),
Chrysale, Ariste

ARISTE

I'm here to speak for young Clitandre, and let
You know of his deep love for Henriette.

CHRYSALE

He loves my daughter?

ARISTE

Yes. Upon my honor,
I've never seen such passion; he dotes upon her.

BÉLISE (*to Ariste*)

No, no; I see what's happened. You're unaware
Of the true character of this affair.

ARISTE

What, Sister?

BÉLISE

Clitandre has misled you, Brother:
The passion which he feels is for another.

ARISTE

Oh, come. He doesn't love Henriette? Then how—

BÉLISE

I'm certain of it.

ARISTE

He said he did, just now.

BÉLISE

Of course.

ARISTE

He sent me here, please understand,
To ask her father for the lady's hand.

BÉLISE

Splendid.

ARISTE

What's more, his ardor is so great
That I'm to urge an early wedding date.

BÉLISE

Oh, how delightful; what obliquity!
We use the name of "Henriette," you see,
As a code word and camouflage concealing
The actual object of his tender feeling.
But I'll consent, now, to enlighten you.

ARISTE

Well, Sister, since you know so much, please do
Tell us with whom his true affections lie.

BÉLISE

You wish to know?

ARISTE

I do.

BÉLISE

It's I.

ARISTE

You?

BÉLISE

I.

ARISTE

Well, Sister!

BÉLISE

What do you mean by *well*? My word,
Why should you look surprised at what you've heard?
My charms are evident, in my frank opinion,
And more than one heart's under their dominion.
Dorante, Damis, Cléonte, Valère—all these
Are proof of my attractive qualities.

ARISTE

These men all love you?

BÉLISE

Yes, with all their might.

ARISTE

They've said so?

BÉLISE

None has been so impolite:
They've worshipped me as one from Heaven above,
And not presumed to breathe a word of love.
Mute signs, however, have managed to impart
The keen devotion of each humble heart.

ARISTE

Damis is almost never seen here. Why?

BÉLISE

His reverence for me has made him shy.

ARISTE

Dorante reviles you in the harshest fashion.

BÉLISE

He's seized, at times, by fits of jealous passion.

ARISTE

Cléonte has lately married; so has Valère.

BÉLISE

That was because I drove them to despair.

ARISTE

Sister, you're prone to fantasies, I fear.

CHRYSALE (*to Bélise*)

Get rid of these chimeras, Sister dear.

BÉLISE

Chimeras! Well! Chimeras, did you say?
I have chimeras! Well, how very gay!
May all your thoughts, dear Brothers, be as clear as
Those which you dared, just now, to call *chimeras*!

SCENE FOUR

Chrysale, Ariste

CHRYSALE

Our sister's mad.

ARISTE

And growing madder daily.
But, once more, let's discuss our business, may we?
Clitandre longs to marry Henriette,
And asks your blessing. What answer shall he get?

CHRYSALE

No need to ask. I readily agree.
His wish does honor to my family.

ARISTE

He has, as you well know, no great amount
Of worldly goods—

CHRYSALE

Ah, gold's of no account:
He's rich in virtue, that most precious ore;
His father and I were bosom friends, what's more.

ARISTE

Let's go make certain that your wife concurs.

CHRYSALE

I've given my consent; no need for hers.

ARISTE

True, Brother; still, 'twould do no harm if your
Decision had her strong support, I'm sure.
Let's both go—

CHRYSALE

Nonsense, that's a needless move;
I'll answer for my wife. She will approve.

ARISTE

But—

CHRYSALE

No. Enough. I'll deal with her. Don't worry.
The business will be settled in a hurry.

ARISTE

So be it. I'll go consult with Henriette,
And then—

CHRYSALE

The thing's as good as done; don't fret.
I'll tell my wife about it, without delay.

SCENE FIVE

Martine, Chrysale

MARTINE

Ain't that my luck! It's right, what people say—
When you hang a dog, first give him a bad name.
Domestic service! It's a losing game.

CHRYSALE

Well, well, Martine! What's up?

MARTINE
                        You want to know?

CHRYSALE

Why, yes.

MARTINE
          What's up is, Madam's let me go.

CHRYSALE

She's let you go?

MARTINE
                  Yes, given me the sack.

CHRYSALE

But why? Whatever for?

MARTINE
                        She says she'll whack
Me black and blue if I don't clear out of here.

ACT TWO, SCENE FIVE ❧ 373

CHRYSALE

No, you shall stay; you've served me well, my dear.
My wife's a bit short-tempered at times, and fussy:
But this won't do. I'll—

SCENE SIX

Philaminte, Bélise, Chrysale, Martine

PHILAMINTE (*seeing Martine*)
                    What! Still here, you hussy!
Be off, you trollop; leave my house this minute,
And mind you never again set foot within it!

CHRYSALE

Gently, now.

PHILAMINTE
        No, it's settled.

CHRYSALE
        But—

PHILAMINTE
                    Off with her!

CHRYSALE
What crime has she committed, to incur—

PHILAMINTE
So! You defend the girl!

CHRYSALE
        No, that's not so.

PHILAMINTE
Are you taking her side against me?

CHRYSALE
                    Heavens, no;
I merely asked the nature of her offense.

PHILAMINTE
Would I, without good reason, send her hence?

CHRYSALE
Of course not; but employers should be just—

PHILAMINTE
Enough! I bade her leave, and leave she must.

CHRYSALE
Quite so, quite so. Has anyone denied it?

PHILAMINTE
I won't be contradicted. I can't abide it.

CHRYSALE
Agreed.

PHILAMINTE
If you were a proper husband, you
Would take my side, and share my outrage, too.

CHRYSALE
I do, dear.
(*Turning towards Martine*)
Wench! My wife is right to rid
This house of one who's done the thing you did.

MARTINE
What did I do?

CHRYSALE (*aside*)
Alas, you have me there.

PHILAMINTE
She takes a light view, still, of this affair.

CHRYSALE

What caused your anger? How did all this begin?
Did she break some mirror, or piece of porcelain?

PHILAMINTE

Do you suppose that I'd be angry at her,
And bid her leave, for such a trifling matter?

CHRYSALE (*to Martine*)

What can this mean? (*To Philaminte*) Is the crime, then,
    very great?

PHILAMINTE

Of course it is. Would I exaggerate?

CHRYSALE

Did she, perhaps, by inadvertence, let
Some vase be stolen, or some china set?

PHILAMINTE

That would be nothing.

CHRYSALE (*to Martine*)

                    Blast, girl, what can this be?
                    (*To Philaminte*)
Have you caught the chit in some dishonesty?

PHILAMINTE

Far worse than that.

CHRYSALE

                    Far worse than that?

PHILAMINTE

                                        Far worse.

CHRYSALE (*to Martine*)

For shame, you strumpet! (*To Philaminte*) Has she been so
  perverse—

PHILAMINTE

This creature, who for insolence has no peer,
Has, after thirty lessons, shocked my ear
By uttering a low, plebeian word
Which Vaugelas deems unworthy to be heard.

CHRYSALE

Is *that*—?

PHILAMINTE

And she persists in her defiance
Of that which is the basis of all science—
Grammar! which even the mightiest must obey,
And whose pure laws hold princes in their sway.

CHRYSALE

I was sure she'd done the worst thing under the sun.

PHILAMINTE

What! You don't find it monstrous, what she's done?

CHRYSALE

Oh, yes.

PHILAMINTE

I'd love to hear you plead her case!

CHRYSALE

Not I!

BÉLISE

It's true, her speech is a disgrace.
How long we've taught her language and its laws!
Yet still she butchers every phrase or clause.

MARTINE

I'm sure your preachings is all well and good,
But I wouldn't talk your jargon if I could.

PHILAMINTE

She dares describe as jargon a speech that's based
On reason, and good usage, and good taste!

MARTINE

If people get the point, that's speech to me;
Fine words don't have no use that I can see.

PHILAMINTE

Hark! There's a sample of her style again!
"Don't have no!"

BÉLISE

O ineducable brain!
How futile have our efforts been to teach
Your stubborn mind the rules of proper speech!
You've coupled *don't* with *no*. I can't forgive
That pleonasm, that double negative.

MARTINE

Good Lord, Ma'am, I ain't studious like you;
I just talk plain, the way my people do.

PHILAMINTE

What ghastly solecisms!

BÉLISE

I could faint!

PHILAMINTE

How the ear shudders at the sound of "ain't"!

BÉLISE (*to Martine*)

With ignorance like yours, one struggles vainly.

"Plain" is an adjective; the adverb's "plainly."
Shall grammar be abused by you forever?

MARTINE

Me abuse Gramma? Or Grampa either? Never!

PHILAMINTE

Dear God!

BÉLISE

What I said was "grammar." You misheard.
I've told you about the origin of the word.

MARTINE

Let it come from Passy, Pontoise, or Chaillot;
It's Greek to me.

BÉLISE

Alas, what *do* you know,
You peasant? It is grammar which lays down
The laws which govern adjective and noun,
And verb, and subject.

MARTINE

Madam, I'd just be lying
If I said I knew those people.

PHILAMINTE

Oh, how trying!

BÉLISE

Girl, those are parts of speech, and we must be
At pains to make those parts of speech agree.

MARTINE

Let them agree or squabble, what does it matter?

PHILAMINTE (*to her sister-in-law*)

Ah, mercy, let's be done with all this chatter!
(*To her husband*)
Sir! Will you bid her go and leave me in peace?

CHRYSALE

Yes, yes. (*Aside*) I must give in to her caprice.
(*To Martine*)
Martine, don't vex her further; you'd best depart.

PHILAMINTE

So, you're afraid to wound her little heart!
The hussy! Must you be so sweet and mild?

CHRYSALE

Of course not. (*Loudly*) Wench, be off!
(*Softly, to Martine*)
Go, go, poor child.

SCENE SEVEN

—•◆•—

Philaminte, Chrysale, Bélise

CHRYSALE

Well, you have had your way, and she is gone;
But I don't think much of the way you've carried on.
The girl is good at what she does, and you've
Dismissed her for a trifle. I don't approve.

PHILAMINTE

Would you have me keep her in my service here
To give incessant anguish to my ear
By constant barbarisms, and the breach
Of every law of reason and good speech,
Patching the mangled discourse which she utters
With coarse expressions from the city's gutters?

BÉLISE

It's true, her talk can drive one out of one's wits.
Each day, she tears dear Vaugelas to bits,
And the least failings of this pet of yours
Are vile cacophonies and non sequiturs.

CHRYSALE

Who cares if she offends some grammar book,
So long as she doesn't offend us as a cook?
If she makes a tasty salad, it seems to me
Her subjects and her verbs need not agree.
Let all her talk be barbarous, if she'll not
Burn up my beef or oversalt the pot.
It's food, not language, that I'm nourished by.
Vaugelas can't teach you how to bake a pie;
Malherbe, Balzac, for all their learnèd rules,
Might, in a kitchen, have been utter fools.

PHILAMINTE

I'm stunned by what you've said, and shocked at seeing
How you, who claim the rank of human being,
Rather than rise on spiritual wings,
Give all your care to base, material things.
This rag, the body—does it matter so?
Should its desires detain us here below?
Should we not soar aloft, and scorn to heed it?

CHRYSALE

My body is myself, and I aim to feed it.
It's a rag, perhaps, but one of which I'm fond.

BÉLISE

Brother, 'twixt flesh and spirit there's a bond;
Yet, as the best minds of the age have stated,
The claims of flesh must be subordinated,
And it must be our chief delight and care
To feast the soul on philosophic fare.

CHRYSALE

I don't know what your soul's been eating of late,
But it's not a balanced diet, at any rate;
You show no womanly solicitude
For—

PHILAMINTE

"Womanly"! That word is old and crude.
It reeks, in fact, of its antiquity.

BÉLISE

It sounds old-fashioned and absurd to me.

CHRYSALE

See here; I can't contain myself; I mean
To drop the mask for once, and vent my spleen.
The whole world thinks you mad, and I am through—

PHILAMINTE

How's that, Sir?

CHRYSALE (*to Bélise*)
Sister, I am addressing *you*.
The least mistake in speech you can't forgive,
But how mistakenly you choose to live!
I'm sick of those eternal books you've got;
In my opinion, you should burn the lot,
Save for that Plutarch where I press my collars,
And leave the studious life to clerks and scholars;
And do throw out, if I may be emphatic,
That great long frightful spyglass in the attic,
And all these other gadgets, and do it soon.
Stop trying to see what's happening in the moon
And look what's happening in your household here,
Where everything is upside down and queer.
For a hundred reasons, it's neither meet nor right
That a woman study and be erudite.
To teach her children manners, overlook
The household, train the servants and the cook,
And keep a thrifty budget—these should be
Her only study and philosophy.
Our fathers had a saying which made good sense:
A woman's polished her intelligence
Enough, they said, if she can pass the test
Of telling a pair of breeches from a vest.
Their wives read nothing, yet their lives were good;
Domestic lore was all they understood,
And all their books were needle and thread, with which
They made their daughters' trousseaus, stitch by stitch.
But women scorn such modest arts of late;
They want to scribble and to cogitate;
No mystery is too deep for them to plumb.
Is there a stranger house in Christendom
Than mine, where women are as mad as hatters,
And everything is known except what matters?

They know how Mars, the moon, and Venus turn,
And Saturn, too, that's none of my concern,
And what with all this vain and far-fetched learning,
They don't know if my roast of beef is burning.
My servants, who now aspire to culture, too,
Do anything but what they're paid to do;
Thinking is all this household thinks about,
And reasoning has driven reason out.
One spoils a sauce, while reading the dictionary;
One mumbles verses when I ask for sherry;
Because they ape the follies they've observed
In you, I keep six servants and am not served.
Just one poor wench remained who hadn't caught
The prevalent disease of lofty thought,
And now, since Vaugelas might find her lacking
In grammar, you've blown up and sent her packing.
Sister (I'm speaking to you, as I said before),
These goings-on I censure and deplore.
I'm tired of visits from these pedants versed
In Latin, and that ass Trissotin's the worst.
He's flattered you in many a wretched sonnet;
There's a great swarm of queer bees in his bonnet;
Each time he speaks, one wonders what he's said;
I think, myself, that he's crazy in the head.

PHILAMINTE
Dear God, what brutishness of speech and mind!

BÉLISE
Could particles more grossly be combined,
Or atoms form an aggregate more crass?
And can we be of the same blood? Alas,
I hate myself because we two are kin,
And leave this scene in horror and chagrin.

SCENE EIGHT

———•◦•———

Philaminte, Chrysale

PHILAMINTE
Have you other shots to fire, or are you through?

CHRYSALE
I? No, no. No more quarreling. That will do.
Let's talk of something else. As we've heard her state,
Your eldest daughter scorns to take a mate.
She's a philosopher—mind you, I'm not complaining;
She's had the finest of maternal training.
But her younger sister's otherwise inclined,
And I've a notion that it's time to find
A match for Henriette—

PHILAMINTE
Exactly, and
I'll now inform you of the match I've planned.
That Trissotin whose visits you begrudge,
And whom you so contemptuously judge,
Is, I've decided, the appropriate man.
If you can't recognize his worth, I can.
Let's not discuss it; it's quite unnecessary;
I've thought things through; it's he whom she should marry.
Don't tell her of my choice, however; I choose
To be the first to let her know the news.
That she will listen to reason I have no doubt,
And if you seek to meddle, I'll soon find out.

SCENE NINE

Ariste, Chrysale

ARISTE

Ah, Brother; your wife's just leaving, and it's clear
That you and she have had a conference here.

CHRYSALE

Yes.

ARISTE

Well, shall Clitandre have his Henriette?
Is your wife willing? Can the date be set?

CHRYSALE

Not altogether.

ARISTE

What, she refuses?

CHRYSALE

No.

ARISTE

Is she wavering, then?

CHRYSALE

I wouldn't describe her so.

ARISTE

What, then?

CHRYSALE

There's someone else whom she prefers.

ARISTE

For a son-in-law?

CHRYSALE

Yes.

ARISTE

Who is this choice of hers?

CHRYSALE

Well . . . Trissotin.

ARISTE

What! That ass, that figure of fun—

CHRYSALE

Who babbles verse and Latin? Yes, that's the one.

ARISTE

Did you agree to him?

CHRYSALE

I? No; God forbid!

ARISTE

What did you say, then?

CHRYSALE

Nothing; and what I did
Was wise, I think, for it left me uncommitted.

ARISTE

I see! What strategy! How nimble-witted!
Did you, at least, suggest Clitandre, Brother?

CHRYSALE

No. When I found her partial toward another,
It seemed best not to push things then and there.

ARISTE

Your prudence, truly, is beyond compare!
Aren't you ashamed to be so soft and meek?
How can a man be so absurdly weak
As to yield his wife an absolute dominion
And never dare contest her least opinion?

CHRYSALE

Ah, Brother, that's easy enough for you to say.
You've no idea how noisy quarrels weigh
Upon my heart, which loves tranquillity,
And how my wife's bad temper frightens me.
Her nature's philosophic—or that's her claim,
But her tongue's sharp and savage all the same;
All this uplifting thought has not decreased
Her rancorous behavior in the least.
If I cross her even slightly, she will loose
An eight-day howling tempest of abuse.
There's no escape from her consuming ire;
She's like some frightful dragon spitting fire;
And yet, despite her devilish ways, my fear
Obliges me to call her "pet" and "dear."

ARISTE

For shame. That's nonsense. It's your cowardice
Which lets your wife rule over you like this.
What power she has, your weakness has created;
She only rules because you've abdicated;
She couldn't bully you unless you chose,
Like an ass, to let her lead you by the nose.
Come now: despite your timid nature, can
You not resolve for once to be a man,
And, saying "This is how it's going to be,"
Lay down the law, and make your wife agree?
Shall you sacrifice your Henriette to these
Besotted women and their fantasies,
And take for son-in-law, and *heir*, a fool
Who's turned your house into a Latin school,

A pedant whom your dazzled wife extols
As best of wits, most erudite of souls
And peerless fashioner of gallant verse,
And who, in all respects, could not be worse?
Once more I say, for shame: it's ludicrous
To see a husband cringe and cower thus.

CHRYSALE

Yes, you're quite right; I see that I've been wrong.
It's high time, Brother, to be firm and strong,
To take a stand.

ARISTE

Well said.

CHRYSALE

It's base, I know,
To let a woman dominate one so.

ARISTE

Quite right.

CHRYSALE

She's taken advantage of my patience.

ARISTE

She has.

CHRYSALE

And of my peaceful inclinations.

ARISTE

That's true.

CHRYSALE

But, as she'll learn this very day,
My daughter's mine, and I shall have my way
And wed her to a man who pleases me.

ARISTE

Now you're the master, as I'd have you be.

CHRYSALE

Brother, as young Clitandre's spokesman, you
Know where to find him. Send him to me, do.

ARISTE

I'll go this instant.

CHRYSALE

           Too long my will's been crossed;
Henceforth I'll be a man, whatever the cost.

Act Three

SCENE ONE

———— •• ————

Philaminte, Armande, Bélise,
Trissotin, Lépine

PHILAMINTE
Let's all sit down and savor, thought by thought,
The verses which our learnèd guest has brought.

ARMANDE
I burn to see them.

BÉLISE
Yes; our souls are panting.

PHILAMINTE (*to Trissotin*)
All that your mind brings forth, I find enchanting.

ARMANDE
For me, your compositions have no peer.

BÉLISE
Their music is a banquet to my ear.

PHILAMINTE
Don't tantalize your breathless audience.

ARMANDE
Do hurry—

BÉLISE
And relieve this sweet suspense.

PHILAMINTE
Yield to our urging; give us your epigram.

TRISSOTIN (*to Philaminte*)

Madam, 'tis but an infant; still, I am
In hopes that you may condescend to love it,
Since on your doorstep I was delivered of it.

PHILAMINTE

Knowing its father, I can do no other.

TRISSOTIN

Your kind approval, then, shall be its mother.

BÉLISE

What wit he has!

SCENE TWO

Henriette, Philaminte, Armande,
Bélise, Trissotin, Lépine

PHILAMINTE (*to Henriette, who has*
entered and has turned at once to go)
Ho! Don't rush off like that.

HENRIETTE
I feared I might disrupt your pleasant chat.

PHILAMINTE
Come here, and pay attention, and you shall share
The joy of hearing something rich and rare.

HENRIETTE
I'm no fit judge of elegance in letters;
I leave such heady pastimes to my betters.

PHILAMINTE
That doesn't matter. Stay, and when we're through
I shall reveal a sweet surprise to you.

TRISSOTIN (*to Henriette*)
What need you know of learning and the arts,
Who know so well the way to charm men's hearts?

HENRIETTE
Sir, I know neither; nor is it my ambition—

BÉLISE
Oh, please! Let's hear the infant composition.

PHILAMINTE (*to Lépine*)
Quick, boy, some chairs.
            (*Lépine falls down in bringing a chair.*)

Dear God, how loutish! Ought you
To fall like that, considering what we've taught you
Regarding equilibrium and its laws?

BÉLISE

Look what you've done, fool. Surely you see the cause?
It was by wrongly shifting what we call
The center of gravity, that you came to fall.

LÉPINE

I saw that when I hit the floor, alas.

PHILAMINTE (*to Lépine, as he leaves*)

Dolt!

TRISSOTIN

It's a blessing he's not made of glass.

ARMANDE

What wit! It never falters!

BÉLISE

Not in the least.
(*All sit down.*)

PHILAMINTE

Now then, do serve us your poetic feast.

TRISSOTIN

For such great hunger as confronts me here,
An eight-line dish would not suffice, I fear.
My epigram's too slight. It would be wiser,
I think, to give you first, as appetizer,
A sonnet which a certain princess found
Subtle in sense, delectable in sound.
I've seasoned it with Attic salt throughout,
And you will find it tasty, I have no doubt.

ARMANDE

How could we not?

PHILAMINTE

Let's listen, with concentration.

BÉLISE (*interrupting Trissotin each time
he starts to read*)

My heart is leaping with anticipation.
I'm mad for poetry, and I love it best
When pregnant thoughts are gallantly expressed.

PHILAMINTE

So long as we talk, our guest can't say a word.

TRISSOTIN

SON—

BÉLISE (*to Henriette*)

Niece, be silent.

ARMANDE

Please! Let the poem be heard.

TRISSOTIN

SONNET TO THE PRINCESS URANIE,
REGARDING HER FEVER

Your prudence, Madam, must have drowsed
When you took in so hot a foe
And let him be so nobly housed,
And feasted and regaled him so.

BÉLISE

A fine first quatrain!

ARMANDE

And the style! How gallant!

PHILAMINTE

For metric flow he has a matchless talent.

ARMANDE

"Your *prudence* must have *drowsed*": a charming touch.

BÉLISE

"So hot a foe" delights me quite as much.

PHILAMINTE

I think that "feasted and regaled" conveys
A sense of richness in so many ways.

BÉLISE

Let's listen to the rest.

TRISSOTIN

Your prudence, Madam, must have drowsed
When you took in so hot a foe
And let him be so nobly housed,
And feasted and regaled him so.

ARMANDE

"Your prudence must have drowsed"!

BÉLISE

"So hot a foe"!

PHILAMINTE

"Feasted and regaled"!

TRISSOTIN

Say what they may, the wretch must go!
From your rich lodging drive away
This ingrate who, as well you know,
Would make your precious life his prey.

BÉLISE

Oh! Pause a moment, I beg you; one is breathless.

ARMANDE

Let us digest those verses, which are deathless.

PHILAMINTE

There's a rare something in those lines which captures
One's inmost heart, and stirs the soul to raptures.

ARMANDE

"Say what they may, the wretch must go!
From your rich lodging drive away . . ."

How apt that is—"rich lodging." I adore
The wit and freshness of that metaphor!

PHILAMINTE

"Say what they may, the wretch must go!"

That "Say what they may" is greatly to my liking.
I've never encountered any words more striking.

ARMANDE

Nor I. That "Say what they may" bewitches me.

BÉLISE

"Say what they may" is brilliant, I agree.

ARMANDE

Oh, to have said it.

BÉLISE

It's a whole poem in a phrase.

PHILAMINTE

But have you fully grasped what it conveys,
As I have?

ARMANDE and BÉLISE

Oh! Oh!

PHILAMINTE

"Say what they may, the wretch must go"!

That means, if people take the fever's side,
Their pleadings should be scornfully denied.

"Say what they may, the wretch must go,
Say what they may, say what they may"!

There's more in that "Say what they may" than first appears.
Perhaps I am alone in this, my dears,
But I see no limit to what that phrase implies.

BÉLISE

It's true, it means a great deal for its size.

PHILAMINTE (*to Trissotin*)

Sir, when you wrote this charming "Say what they may,"
Did you know your own great genius? Can you say
That you were conscious, then, of all the wit
And wealth of meaning we have found in it?

TRISSOTIN

Ah! Well!

ARMANDE

I'm very fond of "ingrate," too.
It well describes that villain fever, who
Repays his hosts by causing them distress.

PHILAMINTE

In short, the quatrains are a great success.
Do let us have the tercets now, I pray.

ARMANDE

Oh, please, let's once more hear "Say what they may."

TRISSOTIN
Say what they may, the wretch must go!

PHILAMINTE, ARMANDE, and BÉLISE
"Say what they may"!

TRISSOTIN
From your rich lodging drive away . . .

PHILAMINTE, ARMANDE, and BÉLISE
"Rich lodging"!

TRISSOTIN
This ingrate who, as well you know . . .

PHILAMINTE, ARMANDE, and BÉLISE
That "ingrate" of a fever!

TRISSOTIN
Would make your precious life his prey.

PHILAMINTE
"Your precious life"!

ARMANDE and BÉLISE
Ah!

TRISSOTIN
What! Shall he mock your rank, and pay
No deference to the blood of kings?

PHILAMINTE, ARMANDE, and BÉLISE
Ah!

TRISSOTIN
Shall he afflict you night and day,
And shall you tolerate such things?

No! To the baths you must repair,
And with your own hands drown him there.

PHILAMINTE

I'm overcome.

BÉLISE

I'm faint.

ARMANDE

I'm ravished, quite.

PHILAMINTE

One feels a thousand tremors of delight.

ARMANDE

"And shall you tolerate such things?"

BÉLISE

"No! To the baths you must repair . . ."

PHILAMINTE

"And with your own hands drown him there."

Drown him, that is to say, in the bath-water.

ARMANDE

Your verse, at each step, gives some glad surprise.

BÉLISE

Wherever one turns, fresh wonders greet the eyes.

PHILAMINTE

One treads on beauty, wandering through your lines.

ARMANDE

They're little paths all strewn with eglantines.

TRISSOTIN

You find the poem, then—

PHILAMINTE

          Perfect, and, what's more,
Novel: the like was never done before.

BÉLISE (*to Henriette*)

What, Niece, did not this reading stir your heart?
By saying nothing, you've played a dreary part.

HENRIETTE

We play what parts we're given, here below;
Wishing to be a wit won't make one so.

TRISSOTIN

Perhaps my verses bored her.

HENRIETTE

          No indeed;
I didn't listen.

PHILAMINTE

The epigram! Please proceed.

TRISSOTIN

CONCERNING A VERMILION COACH, GIVEN
TO A LADY OF HIS ACQUAINTANCE . . .

PHILAMINTE

There's always something striking about his titles.

ARMANDE

They ready us for the wit of his recitals.

TRISSOTIN

Love sells his bonds to me at such a rate . . .

PHILAMINTE, ARMANDE, and BÉLISE

Ah!

TRISSOTIN

I've long since spent the half of my estate;
  And when you see this coach, embossed
  With heavy gold at such a cost
  That all the dazzled countryside
Gapes as my Laïs passes in her pride . . .

PHILAMINTE

Listen to that. "My Laïs." How erudite!

BÉLISE

A stunning reference. So exactly right.

TRISSOTIN

  And when you see this coach, embossed
  With heavy gold at such a cost
  That all the dazzled countryside
Gapes as my Laïs passes in her pride,
  Know by that vision of vermilion
  That what was mine is now *her* million.

ARMANDE

Oh! Oh! I didn't foresee that final twist.

PHILAMINTE

We have no subtler epigrammatist.

BÉLISE

  "Know by that vision of vermilion
  That what was mine is now *her* million."

The rhyme is clever, and yet not forced: "*ver*milion, *her* million."

PHILAMINTE

Since first we met, Sir, I have had the highest
Opinion of you; it may be that I'm biased;
But all you write, to my mind, stands alone.

TRISSOTIN (*to Philaminte*)

If you'd but read us something of your own,
One might reciprocate your admiration.

PHILAMINTE

I've no new poems, but it's my expectation
That soon, in some eight chapters, you may see
The plans I've made for our Academy.
Plato, in his *Republic*, did not go
Beyond an abstract outline, as you know,
But what I've shaped in words, I shall not fail
To realize, in most concrete detail.
I'm much offended by the disrespect
Which men display for women's intellect,
And I intend to avenge us, every one,
For all the slighting things which men have done—
Assigning us to cares which stunt our souls,
And banning our pursuit of studious goals.

ARMANDE

It's too insulting to forbid our sex
To ponder any questions more complex
Than whether some lace is pretty, or some brocade,
And whether a skirt or cloak is nicely made.

BÉLISE

It's time we broke our mental chains, and stated
Our high intent to be emancipated.

TRISSOTIN

My deep respect for women none can deny;
Though I may praise a lady's lustrous eye,
I honor, too, the lustre of her mind.

PHILAMINTE

For that, you have the thanks of womankind;
But there are some proud scholars I could mention
To whom we'll prove, despite their condescension,
That women may be learnèd if they please,
And found, like men, their own academies.
Ours, furthermore, shall be more wisely run
Than theirs: we'll roll all disciplines into one,
Uniting letters, in a rich alliance,
With all the tools and theories of science,
And in our thought refusing to be thrall
To any school, but making use of all.

TRISSOTIN

For method, Aristotle suits me well.

PHILAMINTE

But in abstractions, Plato *does* excel.

ARMANDE

The thought of Epicurus is very keen.

BÉLISE

I rather like his atoms, but as between
A vacuum and a field of subtle matter
I find it easier to accept the latter.

TRISSOTIN

On magnetism, Descartes supports my notions.

ARMANDE

I love his falling worlds . . .

PHILAMINTE

And whirling motions!

ARMANDE

I can't wait for our conclaves. We shall proclaim
Discoveries, and they shall bring us fame.

TRISSOTIN

Yes, to your keen minds Nature can but yield,
And let her rarest secrets be revealed.

PHILAMINTE

I can already offer one such rarity:
I have seen men in the moon, with perfect clarity.

BÉLISE

I'm not sure I've seen men, but I can say
That I've seen steeples there, as plain as day.

ARMANDE

To master grammar and physics is our intent,
And history, ethics, verse, and government.

PHILAMINTE

Ethics, which thrills me in so many respects,
Was once the passion of great intellects;
But it's the Stoics to whom I'd give the prize;
They knew that only the virtuous can be wise.

ARMANDE

Regarding language, we aim to renovate
Our tongue through laws which soon we'll promulgate.
Each of us has conceived a hatred, based
On outraged reason or offended taste,
For certain nouns and verbs. We've gathered these
Into a list of shared antipathies,
And shall proceed to doom and banish them.
At each of our learnèd gatherings, we'll condemn
In mordant terms those words which we propose
To purge from usage, whether in verse or prose.

PHILAMINTE

But our academy's noblest plan of action,
A scheme in which I take deep satisfaction,
A glorious project which will earn the praise
Of all discerning minds of future days,
Is to suppress those *syllables* which, though found
In blameless words, may have a shocking sound,
Which naughty punsters utter with a smirk,
Which, age on age, coarse jesters overwork,
And which, by filthy double meanings, vex
The finer feelings of the female sex.

TRISSOTIN

You have most wondrous plans, beyond a doubt!

BÉLISE

You'll see our by-laws, once we've worked them out.

TRISSOTIN

They can't fail to be beautiful and wise.

ARMANDE

By our high standards we shall criticize
Whatever's written, and be severe with it.
We'll show that only we and our friends have wit.
We'll search out faults in everything, while citing
Ourselves alone for pure and flawless writing.

SCENE THREE

———— • • ————

Lépine, Trissotin, Philaminte, Bélise,
Armande, Henriette, Vadius

LÉPINE (*to Trissotin*)
There's a man outside to see you, Sir; he's wearing
Black, and he has a gentle voice and bearing.

(*All rise.*)

TRISSOTIN
It's that learnèd friend of mine, who's begged me to
Procure for him the honor of meeting you.

PHILAMINTE
Please have him enter; you have our full consent.
        (*Trissotin goes to admit Vadius; Philaminte*
        speaks to Armande and Bélise.)
We must be gracious, and *most* intelligent.
        (*To Henriette, who seeks to leave*)
Whoa, there! I told you plainly, didn't I,
That I wished you to remain with us?

HENRIETTE
                  But why?

PHILAMINTE
Come back, and you shall shortly understand.

TRISSOTIN (*returning with Vadius*)
Behold a man who yearns to kiss your hand.
And in presenting him, I have no fear
That he'll profane this cultured atmosphere:
Among our choicest wits, he quite stands out.

PHILAMINTE

Since you present him, his worth's beyond a doubt.

TRISSOTIN

In classics, he's the greatest of savants,
And knows more Greek than any man in France.

PHILAMINTE (*to Bélise*)

Greek! Sister, our guest knows Greek! How marvelous!

BÉLISE (*to Armande*)

Greek, Niece! Do you hear?

ARMANDE

Yes, Greek! What joy for *us*!

PHILAMINTE

Think of it! Greek! Oh, Sir, for the love of Greek,
Permit us each to kiss you on the cheek.
(*Vadius kisses them all save Henriette, who refuses.*)

HENRIETTE

I don't know Greek, Sir; permit me to decline.

PHILAMINTE

I think Greek books are utterly divine.

VADIUS

In my eagerness to meet you, I fear I've come
Intruding on some grave symposium.
Forgive me, Madam, if I've caused confusion.

PHILAMINTE

Ah, Sir, to bring us Greek is no intrusion.

TRISSOTIN

My friend does wonders, too, in verse and prose,
And might well show us something, if he chose.

VADIUS

The fault of authors is their inclination
To dwell upon their works in conversation,
And whether in parks, or parlors, or at table,
To spout their poems as often as they're able.
How sad to see a writer play the extorter,
Demanding oh's and ah's from every quarter,
And forcing any gathering whatever
To tell him that his labored verse is clever.
I've never embraced the folly of which I speak,
And hold the doctrine of a certain Greek
That men of sense, however well endowed,
Should shun the urge to read their works aloud.
Still, here are some lines, concerning youthful love,
Which I'd be pleased to hear your judgments of.

TRISSOTIN

For verve and beauty, your verses stand alone.

VADIUS

Venus and all the Graces grace your own.

TRISSOTIN

Your choice of words is splendid, and your phrasing.

VADIUS

Your *ethos* and your *pathos* are amazing.

TRISSOTIN

The polished eclogues which you've given us
Surpass both Virgil and Theocritus.

VADIUS

Your odes are noble, gallant, and refined,
And leave your master Horace far behind.

TRISSOTIN

Ah, but your little love songs: what could be sweeter?

VADIUS

As for your well-turned sonnets, none are neater.

TRISSOTIN

Your deft *rondeaux*; are any poems more charming?

VADIUS

Your madrigals—are any more disarming?

TRISSOTIN

Above all, you're a wizard at *ballades*.

VADIUS

At *bouts-rimés*, you always have the odds.

TRISSOTIN

If France would only recognize your merits—

VADIUS

If the age did justice to its finer spirits—

TRISSOTIN

You'd have a gilded coach in which to ride.

VADIUS

Statues of you would rise on every side.
                    (*To Trissotin*)
Hem! Now for my *ballade*. Please comment on it
In the frankest—

TRISSOTIN

                    Have you seen a certain sonnet
About the fever of Princess Uranie?

VADIUS

Yes. It was read to me yesterday, at tea.

TRISSOTIN

Do you know who wrote it?

VADIUS

No, but of this I'm sure:
The sonnet, frankly, is very, very poor.

TRISSOTIN

Oh? Many people have praised it, nonetheless.

VADIUS

That doesn't prevent its being a sorry mess,
And if you've read it, I know you share my view.

TRISSOTIN

Why no, I don't in the least agree with you;
Not many sonnets boast so fine a style.

VADIUS

God grant I never write a thing so vile!

TRISSOTIN

It couldn't be better written, I contend;
And I should know, because I wrote it, friend.

VADIUS

You?

TRISSOTIN

I.

VADIUS

Well, how this happened I can't explain.

TRISSOTIN

What happened was that you found my poem inane.

VADIUS

When I heard the sonnet, I must have been distrait;
Or perhaps 'twas read in an unconvincing way.
But let's forget it; this *ballade* of mine—

TRISSOTIN

Ballades, I think, are rather asinine.
The form's old-hat; it has a musty smell.

VADIUS

Still, many people like it very well.

TRISSOTIN

That doesn't prevent my finding it dull and flat.

VADIUS

No, but the form is none the worse for that.

TRISSOTIN

The *ballade* is dear to pedants; they adore it.

VADIUS

How curious, then, that you should not be for it.

TRISSOTIN

You see in others your own drab qualities.

(All rise.)

VADIUS

Don't see your own in me, Sir, if you please.

TRISSOTIN

Be off, you jingling dunce! Let's end this session.

VADIUS

You scribbler! You disgrace to the profession!

TRISSOTIN
You poetaster! You shameless plagiarist!

VADIUS
You ink-stained thief!

PHILAMINTE
Oh, gentlemen! Please desist!

TRISSOTIN (*to Vadius*)
Go to the Greeks and Romans, and pay back
The thousand things you've filched from them, you hack.

VADIUS
Go to Parnassus and confess your guilt
For turning Horace into a crazy-quilt.

TRISSOTIN
Think of your book, which caused so little stir.

VADIUS
And you, Sir, think of your bankrupt publisher.

TRISSOTIN
My fame's established; in vain you mock me so.

VADIUS
Do tell. Go look at the *Satires* of Boileau.

TRISSOTIN
Go look at them yourself.

VADIUS
                    As between us two,
I'm treated there more honorably than you.
He gives me a passing thrust, and links my name
With several authors of no little fame;

But nowhere do his verses leave you in peace;
His witty attacks upon you never cease.

TRISSOTIN

It's therefore I whom he respects the more.
To him, you're one of the crowd, a minor bore;
You're given a single sword-thrust, and are reckoned
Too insignificant to deserve a second.
But me he singles out as a noble foe
Against whom he must strive with blow on blow,
Betraying, by those many strokes, that he
Is never certain of the victory.

VADIUS

My pen will teach you that I'm no poetaster.

TRISSOTIN

And mine will show you, fool, that I'm your master.

VADIUS

I challenge you in verse, prose, Latin, and Greek.

TRISSOTIN

We'll meet at Barbin's bookshop, in a week.

SCENE FOUR

———————— •• ————————

Trissotin, Philaminte, Armande,
Bélise, Henriette

TRISSOTIN (*to Philaminte*)
Forgive me if my wrath grew uncontrolled;
I felt an obligation to uphold
Your judgment of that sonnet he maligned.

PHILAMINTE
I'll try to mend your quarrel; never mind.
Let's change the subject. Henriette, come here.
I've long been troubled because you don't appear
At all endowed with wit or intellect;
But I've a remedy, now, for that defect.

HENRIETTE
Don't trouble, Mother; I wish no remedy.
Learnèd discourse is not my cup of tea.
I like to take life easy, and I balk
At trying to be a fount of clever talk.
I've no ambition to be a parlor wit,
And if I'm stupid, I don't mind a bit.
I'd rather speak in a plain and common way
Than rack my brains for brilliant things to say.

PHILAMINTE
I know your shameful tastes, which I decline
To countenance in any child of mine.
Beauty of face is but a transient flower,
A brief adornment, the glory of an hour,
And goes no deeper than the outer skin;
But beauty of mind endures, and lies within.
I've long sought means to cultivate in you
A beauty such as time could not undo,
And plant within your breast a noble yearning

For higher knowledge and the fruits of learning;
And now, at last, I've settled on a plan,
Which is to mate you with a learnèd man—
          (*Gesturing toward Trissotin*)
This gentleman, in short, whom I decree
That you acknowledge as your spouse-to-be.

HENRIETTE

I, Mother?

PHILAMINTE
Yes, you. Stop playing innocent.

BÉLISE (*to Trissotin*)
I understand. Your eyes ask my consent
Before you pledge to her a heart that's mine.
Do so. All claims I willingly resign:
This match will bring you wealth and happiness.

TRISSOTIN (*to Henriette*)
My rapture, Madam, is more than I can express:
The honor which this marriage will confer
Upon me—

HENRIETTE
    Hold! It's not yet settled, Sir;
Don't rush things.

PHILAMINTE
    What a reply! How overweening!
Girl, if you dare . . . Enough, you take my meaning.
        (*To Trissotin*)
Just let her be. Her mind will soon be changed.

SCENE FIVE

———————•◦•———————

Henriette, Armande

ARMANDE

What a brilliant match our mother has arranged!
She's found for you a spouse both great and wise.

HENRIETTE

Why don't you take him, if he's such a prize?

ARMANDE

It's you, not I, who are to be his bride.

HENRIETTE

For my elder sister, I'll gladly step aside.

ARMANDE

If I, like you, yearned for the wedded state,
I'd take your offer of so fine a mate.

HENRIETTE

If I, like you, were charmed by pedantry,
I'd think the man a perfect choice for me.

ARMANDE

Our tastes may differ, Sister, but we still
Owe strict obedience to our parents' will;
Whether or not you're fractious and contrary,
You'll wed the man our mother bids you marry. . . .

SCENE SIX

Chrysale, Ariste, Clitandre, Henriette, Armande

CHRYSALE (*to Henriette, presenting Clitandre*)
Now, Daughter, you shall do as I command.
Take off that glove, and give this man your hand,
And think of him henceforward as the one
I've chosen as your husband and my son.

ARMANDE
In this case, Sister, you're easy to persuade.

HENRIETTE
Sister, our parents' will must be obeyed;
I'll wed the man my father bids me marry.

ARMANDE
Your mother's blessing, too, is necessary.

CHRYSALE
Just what do you mean?

ARMANDE
                    I much regret to state
That Mother has a rival candidate
For the hand of Henri—

CHRYSALE
                    Hush, you chatterer!
Go prate about philosophy with her,
And cease to meddle in what is my affair.
Tell her it's settled, and bid her to beware
Of angering me by making any fuss.
Go on, now.

ARISTE

Bràvo! This is miraculous.

CLITANDRE

How fortunate I am! What bliss! What joy!

CHRYSALE (*to Clitandre*)

Come, take her hand, now. After you, my boy;
Conduct her to her room. (*To Ariste*) Ah, Brother, this is
A tonic to me; think of those hugs, those kisses!
It warms my old heart, and reminds me of
My youthful days of gallantry and love.

Act Four

SCENE ONE

━━━━━●◆●━━━━━

Armande, Philaminte

ARMANDE

Oh, no, she didn't waver or delay,
But, with a flourish, hastened to obey.
Almost before he spoke, she had agreed
To do his bidding, and she appeared, indeed,
Moved by defiance toward her mother, rather
Than deference to the wishes of her father.

PHILAMINTE

I soon shall show her to whose government
The laws of reason oblige her to consent,
And whether it's matter or form, body or soul,
Father or mother, who is in control.

ARMANDE

The least they could have done was to consult you;
It's graceless of that young man to insult you
By trying to wed your child without your blessing.

PHILAMINTE

He's not yet won. His looks are prepossessing,
And I approved his paying court to you;
But I never liked his manners. He well knew
That writing poetry is a gift of mine,
And yet he never asked to hear a line.

SCENE TWO

Clitandre (entering quietly and listening unseen),
Armande, Philaminte

ARMANDE

Mother, if I were you, I shouldn't let
That gentleman espouse our Henriette.
Not that I care, of course; I do not speak
As someone moved by prejudice or pique,
Or by a heart which, having been forsaken,
Asks vengeance for the wounds which it has taken.
For what I've suffered, philosophy can give
Full consolation, helping one to live
On a high plane, and treat such things with scorn;
But what he's done to you cannot be borne.
Honor requires that you oppose his suit;
Besides, you'd never come to like the brute.
In all our talks, I cannot recollect
His speaking of you with the least respect.

PHILAMINTE

Young whelp!

ARMANDE

Despite your work's great reputation,
He icily withheld his approbation.

PHILAMINTE

The churl!

ARMANDE

A score of times, I read to him
Your latest poems. He tore them limb from limb.

PHILAMINTE

The beast!

ARMANDE

We quarreled often about your writing.
And you would not believe how harsh, how biting—

CLITANDRE (*to Armande*)

Ah, Madam, a little charity, I pray,
Or a little truthful speaking, anyway.
How have I wronged you? What was the offense
Which makes you seek, by slanderous eloquence,
To rouse against me the distaste and ire
Of those whose good opinion I require?
Speak, Madam, and justify your vicious grudge.
I'll gladly let your mother be our judge.

ARMANDE

Had I the grudge of which I stand accused,
I could defend it, for I've been ill-used.
First love, Sir, is a pure and holy flame
Which makes upon us an eternal claim;
'Twere better to renounce this world, and die,
Than be untrue to such a sacred tie.
Fickleness is a monstrous crime, and in
The moral scale there is no heavier sin.

CLITANDRE

Do you call it fickleness, *Madame*, to do
What your heart's cold disdain has driven me to?
If, by submitting to its cruel laws,
I've wounded you, your own proud heart's the cause.
My love for you was fervent and entire;
For two whole years it burned with constant fire;
My duty, care, and worship did not falter;
I laid my heart's devotion on your altar.
But all my love and service were in vain;
You dashed the hopes I dared to entertain.
If, thus rejected, I made overtures
To someone else, was that my fault, or yours?

Was I inconstant, or was I forced to be?
Did I forsake you, or did you banish me?

ARMANDE

Sir, can you say that I've refused your love
When all I've sought has been to purge it of
Vulgarity, and teach you that refined
And perfect passion which is of the mind?
Can you not learn an ardor which dispenses
Entirely with the commerce of the senses,
Or see how sweetly spirits may be blended
When bodily desires have been transcended?
Alas, your love is carnal, and cannot rise
Above the plane of gross material ties;
The flame of your devotion can't be fed
Except by marriage, and the marriage bed.
How strange is such a love! And oh, how far
Above such earthliness true lovers are!
In their delights, the body plays no part,
And their clear flames but marry heart to heart,
Rejecting all the rest as low and bestial.
Their fire is pure, unsullied, and celestial.
The sighs they breathe are blameless, and express
No filthy hankerings, no fleshliness.
There's no ulterior goal they hunger for.
They love for love's sake, and for nothing more,
And since the spirit is their only care,
Bodies are things of which they're unaware.

CLITANDRE

Well, *I'm* aware, though you may blush to hear it,
That I have both a body and a spirit;
Nor can I part them to my satisfaction;
I fear I lack the power of abstraction
Whereby such philosophic feats are done,
And so my body and soul must live as one.
There's nothing finer, as you say, than these

Entirely spiritual ecstasies,
These marriages of souls, these sentiments
So purified of any taint of sense;
But such love is, for my taste, too ethereal;
I am, as you've complained, a bit material;
I love with all my being, and I confess
That a whole woman is what I would possess.
Need I be damned for feelings of the kind?
With all respect for your high views, I find
That men in general feel my sort of passion,
That marriage still is pretty much in fashion,
And that it's deemed an honorable estate;
So that my asking you to be my mate,
And share with me that good and sweet condition,
Was scarcely an indecent proposition.

ARMANDE

Ah well, Sir: since you thrust my views aside,
Since your brute instincts must be satisfied,
And since your feelings, to be faithful, must
Be bound by ties of flesh and chains of lust,
I'll force myself, if Mother will consent,
To grant the thing on which you're so intent.

CLITANDRE

It's too late, Madam: another's occupied
Your place; if I now took you as my bride,
I'd wrong a heart which sheltered and consoled me
When, in your pride, you'd treated me so coldly.

PHILAMINTE

Sir, do you dream of my consenting to
This other marriage which you have in view?
Does it not penetrate your mind as yet
That I have other plans for Henriette?

CLITANDRE

Ah, Madam, reconsider, if you please,

And don't expose me thus to mockeries;
Don't put me in the ludicrous position
Of having Trissotin for competition.
What a shabby rival! You couldn't have selected
A wit less honored, a pedant less respected.
We've many pseudo-wits and polished frauds
Whose cleverness the time's bad taste applauds,
But Trissotin fools no one, and indeed
His writings are abhorred by all who read.
Save in this house, his work is never praised,
And I have been repeatedly amazed
To hear you laud some piece of foolishness
Which, had you written it, you would suppress.

PHILAMINTE
That's how you judge him. We feel otherwise
Because we look at him with different eyes.

SCENE THREE

Trissotin, Armande, Philaminte, Clitandre

TRISSOTIN (*to Philaminte*)
I bring you, Madam, some startling news I've heard.
Last night, a near-catastrophe occurred:
While we were all asleep, a comet crossed
Our vortex, and the Earth was all but lost;
Had it collided with our world, alas,
We'd have been shattered into bits, like glass.

PHILAMINTE
Let's leave that subject for another time;
This gentleman, I fear, would see no rhyme
Or reason in it; it's ignorance he prizes;
Learning and wit are things which he despises.

CLITANDRE
Kindly permit me, Madam, to restate
Your summary of my views: I only hate
Such wit and learning as twist men's brains awry.
Those things are excellent in themselves, but I
Had rather be an ignorant man, by far,
Than learnèd in the way some people are.

TRISSOTIN
Well, as for me, I hold that learning never
Could twist a man in any way whatever.

CLITANDRE
And I assert that learning often breeds
Men who are foolish both in words and deeds.

TRISSOTIN
What a striking paradox!

CLITANDRE
                    Though I'm no wit,
I'd have no trouble, I think, in proving it.
If arguments should fail, I'm sure I'd find
That living proofs came readily to mind.

TRISSOTIN
The living proofs you gave might not persuade.

CLITANDRE
I'd not look far before my point was made.

TRISSOTIN
I cannot think, myself, of such a case.

CLITANDRE
I can; indeed, it stares me in the face.

TRISSOTIN
I thought it was by ignorance, and not
By learning, Sir, that great fools were begot.

CLITANDRE
Well, you thought wrongly. It's a well-known rule
That no fool's greater than a learnèd fool.

TRISSOTIN
Our common usage contradicts that claim,
Since "fool" and "ignoramus" mean the same.

CLITANDRE
You think those words synonymous? Oh no, Sir!
You'll find that "fool" and "pedant" are much closer.

TRISSOTIN
"Fool" denotes plain and simple foolishness.

CLITANDRE

"Pedant" denotes the same, in fancy dress.

TRISSOTIN

The quest for knowledge is noble and august.

CLITANDRE

But knowledge, in a pedant, turns to dust.

TRISSOTIN

It's clear that ignorance has great charms for you,
Or else you wouldn't defend it as you do.

CLITANDRE

I came to see the charms of ignorance when
I made the acquaintance of certain learnèd men.

TRISSOTIN

Those certain learnèd men, it may turn out,
Are better than certain folk who strut about.

CLITANDRE

The learnèd men would say so, certainly;
But then, those certain folk might not agree.

PHILAMINTE (*to Clitandre*)

I think, Sir—

CLITANDRE

Madam, spare me, please. This rough
Assailant is already fierce enough.
Don't join him, pray, in giving me a beating.
I shall preserve myself, now, by retreating.

ARMANDE

You, with your brutal taunts, were the offender;
'Twas you—

CLITANDRE
More reinforcements! I surrender.

PHILAMINTE
Sir, witty repartee is quite all right,
But personal attacks are impolite.

CLITANDRE
Good Lord, he's quite unhurt, as one can tell.
No one in France takes ridicule so well.
For years he's heard men gibe at him, and scoff,
And in his smugness merely laughed it off.

TRISSOTIN
I'm not surprised to hear this gentleman say
The things he's said in this unpleasant fray.
He's much at court, and as one might expect,
He shares the court's mistrust of intellect,
And, as a courtier, defends with zest
The ignorance that's in its interest.

CLITANDRE
You're very hard indeed on the poor court,
Which hears each day how people of your sort,
Who deal in intellectual wares, decry it,
Complain that their careers are blighted by it,
Deplore its wretched taste, and blame their own
Unhappy failures on that cause alone.
Permit me, Mister Trissotin, with due
Respect for your great name, to say that you
And all your kind would do well to discuss
The court in tones less harsh and querulous;
That the court is not so short of wit and brain
As you and all your scribbling friends maintain;
That all things, there, are viewed with common sense,
That good taste, too, is much in evidence,
And that its knowledge of the world surpasses
The fusty learning of pedantic asses.

TRISSOTIN

It has good taste, you say? If only it had!

CLITANDRE

What makes you say, Sir, that its taste is bad?

TRISSOTIN

What makes me say so? Rasiùs and Baldùs
Do France great honor by what their pens produce,
Yet the court pays these scholars no attention,
And neither of them has received a pension.

CLITANDRE

I now perceive your grievance, and I see
That you've left your own name out, from modesty.
Well, let's not drag it into our debate.
Just tell me: how have your heroes served the State?
What are their writings worth, that they expect
Rewards, and charge the nation with neglect?
Why should they whine, these learnèd friends of yours,
At not receiving gifts and sinecures?
A precious lot they've done for France, indeed!
Their tomes are just what court and country need!
The vanity of such beggars makes me laugh:
Because they're set in type and bound in calf,
They think that they're illustrious citizens;
That the fate of nations hangs upon their pens;
That the least mention of their work should bring
The pensions flocking in on eager wing;
That the whole universe, with one wide stare,
Admires them; that their fame is everywhere,
And that they're wondrous wise because they know
What others said before them, long ago—
Because they've given thirty years of toil
And eyestrain to acquire, by midnight oil,
Some jumbled Latin and some garbled Greek,
And overload their brains with the antique
Obscurities which lie about in books.

These bookworms, with their smug, myopic looks,
Are full of pompous talk and windy unction;
They have no common sense, no useful function,
And could, in short, persuade the human race
To think all wit and learning a disgrace.

PHILAMINTE

You speak most heatedly, and it is clear
What feelings prompt you to be so severe;
Your rival's presence, which seems to irk you greatly—

SCENE FOUR

Julien, Trissotin, Philaminte, Clitandre, Armande

JULIEN

The learnèd man who visited you lately,
And whose valet I have the honor to be,
Sends you this note, *Madame*, by way of me.

PHILAMINTE

Whatever the import of this note you bring,
Do learn, my friend, that it's a graceless thing
To interrupt a conversation so,
And that a rightly trained valet would go
To the servants first, and ask them for admission.

JULIEN

Madam, I'll bear in mind your admonition.

PHILAMINTE (*reading*)

"Trissotin boasts, Madam, that he is going to marry your
daughter. Let me warn you that that great thinker is thinking
only of your wealth, and that you would do well to put off
the marriage until you have seen the poem which I am now
composing against him. It is to be a portrait in verse, and I
propose to depict him for you in his true colors. Meanwhile,
I am sending herewith the works of Horace, Virgil, Terence,
and Catullus, in the margins of which I have marked, for
your benefit, all the passages which he has plundered."

Well, well! To thwart the match which I desire,
A troop of enemies has opened fire
Upon this worthy man; but I'll requite
By one swift action their dishonest spite,
And show them all that their combined assault
Has only hastened what they strove to halt.

(To Julien)
Take back those volumes to your master, and
Inform him, so that he'll clearly understand
Precisely how much value I have set
Upon his sage advice, that Henriette
(Pointing to Trissotin)
Shall wed this gentleman, this very night.
(To Clitandre)
Sir, you're a friend of the family. I invite
You most sincerely to remain and see
The contract signed, as shortly it shall be.
Armande, you'll send for the notary, and prepare
Your sister for her part in this affair.

ARMANDE

No need for me to let my sister know;
This gentleman, I'm sure, will quickly go
To tell her all the news, and seek as well
To prompt her saucy spirit to rebel.

PHILAMINTE

We'll see by whom her spirit will be swayed;
It doesn't suit me to be disobeyed.

SCENE FIVE

Armande, Clitandre

ARMANDE

I'm very sorry for you, Sir; it seems
Things haven't gone according to your schemes.

CLITANDRE

Madam, I mean to do my very best
To lift that weight of sorrow from your breast.

ARMANDE

I fear, Sir, that your hopes are not well-grounded.

CLITANDRE

It may be that your fear will prove ill-founded.

ARMANDE

I hope so.

CLITANDRE

I believe you; nor do I doubt
That you'll do all you can to help me out.

ARMANDE

To serve your cause shall be my sole endeavor.

CLITANDRE

For that, you'll have my gratitude forever.

SCENE SIX

Chrysale, Ariste, Henriette, Clitandre

CLITANDRE

I shall be lost unless you help me, Sir:
Your wife's rejected my appeals to her,
And chosen Trissotin for her son-in-law.

CHRYSALE

Damn it, what ails the woman? I never saw
What in this Trissotin could so attract her.

ARISTE

He versifies in Latin, and that's a factor
Which makes him, in her view, the better man.

CLITANDRE

To marry them tonight, Sir, is her plan.

CHRYSALE

Tonight?

CLITANDRE

Tonight.

CHRYSALE

Her plan, then, will miscarry.
I promise that, tonight, you two shall marry.

CLITANDRE

She's having a contract drawn by the notary.

CHRYSALE

Well, he shall draw another one for me.

CLITANDRE (*indicating Henriette*)

Armande has orders to inform this lady
Of the wedding match for which she's to be ready.

CHRYSALE

And I inform her that, by my command,
It's you on whom she shall bestow her hand.
This is my house, and I shall make it clear
That I'm the one and only master here.

(*To Henriette*)

Wait, Daughter; we'll join you when our errand's done.
Come, Brother, follow me; you too, my son.

HENRIETTE (*to Ariste*)

Please keep him in this mood, whatever you do.

ARISTE

I'll do my utmost for your love and you.

SCENE SEVEN

—————•◆•—————

Henriette, Clitandre

CLITANDRE

Whatever aid our kind allies may lend,
It's your true heart on which my hopes depend.

HENRIETTE

As to my heart, of that you may be sure.

CLITANDRE

If so, my own is happy and secure.

HENRIETTE

I must be strong, so as not to be coerced.

CLITANDRE

Cling to our love, and let them do their worst.

HENRIETTE

I'll do my best to make our cause prevail;
But if my hope of being yours should fail,
And if it seems I'm to be forced to marry,
A convent cell shall be my sanctuary.

CLITANDRE

Heaven grant that you need never give to me
Such painful proof of your fidelity.

Act Five

SCENE ONE

———— •• ————

Henriette, Trissotin

HENRIETTE

It seems to me that we two should confer
About this contemplated marriage, Sir,
Since it's reduced our household to dissension.
Do give my arguments your kind attention.
I know that you expect to realize,
By wedding me, a dowry of some size;
Yet money, which so many men pursue,
Should bore a true philosopher like you,
And your contempt for riches should be shown
In your behavior, not in words alone.

TRISSOTIN

It's not in wealth that your attraction lies:
Your sparkling charms, your soft yet flashing eyes,
Your airs, your graces—it is these in which
My ravished heart perceives you to be rich,
These treasures only which I would possess.

HENRIETTE

I'm honored by the love which you profess,
Although I can't see what I've done to earn it,
And much regret, Sir, that I can't return it.
I have the highest estimation of you,
But there's one reason why I cannot love you.
A heart's devotion cannot be divided,
And it's Clitandre on whom my heart's decided.
I know he lacks your merits, which are great,
That I'm obtuse to choose him for my mate,
That you should please me by your gifts and wit;

I know I'm wrong, but there's no help for it;
Though reason chides me for my want of sense,
My heart clings blindly to its preference.

TRISSOTIN

When I am given your hand and marriage vow,
I'll claim the heart Clitandre possesses now,
And I dare hope that I can then incline
That heart, by sweet persuasions, to be mine.

HENRIETTE

No, no: first love, Sir, is too strong a feeling.
All your persuasions could not prove appealing.
Let me, upon this point, be blunt and plain,
Since nothing I shall say could cause you pain.
The fires of love, which set our hearts aglow,
Aren't kindled by men's merits, as you know.
They're most capricious; when someone takes our eye,
We're often quite unable to say why.
If, Sir, our loves were based on wise selection,
You would have all my heart, all my affection;
But love quite clearly doesn't work that way.
Indulge me in my blindness, then, I pray,
And do not show me, Sir, so little mercy
As to desire that others should coerce me.
What man of honor would care to profit by
A parent's power to make a child comply?
To win a lady's hand by such compulsion,
And not by love, would fill him with revulsion.
Don't, then, I beg you, urge my mother to make
Me bow to her authority for your sake.
Take back the love you offer, and reserve it
For some fine woman who will more deserve it.

TRISSOTIN

Alas, what you command I cannot do.
I'm powerless to retract my love for you.

How shall I cease to worship you, unless
You cease to dazzle me with loveliness,
To stun my heart with beauty, to enthrall—

HENRIETTE

Oh, come, Sir; no more nonsense. You have all
These Irises and Phyllises whose great
Attractiveness your verses celebrate,
And whom you so adore with so much art—

TRISSOTIN

My mind speaks in those verses, not my heart.
I love those ladies in my poems merely,
While Henriette, alone, I love sincerely.

HENRIETTE

Please, Sir—

TRISSOTIN

                    If by so speaking I offend,
I fear that my offense will never end.
My ardor, which I've hidden hitherto,
Belongs for all eternity to you;
I'll love you till this beating heart has stopped;
And, though you scorn the tactics I adopt,
I can't refuse your mother's aid in gaining
The joy I'm so desirous of obtaining.
If the sweet prize I long for can be won,
And you be mine, I care not how it's done.

HENRIETTE

But don't you see that it's a risky course
To take possession of a heart by force;
That things, quite frankly, can go very ill
When a woman's made to wed against her will,
And that, in her resentment, she won't lack
For means to vex her spouse, and pay him back?

TRISSOTIN

I've no anxiety about such things.
The wise man takes whatever fortune brings.
Transcending vulgar weaknesses, his mind
Looks down unmoved on mishaps of the kind,
Nor does he feel the least distress of soul
Regarding matters not in his control.

HENRIETTE

You fascinate me, Sir; I'm much impressed.
I didn't know philosophy possessed
Such powers, and could teach men to endure
Such tricks of fate without discomfiture.
Your lofty patience ought, Sir, to be tested,
So that its greatness could be manifested;
It calls, Sir, for a wife who'd take delight
In making you display it, day and night;
But since I'm ill-equipped, by temperament,
To prove your virtue to its full extent,
I'll leave that joy to one more qualified,
And let some other woman be your bride.

TRISSOTIN

Well, we shall see. The notary for whom
Your mother sent is in the neighboring room.

SCENE TWO

Chrysale, Clitandre, Martine, Henriette

CHRYSALE

Ah, Daughter, I'm pleased indeed to find you here.
Prepare to show obedience now, my dear,
By doing as your father bids you do.
I'm going to teach your mother a thing or two;
And, first of all, as you can see, I mean
To thwart her will and reinstate Martine.

HENRIETTE

I much admire the stands which you have taken.
Hold to them, Father; don't let yourself be shaken.
Be careful lest your kindly disposition
Induce you to abandon your position;
Cling to your resolutions, I entreat you,
And don't let Mother's stubbornness defeat you.

CHRYSALE

What! So you take me for a booby, eh?

HENRIETTE

Heavens, no!

CHRYSALE

Am I a milksop, would you say?

HENRIETTE

I'd not say that.

CHRYSALE

Do you think I lack the sense
To stand up firmly for my sentiments?

HENRIETTE

No, Father.

CHRYSALE

Have I too little brain and spirit
To run my own house? If so, let me hear it.

HENRIETTE

No, no.

CHRYSALE

Am I the sort, do you suppose,
Who'd let a woman lead him by the nose?

HENRIETTE

Of course not.

CHRYSALE

Well then, what were you implying?
Your doubts of me were scarcely gratifying.

HENRIETTE

I didn't mean to offend you, Heaven knows.

CHRYSALE

Under this roof, my girl, what I say goes.

HENRIETTE

True, Father.

CHRYSALE

No one but me has any right
To govern in this house.

HENRIETTE

Yes, Father; quite.

CHRYSALE

This is my family, and I'm sole head.

HENRIETTE

That's so.

CHRYSALE

I'll name the man my child shall wed.

HENRIETTE

Agreed!

CHRYSALE

By Heaven's laws, I rule your fate.

HENRIETTE

Who questions that?

CHRYSALE

And I'll soon demonstrate
That, in your marriage, your mother has no voice,
And that you must accept your father's choice.

HENRIETTE

Ah, Father, that's my dearest wish. I pray you,
Crown my desires by making me obey you.

CHRYSALE

If my contentious wife should dare to take—

CLITANDRE

She's coming, with the notary in her wake.

CHRYSALE

Stand by me, all of you.

MARTINE
Trust me, Sir. I'm here
To back you up, if need be. Never fear.

SCENE THREE

Philaminte, Bélise, Armande, Trissotin, the Notary,
Chrysale, Clitandre, Henriette, Martine

PHILAMINTE (*to the Notary*)
Can't you dispense with jargon, Sir, and write
Our contract in a style that's more polite?

THE NOTARY
Our style is excellent, Madam; I'd be absurd
Were I to modify a single word.

PHILAMINTE
Such barbarism, in the heart of France!
Can't you at least, for learning's sake, enhance
The document by putting the dowry down
In talent and drachma, rather than franc and crown?
And do use ides and calends for the date.

THE NOTARY
If I did, Madam, what you advocate,
I should invite professional ostracism.

PHILAMINTE
It's useless to contend with barbarism.
Come on, Sir; there's a writing table here.
(*Noticing Martine*)
Ah! Impudent girl, how dare you reappear?
Why have you brought her back, Sir? Tell me why.

CHRYSALE
I'll tell you that at leisure, by and by.
First, there's another matter to decide.

THE NOTARY
Let us proceed with the contract. Where's the bride?

PHILAMINTE

I'm giving away my younger daughter.

THE NOTARY

I see.

CHRYSALE

Yes. Henriette's her name, Sir. This is she.

THE NOTARY

Good. And the bridegroom?

PHILAMINTE (*indicating Trissotin*)

This is the man I choose.

CHRYSALE (*indicating Clitandre*)

And I, for my part, have a bit of news:
This is the man she'll marry.

THE NOTARY

Two grooms? The law
Regards that as excessive.

PHILAMINTE

Don't hem and haw;
Just write down Trissotin, and your task is done.

CHRYSALE

Write down Clitandre; he's to be my son.

THE NOTARY

Kindly consult together, and agree
On a single person as the groom-to-be.

PHILAMINTE

No, no, Sir, do as I have indicated.

CHRYSALE

Come, come, put down the name that I have stated.

THE NOTARY

First tell me by whose orders I should abide.

PHILAMINTE (*to Chrysale*)

What's this, Sir? Shall my wishes be defied?

CHRYSALE

I won't stand by and let this fellow take
My daughter's hand just for my money's sake.

PHILAMINTE

A lot your money matters to him! Indeed!
How dare you charge a learnèd man with greed?

CHRYSALE

Clitandre shall marry her, as I said before.

PHILAMINTE (*pointing to Trissotin*)

This is the man I've chosen. I'll hear no more.
The matter's settled, do you understand?

CHRYSALE

My! For a woman, you have a heavy hand.

MARTINE

It just ain't right for the wife to run the shop.
The man, I say, should always be on top.

CHRYSALE

Well said.

MARTINE

        Though I'm sacked ten times for saying so,
It's cocks, not hens, should be the ones to crow.

CHRYSALE

Correct.

MARTINE

When a man's wife wears the breeches, folks
Snicker about him, and make nasty jokes.

CHRYSALE

That's true.

MARTINE

If I had a husband, I wouldn't wish
For him to be all meek and womanish;
No, no, he'd be the captain of the ship,
And if I happened to give him any lip,
Or crossed him, he'd be right to slap my face
A time or two, to put me in my place.

CHRYSALE

Sound thinking.

MARTINE

The master's heart is rightly set
On finding a proper man for Henriette.

CHRYSALE

Yes.

MARTINE

Well then, here's Clitandre. Why deny
The girl a fine young chap like him? And why
Give her a learnèd fool who prates and drones?
She needs a husband, not some bag of bones
Who'll teach her Greek, and be her Latin tutor.
This Trissotin, I tell you, just don't suit her.

CHRYSALE

Right.

PHILAMINTE

We must let her chatter until she's through.

MARTINE

Talk, talk, is all these pedants know how to do.
If I ever took a husband, I've always said,
It wouldn't be no learnèd man I'd wed.
Wit's not the thing you need around the house,
And it's no joy to have a bookish spouse.
When I get married, you can bet your life
My man will study nothing but his wife;
He'll have no other book to read but me,
And won't—so please you, Ma'am—know A from B.

PHILAMINTE

Has your spokesman finished? And have I not politely
Listened to all her speeches?

CHRYSALE

                    The girl spoke rightly.

PHILAMINTE

Well then, to end all squabbling and delay,
Things now shall go exactly as I say.
                    (*Indicating Trissotin*)
Henriette shall wed this man at once, d'you hear?
Don't answer back; don't dare to interfere;
And if you've told Clitandre that he may wed
One of your daughters, give him Armande instead.

CHRYSALE

Well! . . . There's one way to settle this argument.
                    (*To Henriette and Clitandre*)
What do you think of that? Will you consent?

HENRIETTE

Oh, Father!

CLITANDRE
Oh, Sir!

BÉLISE
There's yet another bride
By whom he might be yet more satisfied;
But that can't be; the love we share is far
Higher and purer than the morning star;
Our bonds are solely of the intellect,
And all extended substance we reject.

SCENE FOUR

*Ariste, Chrysale, Philaminte, Bélise, Henriette, Armande,
Trissotin, the Notary, Clitandre, Martine*

ARISTE

I hate to interrupt this happy affair
By bringing you the tidings which I bear.
You can't imagine what distress I feel
At the shocking news these letters will reveal.
(*To Philaminte*)
This one's from your attorney.
(*To Chrysale*)
And the other
Is yours; it's from Lyons.

CHRYSALE

What news, dear Brother,
Could be so pressing, and distress you so?

ARISTE

There is your letter; read it, and you'll know.

PHILAMINTE (*reading*)

"Madam, I have asked your brother to convey to you this
message, advising you of something which I dared not come
and tell you in person. Owing to your great neglect of your
affairs, the magistrate's clerk did not notify me of the pre-
liminary hearing, and you have irrevocably lost your lawsuit,
which you should in fact have won."

CHRYSALE (*to Philaminte*)

You've lost your case!

PHILAMINTE

My! Don't be shaken so!
I'm not disheartened by this trivial blow.

Do teach your heart to take a nobler stance
And brave, like me, the buffetings of chance.

"This negligence of yours has cost you forty thousand
crowns, for it is that amount, together with the legal expenses,
which the court has condemned you to pay."

Condemned! What shocking language! That's a word
Reserved for criminals.

ARISTE
True; your lawyer erred,
And you're entirely right to be offended.
He should say that the court has *recommended*
That you comply with its decree, and pay
Forty thousand and costs without delay.

PHILAMINTE
What's in this other letter?

CHRYSALE (*reading*)
"Sir, my friendship with your brother leads me to take an
interest in all that concerns you. I know that you have put
your money in the hands of Argante and Damon, and I regret
to inform you that they have both, on the same day, gone
into bankruptcy."

Lost! All my money! Every penny of it!

PHILAMINTE
What a shameful outburst, Sir. Come, rise above it!
The wise man doesn't mourn the loss of pelf;
His wealth lies not in things, but in himself.
Let's finish this affair, with no more fuss:
(*Pointing to Trissotin*)
His fortune will suffice for all of us.

TRISSOTIN

No, Madam, urge my cause no further. I see
That everyone's against this match and me,
And where I am not wanted, I shan't intrude.

PHILAMINTE

Well! That's a sudden change of attitude.
It follows close on our misfortunes, Sir.

TRISSOTIN

Weary of opposition, I prefer
To bow out gracefully, and to decline
A heart which will not freely yield to mine.

PHILAMINTE

I see now what you are, Sir. I perceive
What, till this moment, I would not believe.

TRISSOTIN

See what you like; I do not care one whit
What you perceive, or what you think of it.
I've too much self-respect to tolerate
The rude rebuffs I've suffered here of late:
Men of my worth should not be treated so:
Thus slighted, I shall make my bow, and go.

(He leaves.)

PHILAMINTE

What a low-natured, mercenary beast!
He isn't philosophic in the least!

CLITANDRE

Madam, I'm no philosopher; but still
I beg to share your fortunes, good or ill,
And dare to offer, together with my hand,
The little wealth I happen to command.

PHILAMINTE

This generous gesture, Sir, I much admire,
And you deserve to have your heart's desire.
I grant your suit, Sir. Henriette and you—

HENRIETTE

No, Mother, I've changed my mind. Forgive me, do,
If once more I oppose your plans for me.

CLITANDRE

What! Will you cheat me of felicity,
Now that the rest have yielded, one and all?

HENRIETTE

I know, Clitandre, that your wealth is small.
I wished to marry you so long as I
Might realize my sweetest hopes thereby,
And at the same time mend your circumstances.
But after this great blow to our finances,
I love you far too deeply to impose
On you the burden of our present woes.

CLITANDRE

I welcome any fate which you will share,
And any fate, without you, I couldn't bear.

HENRIETTE

So speaks the reckless heart of love; but let's
Be prudent, Sir, and thus avoid regrets.
Nothing so strains the bond of man and wife
As lacking the necessities of life,
And in the end, such dull and mean vexations
Can lead to quarrels and recriminations.

ARISTE (*to Henriette*)

Is there any reason, save the one you've cited,
Why you and Clitandre shouldn't be united?

HENRIETTE

But for that cause, I never would say no;
I must refuse because I love him so.

ARISTE

Then let the bells ring out for him and you.
The bad news which I brought was all untrue.
'Twas but a stratagem which I devised
In hopes to see your wishes realized
And undeceive my sister, showing her
The baseness of her pet philosopher.

CHRYSALE

Now, Heaven be praised for that!

PHILAMINTE

      I'm overjoyed
To think how that false wretch will be annoyed,
And how the rich festivities of this
Glad marriage will torment his avarice.

CHRYSALE (*to Clitandre*)

Well, Son, our firmness has achieved success.

ARMANDE (*to Philaminte*)

Shall you sacrifice me to their happiness?

PHILAMINTE

Daughter, your sacrifice will not be hard.
Philosophy will help you to regard
Their wedded joys with equanimity.

BÉLISE

Let him be careful lest his love for me
Drive him, in desperation, to consent
To a rash marriage of which he will repent.

CHRYSALE (*to the Notary*)
Come, come, Sir, it is time your task was through;
Draw up the contract just as I told you to.

An Interview with the Translator
By Dana Gioia

No major modern American poet had a longer or closer relationship with theater than Richard Wilbur (1921–2017). He was active in the field for six decades—starting with his translation of Molière's *Misanthrope*, which opened in 1955 at the legendary Poets' Theatre in Cambridge, Massachusetts, and continuing until the final decade of his long life. But Wilbur's sustained and prolific involvement in theater was unusual. He did not write plays, not even verse drama. All of Wilbur's theatrical works, with the notable exception of lyrics for one Broadway musical—Leonard Bernstein's *Candide*—are translations of classical French theater, especially the comedies of Molière.

The son of a painter, Wilbur was born in New York City in 1921 but was raised in rural New Jersey. He attended Amherst, where he chaired the college newspaper—an activity that seems typical for a future writer—but he also spent two summers riding the rails in Depression-era America. Graduating in 1942 as America entered World War II, Wilbur married his college sweetheart, Charlotte Ward, and joined the U.S. Army. He initially trained as a cryptographer, but his leftist associations led the army to transfer him to infantry. For the next three years he experienced some of the war's most brutal combat, from the Allied landing on the beaches of Italy to the final push into Germany. He often read in the lulls between battles and once even wrote a poem in a foxhole.

After the war Wilbur started graduate school at Harvard, where he became friends with Robert Frost. Wilbur had written poems since childhood, but the aspiring scholar now began working on them seriously. His literary success was almost immediate. He was from the first a natural poet with a distinctive and powerful personal style. With the publication of his first two books, *The Beautiful Changes* (1947) and *Ceremony* (1950), Wilbur was recognized as one of the finest poets of his generation, a judgment that has never been seriously challenged. Even his detractors recognize his abundant talent; their complaint is only that he was not sufficiently ambitious in exploring it. His champions have no hesitation in acclaiming him one of the major American poets of his age.

Awards came early in his career and continued almost until his death. Wilbur won the Pulitzer Prize twice—in 1957 for *Things of This World* and in 1989 for *New and Collected Poems*. He was also awarded the National Book Award in 1957 for *Things of this World*, and his translation of *Tartuffe* won the Bollingen Poetry Translation Prize in 1963. In 1971, he won a second Bollingen Prize, this time for his poetry collection *Walking to Sleep*. In 1983, he won the Drama Desk Award for his translation of *The Misanthrope*, and the same year he took home the PEN Translation Prize for *Molière: Four Comedies*. In 1987, he was named U.S. Poet Laureate. In 1994, President Clinton awarded him the National Medal of Arts. And in 2012, Yale University conferred on him an honorary Doctor of Letters.

Wilbur's work is elegantly formal and deeply intelligent—two literary qualities that in a lesser talent might undercut the poetry's emotional immediacy or lyric force. But Wilbur's language is so fresh and sensuously alive that his poems never seem stiff or preordained. He possessed the lyric poet's irreplaceable gift of bringing the reader directly into an experience in all its heady complexity. While Wilbur is alert to the dark side of human existence, he is more receptive to the brighter emotions of compassion, love, and joy. Few American poets since Walt Whitman have offered such compelling optimism.

Wilbur's involvement with the theater began in 1952 when he won a Guggenheim Fellowship to write an original verse drama. Working on his own plays, he despaired. "They didn't come off," he later admitted. "They were very bad, extremely wooden." To learn the craft of verse drama, Wilbur decided to translate an acknowledged masterpiece of the genre, *The Misanthrope* by Jean-Baptiste Poquelin Molière. Little did he guess that he had begun what would eventually grow into a major part of his life's work as well as one of the great translation projects in American literature.

Over the next forty years Wilbur produced lively, sophisticated and eminently stageworthy versions of Molière's verse comedies: *The Misanthrope* (1955), *Tartuffe* (1963), *The School for Wives* (1971), *The Learned Ladies* (1978), *The School for Husbands* (1992), *Sganarelle, or The Imaginary Cuckold* (1993), *Amphitryon* (1995), *Don Juan* (1998), *The Bungler* (2000) and *Lovers' Quarrels* (2009). The only Molière verse play that escaped his grasp is *Dom Garcie de Navarre*, which Wilbur conceded is "universally considered a lemon." From the moment his first Molière translation was staged, his versions have delighted and impressed audiences. Widely produced from Broadway to college campuses, Wilbur's versions helped create a Molière revival across North America that continues to this day. He also translated two neoclassical verse tragedies by Racine: *Andromache* (1982) and *Phaedra* (1986). He subsequently turned his attention to the works of Corneille: *The Theatre of Illusion* (2007), *Le Cid* (2009), and *The Liar* (2009).

It would be hard to overpraise Wilbur's special genius for verse translation. Whether re-creating the witty badinage of Molière or the high tragic music of Racine and Corneille, Wilbur has the uncanny ability to create English versions that never feel like translations. They read and play as if they were originally written in English. The same virtue is equally evident in his extensive translations of lyric poetry from French, Italian, Russian, and Romanian. (One famous poet told me that Wilbur's translations were as good as her originals—and this was a writer not given to flattery.) The distinction, variety, and extent of his efforts earned him a position as one of the greatest translators in the history of American poetry. His French translations alone fill half a bookshelf.

Happy to leave the drama on the stage, Wilbur led a generally quiet and settled life, making homes in Cummington,

Massachusetts, which he moved into with his wife and family in 1965, and Key West, Florida. He died at ninety-six on October 14, 2017, in Belmont, Massachusetts.

Dana Gioia: How did you first become interested in Molière?

Richard Wilbur: It wasn't in school, where my French studies were all about grammar, a subject to which I've always had a foolish resistance. During World War II, when my division landed in southern France and swept north, I became a halting interpreter for my company, and picked up a book or two to read in transit: something by Pierre Louÿs, some poems of Louis Aragon. After the war, when I went to Harvard on the G.I. Bill, my friends André du Bouchet and Pierre Schneider got me to reading such Frenchmen as Nerval and Villiers de l'Isle-Adam. But it wasn't until 1948, when my wife and I went to Paris on leave from Harvard's Society of Fellows, that I encountered Molière, in a stunning performance of *Le Misanthrope*, starring Pierre Dux, at the Comédie-Française.

What prompted your first translation of Molière?

By 1952, T. S. Eliot and Christopher Fry had brought verse drama to Broadway, and in Cambridge the Poets' Theatre was in high gear. I proposed to the Guggenheim Foundation that I write a verse play, but once I was funded, and established in an adobe study in New Mexico, I proved unripe for the task. It then occurred to me that by translating *The Misanthrope* I could keep my word and learn something.

Can you describe your process of translating Molière?

I read the play, mostly unassisted by scholarship or criticism, and get to know its characters and milieu. Then I render it couplet by couplet, aiming for a maximum fidelity to sense, form, and tone. My chief virtue as a translator is stubbornness: I will spend a whole spring day, a perfect day for tennis, getting one or two lines right. Now that I have seen some splendid productions of my Molière translations, I render them in what I hope is the manner of Brian Bedford or Sada Thompson.

What is the hardest part of translating Molière?

The hardest thing is to find, playing with and against the pentameter, just the right timing for a witty or comical line.

Do the rehearsals and production process change your work?

Because my translations are so slavish, I am not asked to do any rewriting at the rehearsal stage. But attending rehearsals and productions has gradually improved my ability to think and feel theatrically.

As a poet, do you think you approach translating Molière differently from the way a playwright might?

I'm sure that a playwright would more quickly visualize the scene, the action, the choreography, the authorized "business." But I would not defer to him about the text. Because Molière's comedies are so thoroughly *written*, I am not likely to be wrong about his drift and tone.

Poetry tends to be a very personal art, while theater is necessarily collaborative. How has the experience in the theater affected your work?

My lyrics for the musical show *Candide* were collaborative, and I enjoyed working with Lenny Bernstein, but I think that my poems were not altered by the process. In doing the Molière translations, however, I know that I have changed as a poet: I am readier to speak out of a single mood or mask, as in "Two Voices in a Meadow" or that long monologue "The Mind-Reader."

How does Molière speak to contemporary American audiences?

Molière's language is readily understood by any American audience. So are the plots of his major comedies, which study the effect of an unbalanced central figure on those about him. Molière's idea of what is normal, natural, or balanced is very much like our own, and so there is no need for "updating." I have no patience with the sort of director who, thinking to render Alceste accessible, has him dress and behave like a hippie who "tells it like it is." That did happen once, and I have not forgotten it.

You have also translated plays by Racine and Corneille. Is the old actor's adage true for translation, that playing comedy is harder than tragedy?

I've found it easier to translate Molière's comedies. The spare nobility of Racine is very challenging, and in rendering a heroic play like Corneille's *Le Cid* one has to be careful not to slip into the oratorical.

Have there been particular productions of Molière or your other theatrical works that remain particularly memorable?

There have been fine productions in big towns and small, and throughout our splendid galaxy of repertory theaters. Of course, no later performance could so amaze me as *The Misanthrope*'s premiere at the Poets' Theatre in 1955, in which the poet Peter Davison played the lead. To my great joy, the demand for tickets was such that the show had to be moved from its original garret-like venue to MIT's new auditorium. And then there was the next year's New York production, directed by Stephen Porter at Theatre East, and starring Ellis Rabb and Jackie Brookes.

Has working with any particular actor influenced your approach to translation?

Yes. Brian Bedford has been my friend for many years, and I have seen him in many roles. He was unforgettable as Richard II, to mention but one of his triumphs, and he has been the life of many Molière productions. If I think of him while translating, it enlivens the words and gives me a more palpable sense of the work.

Were there other translations or classical theater that inspired the direction of your own work?

When I was fifteen or so, I saw Walter Hampden do *Cyrano* at some New York playhouse. Whose translation was used I don't know, but I think the experience may have implanted in me the notion that old French plays could be viable in contemporary American theater.

What literary translators do you most admire?

The last century has been a great age of translation, and the list of heroes is too long to recite. Let me say just this: Yesterday I came upon a translation by Miller Williams of a poem by the great Trastevere poet Belli, and said to myself, That's it. It will never have to be translated again.

The translators whom I most esteem are those who do not translate *pro tem*, but work in the wild hope of doing the job once and for all.

You are a singularly remarkable translator of poetry. Why do you devote so much creative energy to translation?

Translation must be faithful, and so it can't be creative *ab ovo*. But at the very least it uses a poet's abilities between the visits of his Muse. I think it can limber his voice and range, and give him great satisfactions and, with luck, can bring him royalties.

Why are there so few literary translations published in the U.S.?

As chairman of the National Endowment for the Arts, you would know better than I whether publishers are reluctant to bring out literary translations. If that is true in all genres, they should be ashamed. As a translator of classic French drama, I have of course often heard the editorial adage, "Plays don't sell."

Do you have any advice for poets or playwrights who want to translate or produce classical theater?

I would urge such translators to do their work faithfully and straight, and to insist on the same qualities in any production. Death to adaptations and adulterations.

Poet Dana Gioia served as chairman of the National Endowment for the Arts from 2004 to 2009. This article was funded by the Sidney E. Frank Foundation. It first appeared, in a slightly different version, in American Theatre *magazine in April 2009.*

The text of the book is set in 10½ point Adobe Garamond, a digital typeface designed by Robert Slimbach in 1989 for Adobe Systems and inspired by a hand-cut type created in the mid-1500s by Claude Garamond, as well as the italics produced during the same period by Robert Granjon. The chapter headings and dramatis personae are set in Garamond Premier, a new interpretation of Claude Garamond's font issued fifteen years later by Slimbach and Adobe and touted by typography expert Thomas Phinney as "a more directly authentic revival."

The paper is acid-free and exceeds the requirements for permanence established by the American National Standards Institute. The binding cloth is Verona, a woven rayon fabric manufactured by LBS, Des Moines, Iowa. Text design and composition by Gopa & Ted2, Inc., Albuquerque, New Mexico. Printing and binding by Lakeside Book Company, Crawfordsville, Indiana.